The Baroque Night

The Baroque Night

✦

Spencer Golub

NORTHWESTERN UNIVERSITY PRESS
EVANSTON, ILLINOIS

Northwestern University Press
www.nupress.northwestern.edu

Printed in the United States of America

10 9 8 7 6 5 4 3 2 1

ISBN 978-0-8101-3781-3 (paper)
ISBN 978-0-8101-3782-0 (cloth)
ISBN 978-0-8101-3783-7 (ebook)

Cataloging-in-Publication data are available from the Library of Congress.

To those with too much grist for the mill.

To Jeanie, for the days.

We think by means of synthetic images that follow each other at great speeds, landing every now and then on linguistic fields (i.e., natural languages), though never staying there for too long, and flying off again to return to a grammatical airport.

—Polish mathematician Stanislaw W. Ulam

CONTENTS

1

Noir

> I could not find sleep.
>
> —Maurice Blanchot, *Aminadab*

Following a blackout in André de Toth's 1954 film noir *Crime Wave*, three police detectives break down the door to an apartment and plunge into the darkness of a room we are already in. We "know" this now owing to the intrusion of light and shadow. If movies in general are, as the filmmaker Raúl Ruiz contends, "really just special shadows that give out light," shadows in film noir alert us to the manifestness of unseen, "nocturnal light."[1] The three detectives are Plato's ghosts breaking down the nominal frame to set the scene as an equally unreal "scene." The prior (a priori) darkness is an anticipatory presence already in place but not yet *as* place. I don't really know if I am inside (or) out. "A guy with imagination gets pictures in his head, he gets scared," some noir-guy (maybe myself) cautions me, and I realize that I am awake inside my sleep body.[2]

In the pre-life of film, Leibniz marked down "the things that are thought to come into being and perish" to appearance and disappearance, similar to flashes on a screen, a simile he did not, however, use.[3] Nevertheless, the baroque as analog noir is where we enter, how we break down the door so as to illuminate the darkness of un/reality that confuses inside and outside. What follows is a baroque mise-en-scène lying anamorphically in the surface of my nighttime mental theater. I extend and distend scenic images and linguistic ideas to suffer constraint, so as better to see the model, the game, the puzzle. I am attempting a baroque "*artificialization*" that captures the semantic unease of parts of speech, sentence and syntax, words and ghost words—in short, of language with its true and false etymologies, neologisms and hyperbole.[4] I see waking life better in the figurative dark where abstractions come more often to mind and whisper that they are part of a larger plan. For the narrators of films noir, the narration says "I can" *only* in relation to the past tense and as a means of clarifying why the subject *cannot* even contemplate a future. Death haunts the subject's narration like a shadow, which is why the narration is performed in the spectral mode of the voice-over. The noir voice-over articulates being's intrinsic other-than-self-ness, ventriloquizing a death that is a priori and yet unreal, the affect of "an *inauthentic* cogito," like the one that is writing this book.[5]

In lieu of offering the reader a working definition of film noir, I offer here a brief synopsis. In a famous essay, Paul Schrader argues for the tonal (dark, sardonic, fatalist) rather than the genre identification of film noir, which he says is a production of post–World War II disillusionment and the desire to present American culture with stark realism, the influence of 1920s and 1930s German expressionism which landed in Hollywood with German émigré filmmakers fleeing fascism at home, and the tradition of hard-boiled American detective fiction. Although the history of film noir is generally dated from *The Maltese Falcon* (1941) to *Touch of Evil* (1958), it has many predecessors and successors with which it shares characteristics. Even in its heyday, the formula for producing a film noir was not exact. They were not *all* set in cities or mostly at night, nor did they all (although many of them did) feature oblique camera angles, continuous cigarette smoking, femme fatales, flashbacks, or voice-over narration. There were noir westerns, country noirs, and even melodramas that featured qualified happy endings. The films that I discuss (not all of which would be classified by others as being films noir) mostly share what Schrader calls "a complex chronological order" delineating a furtive rather than an ostensible temporal logic. These films are informed by and infused with a dread upon which is imprinted a "fear of the future," whenever that is, cultivated and accentuated by memories of the past, whatever that was as recalled by the narrator-protagonist, whoever he might be.[6] You cannot trust a film noir to tell the truth, which is why it speaks to me.

Film noir's shadows, along with their aural and visual correlates, voice-overs and flashbacks, constitute the currency (the walking-around money) of seeing the phenomenon of lived reality in aspects, from different points of view, which is what reality is. These devices are the phantom footsteps that engage with the rest of life which is rumored to be beyond our direct, perceptual experience, Schrödinger's cat in different modes of thought and fantasy that encapsulate Husserlian intentionality-defined consciousness. These performative modes of "walking around" project the "aboutness" of consciousness as regards something (and possibly, though not essentially, some *thing*). This is one philosophical way of accounting for the malaise that engorges noir, the sense of sensory perception being inadequate in all the ways that it is in real life, only more so. The conscious(ness) prompts, tics, and representations that one finds in noir speak as well to this inadequacy, or more damningly, to the *adequacy* of consciousness being only what it wants to do in the still shadowy face of possible self-transcendence, the breaking free (from and to what?).

Husserl conceived consciousness on a primary level that renders in/dependence in respect to the world irrelevant, which in turn renders subject and object abstract.[7] One does not have to embrace Husserlian phenomenology to see the value in his bracketing the subjective in thinking through intentionality, even though Husserl kept his fair share of vagueness (his "blur") as regards this theme in play through considerations, for example, of the ego's relationship to consciousness. The protagonists in film noir seldom (but not never) ask, "Who am I?" asking instead "What have I done?" In this alternative question, the "I" is presupposed as a marker against which to judge action and intention. Additionally, the second question speaks to the something or someone that "got me into this," the "this" here being not just a particular situation but a performance mode and a world transcending the subject's personal experience (seeing oneself *as if* from the outside). It is why the protagonist's inner ear detects the sound of phantom footfalls that are now his own. Subjectivity, then, has not been negated so much as redefined (and un-reified) as the achievement of an intentionality, which the mind could not previously fathom. A new attentiveness renders noir shadowing and foreshadowing intelligible to a consciousness that transcends even and especially the perception of self-knowing. I *was* my own double, but I no longer even am who my double thought he/I was.

I imbricate the baroque in film noir and its stages of performance in and through folds and overlays; voice-overs; semi-effacements and visible erasures; visual and verbal neologisms; correspondence and compression; suspension and syncope; transference and transformation; aporias; anamorphosis; and depth of surface. Each category extends its body of meaning (as Descartes might say) from an ostensibly limited idea into different modes of performance. Thus, waiting is a nonvisual anamorphosis, a hidden dimension of interior(ized) time within the subjective expectation of an objective end. Time in waiting is infinitely expandable within a real limit that is (finitely) the opposite. (This introductory chapter constitutes just such a waiting, bearing the weight of philosophical argument meant to prepare you for the arrival and landing of fully voiced, idiosyncratically synthesized cine-images that might otherwise miss seeing the runway.) Awareness of the aporia produces an astigmatism in the mind's eye that sees the end not as a destination but rather as a metastatic point, a (re)cycling of ending. Anamorphosis can in turn be seen not just in pictures but as eye floaters, brain floaters, as the idea of the aporia shedding (which is not to say losing) its malignant cells as a mode of presentation. Recall the mad Prince Prospero in Poe's "Masque of the Red Death" (1842), who brought death inside the palace walls as a masker, already eaten away internally like a living cancer. "The apparition is a mask behind which no one exists, behind which nothing really exists other than nothing. Nothing rather than something." (Leibniz had famously asked, "*Why is there something rather than nothing?*")[8] So said Deleuze, at which point unspecified in historical time, the world passed, as it did in the baroque period, from reason into neurosis and began to fold in on itself. A world of appearance and disappearance, of *fort/da*, is a baroque world, wholly subjective and finite in an abstract way of knowing what is and is not here or there.

The baroque, as I am employing it, asks "what," not "why," in a manner that is unscientific, undemanding of proofs. Its logic is contrived. Its contrivance is an article of faith in the doing of the thing, as per Wittgenstein's "doing philosophy," and not merely in accordance with a system that demands doing according to rule(s), which I cannot abide any more than I can "truth" and "reality," except in scare quotes.

This, then, is not a book *about* the baroque. It is, instead, a book made of what I consider to be baroque materials, themes, structures, and sources. It is a baroque tale of function determining form, "baroque" in my usage being synonymous with the very function of unreality's intervention to create a new real, if not a new reality, since the latter assumes a wider social acceptance or even determination than I am espousing here. The baroque that I have in mind is subjectivism in search of a self, solipsistic and yet at the same time theatrical, a performance misperceived by the one and the many. *My* baroque is not merely, as Deleuze might assume, "an order of thought." It is the disorderliness of an order of thought, its openness to new and even foundationless architectures of seeing through rooms that may be corridors that make it suspect. My baroque's being suspect is the source of its power. It measures what Georges Poulet called "the interior distance," which paradoxically resists being contained. It is the darkness (noir) of thought that brings the truth in all its nonabstract variations (in)to light. But "truth," according to Nietzsche, is "a mobile army of metaphors, metonymies, and anthropomorphisms." And "thinking," Deleuze asserts, "does not simply exist; it must be created."[9] And this creation derives from the contrarian impulse, which says that thinking is thinking *differently*. I want to trouble thought where it throws off dark shadows, thought itself constituting a sort of baroque noir of disillusioned illusion that does violence to itself in the ways in which reality materializes itself and unreality dematerializes life itself.

My choice of materials to discuss in this book is guided by personal idiosyncrasy and baroque irregularity, its fraternal twin. I construct the book's large puzzle from many different kinds and shapes of pieces, some of which contain recognizably useful details in helping to see the whole, while others show us only what appear to be pieces of the sky. I evolve an anamorphic isomorphism of thought looked at as personal design in order to reconstruct the unreality of our lives. As we age, memory grows problematic not because of all that has been forgotten but because misremembering reveals deeper truths about who we have always been, the thoughts and mental tendencies that shaped us. We come in time to realize that the scenic route which memory provides has, as often as not, blocked the view. We come instead to see people inverted by surfaces, animated pictures inside of frames, and to hear sudden laughter at life's hidden circumstances. One sees this in Ruiz's baroque multi-mystery cine-narratives of life lived as multiplicity, which I knew of but did not *know* until *after* I wrote this book—a sequencing of events of which he would no doubt have approved. What we share is a sense of the image(s) inside the image and the secret(s) inside the film, the sense of film as phantasm, the interpenetration of one film by another, and the interrogation of narrative by structure. Above all, I believe, as does Ruiz (whose films and critical works I now esteem), that "the world is nothing more than an image of the world." The spectator is to Ruiz what the reader is to me, the point at which the perspectival lines of the work meet *outside the frame* so that he or she is always on *the inside* of what is happening, "anamorphically reflected."[10]

We experience the inside and outside of ourselves and/as the wor(l)d, which may be, says Nietzsche, as fictional as we. We are the very picture-text of self-containment while at the same time gaining passage through the world via metaphor, which, unlike simile, is an open container. That is, we are not so much actively "like" what we see, even while engaging the world with our and its own fictional likeness. I am my own model of the world (Husserl's "each appearance [that] contains the whole thing") and yet I am also "a body among bodies" that together constitute the world that either writes in or writes out the word "only," as in "only a body among [other] bodies" having no particular ownership of that world's creation nor even a possible "ownness" except to the subject's ear.[11] A central question asked by philosophy is whether such ownness can be contained or even if it is a container in itself.[12] Containment defines and embodies limit, and yet, Rémi Brague argues that "presence in the world is such that we find ourselves in an inside, whose threshold we have never crossed, an inside that has no outside. This is why this inside is defined by the continuity, the impossibility of reaching, starting from within, any sort of limit at all."[13] William H. Gass calls placing consciousness inside a container, a box, "from which words might be taken in or out," "a crime against the mind."[14] The way to prevent this crime (wave) from happening on our watch in our dark room is to employ metaphor in ways that allow us to think figuratively through words and their objects so that they float before our eyes as appearances that capture immanence and hidden intentionality.

I was walking along a beach in the daylight when a small airplane appeared at a relatively near distance in the sky. For some unknown reason, I assumed upon seeing the flying object that it was a model plane or some kind of drone made to look like a plane, and so I saw no need for a designated landing strip. As the plane headed toward a wooded area, a clearing appeared where it could land. I was convinced that before it could do so, however, the plane would crash into a tree in the wooded area and be destroyed. My concern quickly transformed into terrified confusion to see the plane land safely on the airstrip in the clearing. Why terror? Because the plane had miraculously become full-sized and fit the landing strip for which it was intended. It was no longer a model plane but had become some sort of impossible object that could be a smaller model when nearer and the full-size real thing when farther away from me as the viewing subject. How could my mind be so deceived? Then I thought, what if my mind was not so much deceived as bearing witness to some unreality that is in its own way as true or truer than what most normative perception would admit as being content *without* intent? Was I experiencing a "metaphysical certainty not yet defined in time" or experiencing horizons as "the intentionally predelineated potentialities" that Husserl said they are, but which experience teaches is "unsurpassable limit"? Was I looking not at a plane traversing the real sky but rather a plainisphere, a sky map on which were depicted the rotation of representations that subverted "habitual perceptions of space"? Perception speaks to something appearing in space while acknowledging that our attention is what makes it appear. We make the language that makes this metaphorically clear: "the plane from which things appear" reveals and is revealed by the appearance of a plane. Our intentionality renders the thing intelligible even as our attentiveness and our inattentiveness battle to keep it in and out of sight. Just how long have I been thinking, dreaming of this plane that I am on as one phantom being (or) another, and will the fullness of my consciousness appear to me in time?[15]

Upsetting appearance appears to puncture reality, or to paraphrase Žižek, reality is enframed by a part of itself that has broken off and broken through the very thing we call reality.[16] Cartesian skepticism or radical doubt is appropriated to entertain a negative idealism of there being something ontologically bigger than life, something for which the concept of the frame is symptomatic in all places big and small but which is at the same time uncontainable as content. Where we see connections, there are frames that gesture toward the inability to posit a frame of such size that skepticism can be dismissed and idealism can peacefully return to the realm of the positive and transcendental, where spirit, faith, and purposiveness (are said to) reside. Kant's argument that "we cognize nature only as [one-sided] appearance" accounts for our misunderstanding of all that we see as being what is there independent of our understanding.[17] Thomas Nagel argues that we need to learn to take ourselves out of the picture, since the picture is bigger than our subjective frame allows. I read this as being not a call for objectivity, which is impossible, so much as an acknowledgment of the limits of our understanding of nature's purposiveness.[18] I know too—although by knowing this personally I know it subjectively—that taking oneself out of the picture simply puts you into another picture that is alternative to the one we call "the here and now." Is nature trying to tell us something, and is our cognizing nature only as appearance our response to nature's unresponsiveness to our need to know and our being obsessed (with being)? Kant defines purposiveness as "the causality that a *concept* has with regard to its *object*." An object can, of course, be mental, and its "acts purposive even if its possibility does not necessarily presuppose the presentation of a purpose," as passive-aggressive behavior does/not assert. Purposiveness is explainable by a will whose purpose is not necessarily traceable back to a point of origin, an inciting thought, feeling, or decision. Hamlet, it is said, cannot make up his mind to act and yet in the end acts as if he *has* made up his mind. This is not simply a matter of chronology but of form.[19]

The play called *Hamlet* would contest its very name and the name "Hamlet" would not outlive Horatio's publicity of it if Hamlet's death had only purpose but no purposiveness, no form performing its/as function. By framing its form, the play *Hamlet* speaks its mind hypothetically, hauntingly like Hamlet, melancholically self-haunted by the Ghost while in some future anterior tense (e.g., "Life will have been so short") trying to build a better mousetrap (play) to catch consciousness itself in the interiorized shadow of death.[20] Hamlet so disturbs his own trope of self-invention/self-interrogation that Shakespeare named *Hamlet* after him whose mind swallows and regurgitates it whole. *Hamlet* is a play whose after-ness comes before in the form of a ghost, who is a cognitive contrivance, a conventional representation of transcendental thinking inside a theatrical frame (as opposed to a mere motivational source for the Prince)—a familiar way of seeing the thing that we do not really know but suspect is real if not, given the lack of material evidence, true. Hamlet, as they say in noir, was on the case and late on the scene. Being (performatively) the son of his father's ghost, Hamlet is ontologically antic. He plays the a priori nature, the givenness *of* his condition, speculatively—(con)testing the evidence of a confused before and after. That is, Hamlet cannot fully grasp his late father's manifest spectrality, his intelligible unreality as the object giving itself to him so as to be seen. This "'self-givenness' of the object itself" undoes Hamlet's own givenness, and so renders him "mad," but only in the sense that logic and vocabulary tell us that a hawk is *not* a handsaw (which it is).[21]

For Hamlet to play at being mad means "putting out of play" or bracketing his father as being "unreal" in the conventional sense of being merely fictive and illogical. Hamlet's *stage* death inherently obscures our (and perhaps his own) understanding of whether he has moved beyond self-fulfillment to an apprehension of self-givennness that makes his dead father something much more in the sense of different to him than the more-and-lessness Hamlet ascribed to his stepfather ("a little more than kin, and less than kind"; 1.2.65) when the play began. Hamlet's death inside the frame of his own un/making brings forth only the briefest of denouements in which silence is spoken of without any additional understanding of what silence (as in death and ineffability) is. It is a memorial silence intended to hearken our minds back to an unreasonable beginning that offers no resolute end. Hamlet begins as he ends, as his father's death whose name the son carries not forth, not anywhere, alive only in the purposiveness of something else unnamed. His death is caused but is merely a small frame within a bigger teleological picture of final causes he can, as a theatrical figure, only affect in and as a baroque play of dis/appearances: *Noir Hamlet: D.O.A.*

Applying a representational frame counters intuition by rendering bigger-than-life unreality intelligible even as it makes life artful and smaller, more (like) a model than the real thing. ("The model," Ricoeur suggests, "belongs not to the logic of justification or proof, but to the logic of discovery.")

"Philosophy," Kant says, "consists in knowing one's limits."[22] That being said, philosophy intuitively knows theater, perhaps even better than theater knows itself. Theater is not just historically but intuitively framed, although this intuition is too often equated with reduction and the unseen merely with the un-staged, the un-appeared. Theater too often values what is made real rather than what is and values appearance over the unreality that speaks of the bigger than life. Nevertheless, theater's ontology knows better. It says so in film in which the theatrical troping characteristic of particular genres does a better job speaking by contrast about what is in frame in the literal and figurative sense and what is out of frame. But the "reduction" of the stage, as of the airplane, is itself not just a (mis)representation of something (else), it is a Husserlian "bracketing" (*epoché*) on the philosophical plane, a "putting out of play" of the naive natural attitude toward the world (as Wittgenstein's "everything that is the case") and its too often attendant naturalism.[23] As such, it is a turning away from givenness and toward at least the possibility of metaphor, away from psychology and its attendant forms of madness and toward the madness of the day that is life seen openly, without limit for which and to which "I" am bound.

My Representations

> I am conscious of my representations, and hence they exist as well as I myself who have these representations.
>
> —Kant, *Critique of Pure Reason*

This book oscillates between Kant's "mere representation" and (his) "my representations," the latter being the clearinghouse for all species of thought and appearance, all externality. Kant defines appearance as "the undetermined object of an empirical intuition," which is given to us only a posteriori. He attaches the word "mere" not so much as a pejorative but as a qualifier to "positings" (realities) and "intelligible beings," as well as to "representations." "Mere" is that minimum capacity to affect something real (e.g., consciousness of my own existence) and is perforce expressive of and limited by the empirical. The "mere" is never the thing-in-itself, which we cannot know. We are our representations, the source of which is some "residuum of reality" we cannot understand. Our reality, empirical and otherwise, is unreal, in that our experience of it is at once enabled and disabled by our own mental conceptualization.[24]

The thinking subject adores its own unknowability and immateriality, so much so that representation itself dissolves into thought whose origin and locality remain indeterminate. Still, "without some empirical representation, which supplies the material for thought, the act," Kant thinks, "would not take place; and the empirical element is the only condition of the application or of the use of the pure intellectual faculty." All discussions of possibility and limit are in service to degrees of reality, with the purely speculative highest reality being God, who stands as a priori reality's strongest affirmation, for example, in baroque philosophy. The argument Kant makes in his two-sided consideration of whether God or a highest being exists may be applied to reality itself. In each case, we go looking for "the existence of a cause proportionate to . . . the order and purposiveness of the world" and, by extension, the subjective purposiveness that attends, which is to say that all purposiveness, including that we see or intuit to be in nature, is subsumed by the subjective. This results in the creation of "only relational representations of the magnitude of an object, which the observer (of the world) compares with himself and his own power of comprehension." There is in none of this a "determinate concept," only an assumption that this thing we posit is "absolutely necessary." This requires some idea of definitiveness, even of perfection, which grows more rarefied and more speculative as the object becomes more generalized, yet simultaneously more concretized as it becomes in our minds more unified, as our minds make it into *a more unified idea.*

This last stage actually moves the object outside our own personal experience, even making it unreachable by experience. The by now abstract shapeliness of the idea of what the object is becomes self-limiting in the same way that Kant defines shapes representing (only) the limits of space. The positive repurposing of this argument is that thinking beyond the limits of possible experience is an illusion necessary for the instantiation of manifold knowledge and range of motion in both a personal and philosophical sense.[25] There is, of course, no disproving reality, nor is there any proof of unreality. There is only the critique in and of the reasoning process that posits the one or the other, or the one *as* the other. So, although there is no proof, there is always a trial. We fear being (thought to be) unreasonable, because reason not only has its laws: reason *is* the law. By embracing unreality we will surely not be awarded judgment and may even realize our greatest fear, which is to lose custody (of ourselves). We risk this, though, because we must learn from anything and everything that can teach us to deadline.

More so than speculative reality, which derives from categories of realistic thought, "imaginary concepts . . . cannot receive the character of their possibility *a priori*."[26] The world is always appearance (and "a thoroughgoing coherence of appearance"), although only sometimes illusion, as when our perception is in error, that is discordant with "the laws of our understanding." Kant writes, "It would be my own fault if I made a mere illusion out of that which I ought to count as appearance." Levinas says something similar, substituting for "mere illusion" "the ambivalence of apparition."[27] Everything is an iteration or apparent elevation or diminution of everything else. "Between reality and negation there is a continuous coherence of possible realities and of possible smaller perceptions." We not only hold these perceptions. We *are* these perceptions. We are born into a world of our making and die in it too, so that "*if we remove the thinking subject then the whole corporeal world would have to vanish, because it is nothing but the appearance in the sensibility of our own subject and a certain kind of its representations.*" Consciousness is itself just another form of representation, not a particular object but a general form.[28] I am both my own subject *and* my own predicate. What seems logical need not be real, since "logic abstracts from all content" and so is the master of illusion.[29] I do not rule the world, but nor am I undone by rules that are external and by logic that is illusory to myself and who I am, as determined by my inner sense. I accept unreality on my own terms. I care not for what is true or false, only for what is possibly intelligible, imaginatively and intuitively representable, whether with or without an object, a negative idealism that accepts a transcendent knowing that is *inside* ourselves, in the darkness.[30]

The Usual Subject: Nietzsche contra Kant and the World

> It is not with judgment that truth begins.
>
> —Emmanuel Levinas, *The Theory of Intuition in Husserl's Philosophy*

Baroque criminals like us like Nietzsche, and Nietzsche in his own way likes criminals and not just the "lifers" who gain sustenance from his philosophical body-building "will to power" as a disciplined and disciplinary way of unseating a world that has been weakened by logic's law and order. "In fact," the madman Nietzsche's brand of mind over matter recasts the body as a more primordial "mentality" that the conscious mind has almost succeeded in thinking out of primacy, if not existence. Our overlooking the body (despite "the foolish fact that the body has not gone away") analogizes to our derealization of the outside world as being the mere source of our impressions (of it). We believe that the effect is the origin of the cause. As a result, all (the world) is lost and the only way we can think to retrieve it is through memory, because memory is constructed from the same "erroneous causality" of thought feeding upon its own chronology, its own constructed "language of the past." Memory is not factual but rather the form that thought gives to interpretation—interpretation that is not only possible minus input from the outer world, but that seeks to distance that world from the appearance of truth that is memory's desired end. Memory's engine, the "I," says Nietzsche, is "set up . . . at the point at which our ignorance begins." Nietzsche is here arguing against both the a priori subject and the "reality *in itself*" of the Cartesian *cogito* and its "*ergo sum*," against not only the desiring subject but against Cartesian subject-desire.[31]

In arguing contra Kant's a prioris—the laws of logic, identity, and contradiction constituting a pure knowledge that precedes all experience—Nietzsche (unconsciously) aligns himself with the criminal who is dragged into a lineup owing to his "priors." These "priors" allow for the law's reasonable presupposition, though not yet proof of the guilt of "the usual suspect [subject]" who in alibiing himself asserts a consistently simple, unitary (recidivist) self as being a fiction in the face of the law's effort to render him, itself, and its bases as intelligibly true reads. They say that the criminal always returns to the scene of the crime, but it might be better to say that the scene returns to line up the subject's criminality, criminalizing the self by categorizing it according to a judgment that refuses to recognize the self's multiplicity, to be other than how it appears. A bad man can be innocent, just as a good man can be guilty under the law whose judgment is final but not morally absolute. Man's judgment, according to Nietzsche (and, I would add, legal precedent in case law), "works under the presupposition that identical cases exist." The presumption of self-incrimination marks the point at which "the concept 'reality,' 'being,' is taken from our feeling of the 'subject.'" In that the subject must be self-consistent, his guilt is, in a "real" sense, syllogistic. (Nietzsche: "An assumption that is irrefutable—why should it for that reason be 'true'? . . . Everything simple is merely imaginary, is not 'true.' But whatever is real, whatever is true, is neither one nor even, reducible to one.")[32] The thus already imprisoned self is returned to his manifestly physical cell where he is further reduced to a number, which is law and order's way of knowing as a "perspective form." Nietzsche offers the following as an alternative to the basis in/of logic: "Supposing there were no self-identical '*A*,' such as is presupposed by every proposition of logic (and of mathematics), and the '*A*' were already mere appearance, then logic would have a merely apparent world as its condition." By letting "*A*" *not be* "*A*" we enter into an illusion of our own choosing that we may confidently label "my reality," reality as we know it by whatever means we know it and according to what "reality" for us really means.

Kant (says Nietzsche) "*believes* in the fact of knowledge," whereas he (Nietzsche) ascribes "factuality" to the habit of thinking from a certain "perspective illusion."[33] In so doing, of course, Nietzsche falls into the same trap of grouping philosophers on the basis of *their* "priors," ideas that appear not so much to evolve as to repeat themselves from a set of presuppositions that they mistake for original and originary thought. Nietzsche's argument is with the misperception (the false identification) of logic as truth and the confidence that is therefore placed in logic's henchman, causality, to define before and after, crime and punishment. Logic gives man confidence, at the same time making him into a confidence man, an agent of (self-)delusion. In considering the error-prone logic of identification, Nietzsche in no way eschews the value of comparison but not without its sometime partner, contradiction. It is not so much the criminal but the philosopher who is responsible for the fallen world of stasis and oversimplification, the two-pronged retardation of moment-to-moment (be)coming into continuous and consistent being. "The principle of identity," Nietzsche contends, "has behind it the 'apparent fact' of things that are the same."[34] If someone or something (subject or object) stands still long enough, logic aligns with and (mis)appropriates meaning, whereby means are mistaken for ends that facilitate judgment, the illusion of certainty where only doubt should exist, if truth be told.

The narrowness of social, including legal, mechanisms derives from the reduction of the world to what Nietzsche dismisses as being "the facts of consciousness," the truth-making that enables us to categorize reality and construct an inhabitable and knowable world that misrepresents a fragment as a (unified) totality. In this formula, the "unknowable" is consigned to a higher intelligence (i.e., God, the Absolute, Kant's "Pure Reason/Judgment," essences, "things-in-themselves"—all of which Nietzsche rejects) that further defines human and world-limit. Because he believes that "the 'apparent *inner* world' is governed by just the same forms and procedures as the 'outer world,'" Nietzsche (whose philosophy practices a kind of clarity that he rejects in other philosophies as being overly simple) cannot abide any claim for consciousness being factual or even thinking as being an authentic form of anything other than form, "an artificial arrangement of the purpose of intelligibility." Nietzsche contends that "nothing is more erroneous than to make of psychical and physical phenomena the two faces, the two revelations of one and the same substance," the equally compelling, unequally illegible "real" and "unreal." This contention will for me recall Hitchcock's vanished lady, "Miss Froy," whose disappearance insinuates a consciousness she did not know she had into a heterotopic un/reality that logic does not define or control on a train that runs afoul of its own timetable as it passes through a landscape of scenic miniatures. "Becoming obscure," argues Nietzsche, "is a matter of perspective of consciousness," but given that this consciousness is itself responsible for the world's ("this perspective world's") "psychological reduction," our "grades of appearance" and "degrees of reality" (along with our representational art, "repeating in miniature, as it were, the tendency of the whole"), it cannot help but model infinite regress and system stress.[35]

"You realize what you've done to my wife?" An unassuming musician asks this question of a criminal for whom he has been mistaken (owing to eyewitness misidentification), their previous facial overlay (literalized by the film camera) now separating into a face-to-face confrontation. The wrong man's innocence survived the dumb mechanics of the system that drove his wife mad with doubt and fear. The docudrama *The Wrong Man* (1956) is that rare Hitchcock film in which the director does not appear in a cameo. Perhaps he did not want the impossible standard of his authentic self-doubling to undermine the consequentiality of his two characters' merely coincidental resemblance. Eyewitnesses' inability to disengage subjecthood from surrogacy casts what Ricoeur calls "the relational character of identity" in an alternative, negative light. In the grammar of thought, the musician who, on the basis of superficial appearance, is mistaken for a criminal, is like a metaphor taken for a less nuanced simile, the "to be" confused with the "to be *like*."[36] In *The Lineup* (dir. Don Siegel, 1958), an unlettered hit man discovers in a borrowed copy of *English Grammar and Usage* that he has been using the subjunctive in error: "'If I was you,' you know? That's all wrong. It says here, 'If I *were* you.'" Here the "you know?" of rhetorical ("you"-as-"I") self-questioning interrupts a self-correcting grammatical construction that forges the hypothetical agreement of two subjects—"you" and "I"—with which the hit man cannot professionally engage. His misidentification of what his speech really connotes makes him an unreliable witness even (or especially) to his own confession. His unlettered-ness speaks to the disarticulation of image as meaning's legible sign. We hallucinate meanings *as if they were* images.[37] The musician's wife's internalization of her husband's ordeal to which her momentarily doubting him—itself a form of false witnessing—contributes, represents a hallucinatory systemic stress. She believes in his innocence and yet cannot help but *see an image of him* as being guilty. By comparison, any possible doubt in the hitman's mind is momentary, grammatical, and non-systemic as evidenced by the fact that he places the stress elsewhere.

There is, in the discussion of testifying to what is true, the question of doubt but also that of false belief that emulates certainty minus the truth that is conditioned by "errant recollection" when it overrides perception.[38] The (mis)identification of "the wrong man" suggests an unconscious substitution of a priori justification for a priori knowledge, resulting in the expressed certainty of what is in fact "justified false belief." Husserl states that the merely "adequate givenness" of "a positional consciousness" that "excludes the possibility of being otherwise" is "an act of reason" that is not necessarily insightful ("insight" and "evidence" are often mistakenly assumed to be synonymous). (Husserl points out that "we can, for example, 'blindly' predict that 2 + 1 = 1 + 2, but we can also make the same judgment with insight.")[39] Bad eyewitnesses (whose evidence is non-apodictic, neither necessary nor incontrovertible) unknowingly enact the Kantian a priori that is independent of experience while predicating their unacknowledged justified false belief (as per Husserl) on the very experience that this a priori denies. They are philosophically playing both ends against an absent middle in which something was actually seen as being true. Although, philosophically speaking, "seeing" can be defined metaphorically.[40] The words "I see this" offer no trace evidence of what has been elided in the sentence, "I see [like] this." Knowledge is here intuited, and the episteme that knowledge is has become too absorbed in knowing to consider what is actually known.

My Blue Metaphor

"Metaphor," wrote Aristotle, "consists in giving the thing a name that belongs to something else."[41] Our language, then, promotes misidentification, albeit in the name of likeness. A witness would never be moved to say regarding his identification of a suspect, "I mean this, of course, metaphorically." He is prevented from doing so knowing that the suspect will have the legal right to face him in court. There is a particularity and an intimacy in the face-to-face relationship. It behooves metaphor to keep two thought-to-be dissimilar faces apart, since doing so allows for the mechanism of likeness to be unveiled and the effect of wonder to be absorbed. There is a trace of instrumentalism in this insofar as efficacy is set before reality's truthful depiction. Metaphor is a problem-solving function that becomes the problem where mimesis is concerned. Mimesis is the fictional recall of whatever world one deems to be real, with metaphor doing much of the heavy lifting to make this happen. But metaphor's "borrowed meaning [as opposed to] the proper meaning, that is, to the meaning that 'really belongs' to a word by virtue of being its original meaning," makes it "impossible to talk about metaphor non-metaphorically (in the sense implied by borrowing); in short, . . . the definition of metaphor returns on itself." So, if "the displaced meaning comes from somewhere else" and metaphor's "place of origin or of borrowing" [the "from . . . to . . ."] is always potentially identifiable, it, in effect, moves along inside its own frame. Metaphor's poetic reach is further than that of metonymy, which also deals in purposeful misnaming, misidentification, and furthermore, in generalized reduction.[42]

I mention this to suggest that my viewing of the airplane from the ground may have been a kind of metaphoric witnessing of said ground moving from a physical to a philosophical domain. My "I" then says what my eye cannot and still clear the bar of reliable witnessing: "I mean this, of course, metaphorically." The metaphorical figure of "aberrant attribution," says Ricoeur, "disturb[s] a whole network by means of an aberrant attribution."[43] I feel here like Thomas, the protagonist of Maurice Blanchot's novel *Aminadab* (2002), who exclaims, "I entered this house inadvertently. I was passing by on the street outside when someone made a sign to me . . . My situation . . . has not yet been officially defined." Thomas is nominally—that is, through his own accounting—called, but not so much to the thing (in his case the noir figure of the woman in the window) as to the *image* of the thing. The entrance to the house he enters is clearly labeled "*The entrance is here*," but only on the inside and only then above a door "covered in thick curtains," suggesting that all he encounters is baroquely framed, perhaps even baroquely formed. Thomas finds himself in rooms that appear to be proportionately (relationally) too small for the framed painted images of the objects they configure. A door changes its look, a window opens "only from the outside," and "[the] room where you are now," Thomas is told, "is much larger than you would think at first" (in the so-called "here and now"). This last statement is prefaced with, "I will tell you about the portrait," drawing our attention to how the representational image enlarges, even while it appears to reduce life's dimensions, creating the appearance, for example, that a room is bigger on the inside. But here outside and inside are purposely confused in the mind of the protagonist's unreliable witnessing of what is clearly a mental event.[44]

W. V. Quine has suggested that "in an obvious way [the] structure of interconnected sentences is a single connected fabric including all sciences, and indeed everything we ever say about the world." But can this extended sentence be said to encompass conceptually an outside and an inside and, assuming that it can, does one or the other aspect more strongly s(t)imulate its (own) connectedness?[45] Is there a place, even conceptually defined, from whence analogy springs? The airplane writing that I posit and affect is like Blanchot's house entrance, which is either sited on the outside but cited on the inside or only cited on the outside but really sited on the inside. *"The entrance is here."* Wherever "*here*" is, or wherever here "*is*." Or, in the face of the one extended (and in the case of Blanchot's house, wraparound) sentence, are both siting and citing the same two-sided question of the unspoken being somehow the unreal?

Where is the ground, as philosophy asks, do we need to know, and how do we know? (And is knowing ever enough?) This is another way of asking not so much what is real as what informs the thing we call "real" and whether it can be contained in language (and if so, in what form of language—written, verbal, object, image), including the language of the a priori. Wittgenstein famously removed naming from any a priori claim to authenticating a subject or object while making philosophical common cause with ordinary language, as did Heidegger with the ordinary objects with which said language engages and to which it (only) appears to correspond.[46] Heidegger (after Wittgenstein) upturned the ground by defining the latter as reason and ground/reason as Being. And as Being is essence it is a priori (fundamentally ontological) and so cannot be grounded on or in anything else: "What presences as basis does not need the ground."[47] But if there is not anything like, only something *called* "absolute truth," what happens to the claim for Being as its own essential ground that cannot elsewhere or otherwise be grounded? Being rests on nothing. It is, as Lee Braver notes, groundless. It might be more pertinent, then, to ask not about ground but rather, about this "nothing." To be nothing or not to be nothing, *that* is the question. Prior to Hamlet's much puzzled-over soliloquy, the Ghost asks this question in its theatrical-actual self-presencing. It speaks in the voice(-over) of Joe Gillis rising up from Norma Desmond's in-ground swimming pool in Billy Wilder's film noir *Sunset Boulevard* (1950), which is no ground, only an over-large watery grave *and* rebirthing site.

In his short narrative "The Dressmaker's Dummy," Alain Robbe-Grillet uses objects (coffeepot, table, owl-imprinted trivet, etc.) to make appearance apparent.[48] It takes the givenness and neutrality of appearance (which is more a Husserlian givenness of something *to* someone than a Wittgensteinian givenness *of* an a priori truth) and makes this givenness something to be actively achieved by prompting our minds to consider the object's and with it the scene's ontic and ontological *will to be real*. Robbe-Grillet accomplishes this by presenting the reader with a series of observation sentences ("The coffeepot is on the table. It is a four-legged round table," etc.), which Quine tells us, suggest to philosophers "the datum sentences of science." These sentences are vouched for by agreement among "well-placed observers," objects that model in advance and in part Nagel's notion of "particular things [that] can have a noncompetitive completeness." More often than not, though, we as readers of what appear to us to be small figures of speech and their objects fail to see what the object is and what the object can see.[49] We are unreliable witnesses. Even our analysis is dependent upon a descriptive view of reality that undermines observation. For example, I misread one of Quine's follow-up statements, "This immunity to error is, however, like observationality itself," as "This immunity to error is, however, *the* observationality itself." The meaning has now become that observation is its own truth. This transposition of meaning is oddly but not unpredictably confirmed by Quine's intervening reference to "the philosophical doctrine of infallibility of observation sentences" that my mind carried forward to the misread sentence.[50] Here observationality attends to misreading, to unreliable witnessing.

The airplane that appeared to change not so much its size as its scale in relation to context may be said to constitute and to be brought back to life as a "proportional metaphor," and not merely as an instantiation of the problematic philosophical proposition of "the adequation of thought to things that is possible only in a homogeneous sphere." Even though perception is a multiplicity, it does not necessarily bring a higher level of non-representable being (in)to consciousness nor allow us in itself to render a truth judgment in the way that "I see it" referring to intuitive vision would.[51] I am not there yet. In the airplane's approach, "approximation (bringing close) meets the resistance of 'being distant.' " It is not about analogy but transference (after Aristotle), or even, we might say, the rumor of transference overseen by the eye/"I," but only in the sense that her own spectation may have been overheard by death-sleeping Psyche, or, for that matter, by Joe Gillis and the self-presencing *Hamlet* Ghost.[52] I see the airplane twice because I am, as always, checking to see not just whether but *how* I saw it the first time, whether it will be the same when I check it again, whether I am still grounded both in my seeing and in my "seeing as," my spontaneous and intuitive experiencing of the world. We go back to look at a sign or a mirror image to bear witness to our relationship to it. This act of "epistemic overdetermination" marks our need for corroboration that distrusts memory or perception alone. Sight, to paraphrase John L. Pollock, "is a *self-correcting* source of justified beliefs, that is, one that can correct its errors. Consider an elementary case of visual self-correction. I notice a sheet of paper on my desk, look at it, and form the belief that it is square. However, upon subsequent examination, one of its sides appears longer than another, and as a result I come to believe that the sheet is rectangular. If we add the further assumption that the sheet is rectangular, then we have a case of visual self-correction."[53] So, maybe it's (just) an exceptionally well-made paper airplane that I saw, that is, metaphorically speaking. And just maybe the (paper) airplane has nothing but ghost writing on the inside, as Freud "posthumously" indicated it could. Maybe the folded paper airplane contains this book.

Is the airplane that I "saw" change size and scale merely a trick of the eye, that is, perceptual, or was it (also) a sign to look beyond appearance(s) in and of the world, "the general idea of the world itself"? Was it just a reminder that representation is by definition a reduction of some idea and that there really *are* noumena, that is, things we can only think, even though here too we cannot think outside of thought-constructed limits such as size, scale, time, and space, and even (and especially) reason (all part of the composite frame fatale), which render all of our thoughts at least somewhat arbitrary in the invisible shadow thrown by the "big picture" (itself a limit-term)? Can thought as thought ever really be made intelligible, or does it slip the noose of intelligible reality? And if this is so, why would the seemingly antonymic concept of unreality be any more valid or authentic, except as just another attempt to make sense, or as per Wittgenstein, make nonsense out of human experience? Or is there, as Kant suggests, a supersensible or transcendent "structure beyond all possible experience," which, of course, returns us to the noumenal, which exists only as thought devoid of time and place?[54] Did the big-but-small airplane announce the coming into being, however momentarily, of an intuition hitherto unacknowledged in this fashion—a theoretical cognition of a plane's what-if-ness elided with the more ordinary *as*-if-ness of image? I am thinking here of the godlike oligarch Grigory Arkadin piloting his airplane (*Mr. Arkadin*, dir. Orson Welles, 1955), where suddenly in the absence of disappearance there is no pilot, only the plane persisting in flight as image's spatial doubt.[55]

What if empirical cognition is wrong and the large plane is small in the air no matter how close and is big on the ground no matter how far? Werner S. Pluhar reminds us that for Kant "theoretical cognition *is* knowledge, rather than the process that yields it," and "only theoretical cognition is insight."[56] This insight or intuition is in search of a concept to house it, but like the beach sand under my feet that washes away, it resists the solidity and limit that the mind imposes (even) though it entertains thought not only as process. Intuition or intuitive understanding "permits us to *think* of the 'contingency' of the particular as being only a *seeming* contingency, a 'contingency for' our understanding with its particularity, but as in fact being a *necessity*." Furthermore, "our a priori concepts and intuitions *are* the forms that we give to all objects of appearance."[57] We intuit the world as a necessary truth, not as an explanation. Alternatively, consistent with Kant's paraphrased argument that "anything in nature, as long as our imagination can apprehend it in an intuition, can be judged aesthetically," one may allow that the bigness and smallness of an object are merely forms of our aesthetic judgment.[58] The airplane that I see change size is not a functional object in my mind's accounting and so serves some other aesthetic purpose in my mind's design.

What is important here is not what a plane is but what it *looks like*. That said, the plane first appears not only as image but as metaphor, a formal construction of connection, part of a bigger series to which the plane that discovers/creates a landing strip likewise belongs. And as a metaphor, it travels through nature in its own frame, its own (air)space and its own time, awakening at least in me Kant's "feeling of the sublime" and with it "a mental agitation, connected with our judging of the object." "We call *sublime* what is absolutely *large*. To be large and to be a magnitude are quite different concepts." To be absolutely large is to be without comparison, whereas to say of something or someone that they are small, medium, or large moves the discussion from pure concept to subjective judgment, even if or though said judgment is based on the "fact" of physical appearance.[59] This, Kant argues, is a slippery slope. If I was experiencing the sublime as/on another plane, was the size comparison manufactured by my mind in an effort to make sense of what is inherently unreasonable, contra-reason, unreal in a sense that normative cognition disallows except as nonsense, the appearance of an impossibility, an oxymoron? If the sublime makes everything else comparatively small, then the airplane becoming small upon landing announced a moment of re-grounding of purposiveness in purpose, simultaneous with the landing of my idea of how representation had changed from "mere" to "my." At the very least, I experienced a moment of apparently irreconcilable comparison, or rather an incomparable idea that exploded comparison without making its functionality disappear.

Intelligibility

> For the moment let us note the essential correlation of intelligibility and representation.
>
> —Kant, *Critique of Judgment*

There is an outside to everything, including the self, which, as Ricoeur attests, is narrated, emplotted, made comprehensible only in relation to structure. With this in mind, the flashback voice-over in film noir demonstrates this outside-ness in the form of "a new narrative intelligence." Character being, in Ricoeur's definition, "the self under the appearances of sameness" ("the reidentification of a human individual as being the same"), the voice-over cites a narrative beginning and ending, a causality that is outside the normative historical structure and so contests the notion of "the 'I' as the world-limit."[60] The voice-over, which is often that of a dead or dying man, is a catch-and-release strategy whereby an illusory freedom is performed in relation to the life-narrative with which it ultimately syncs up and in catching up to it is inevitably caught by it and released from its so-called freedom. And yet, says Ricoeur after Kant, the human capacity to begin not in time but in causality co-opts from nature a voice that is recognizable as belonging to a man speaking outside of his own mortality.[61] The body lying face-down in Norma Desmond's swimming pool in *Sunset Boulevard* is, says the disembodied voice of Joe Gillis, "*a* body which is also *my* body" performing a narrative resurrection outside of "real" space and time that is the brain of (the) film speaking. The disembodied voice, Gillis's voice-over speaking over his own dead body, makes the "I's" contestation of the world-limit ("the constraint of the corporeal and terrestrial condition" but also "the *environing world* as the correlate of the body-flesh") intelligible as a performance of an outside, which, like the voice of Hamlet's father's Ghost, has no known provenance (other than the medium itself) and so identifies the world as we know it as being only a quasi-causal model of what *its cogito* cannot contain.[62] In the absence of the subject, the corpse is death's objective voice-over. It speaks from a groundless horizon in which nothing but the illusion of life comes into being and comes to pass.

What Ricoeur calls "the otherness of the otherness of self" (i.e., the foreignness ascribed to our being an other to or outside who we are and not solely to another) is a function of our mental encapsulation inside "the circle of sameness-identity" or "*idem*-identity" as opposed to the broader sense of selfhood he calls "*ipse*-identity." His notion of "oneself inasmuch as being other" contests Levinas's insistence on the outside other being essential to our selfhood (ipseity) as a construct.[63] "An abiding epoché" or (self-)bracketing simultaneously dis/engages me.[64] As such, the voice-over is for me a positional un/reality. It ventriloquizes a distracted subject-object relationship, which makes life (merely) lifelike. As memory does not so much fail as fictionalizes, a truth about knowing is revealed. The distance traveled is distance measured, articulated as such, a gapping set off in brackets, as "thoughts about" that are and have always been secondary to knowing life in an active sense. In describing positional versus the neutral subject-object relationships, Husserl effectively articulates the dis/embodied philosophy of the voice-over in the unreal time of presence and of flashback:

> A stereoscopic, cinematographic semblance stands before me. 1) At first I lose myself in as-if contemplation; I contemplate the events as if they were actually happening. This is neutrality consciousness (phantasizing). 2: Taking a position, I posit the semblance image as reality, as "what is seen" in this *quasi*-seeing. I establish a second Ego, which does not take part in the *quasi*-believing, in the *quasi*-occurring, but contemplates it and the "noema," the "image" in it, reflectively.[65]

Husserl's description of the real-life "I" as the perceiving subject of real life's "as if-ness" partners well with the noir "I's" self-cynical rendering of this same "as if-ness" applied to his own "real life." This acknowledgment of "phantastic" positionality in the noir speaker's voice acknowledges that you cannot really tell what is actually hard-boiled until you crack the shell and consider the interior form. The voice-over, which says that the speaker has taken himself out of play, exposes the reality of such bracketing as being not so much a choice but a relationship between "in" and "out" in which there really are no neutral parties, least of all (despite his professional and personal predisposition) himself. The hard-boiled speaker simply wears his voice-over like a second ego, a second shell.

But here we must further ask after Husserl, whether voice-over and flashback define "content" in the same way. There is a sense in which flashback's more legible structure speaks directly to its inability to apprehend empty content, whereas the voice-over carries the idea of empty content (the voice as a non-structure) within it. To voice over something does not define restructure so much as it offers an aural instantiation of reflection, even self-reflection, since it cannot help but talk of itself, speak its own name. Structure renders intelligibility structural, that is, structure is self-enabling: "Intelligibility signifies, as much as does manifestation, the arrangement into a system in which beings signify." This being the case, "the subject will think that he has invented something whereas he has only allowed the system to realize its own arrangement [*arrimage*]." What this leads us to is Levinas's statement that "if something came from consciousness, it would only be a delusion." We are here confronted with the baroque paradox that, "led to seek this intelligible arrangement, the thinking subject interprets itself, despite all its spontaneity, as a detour that being must take to truly appear. It is thus that intelligibility is immanent in being . . . Understood this way, subjectivity is subjection to being before which it effaces itself."[66] We are and are not ourselves at every turn or film noirish recurring detour in our labyrinthine being that is so monstrous in its monstration. Can we affect "a nonthematizable intelligibility" to break the stranglehold of the Sphinxian self, to affect an *irrational* intelligibility, even though "even in the first person, the I [*Moi*] is [also] a concept"?[67] In attempting this, we cannot fail to demonstrate the many detours that monstration takes and produce the many reductions to which the events of death and ontology respond.

Kant asserts that "space consists of spaces only, times of times. Points and instants are only limits, mere places of their limitation. But places always presuppose these intuitions [the best and most essential part of what we are] which they are meant to limit or to determine."[68] Baroque noir manifests a fear of nature's immensity and, after Kant, "the inadequacy of our ability to adopt a standard proportionate to estimating aesthetically the magnitude of nature's *domain*." We model the fear of the too-big by making it small, into a model of self-conscious aesthetic dominance, which in turn speaks to "the sublimity of our intellectual ability" to think beyond mere exhibition, to cognize. The aesthetic model buys us a distance and perspective from which we can judge nature. This judgment inherently self-authenticates as being not only necessary to understanding nature but necessary *to* nature as well.

Baroque noir (and the theater it attends) exhibits the subjective purposiveness of our mind to model the shapeliness of a totality bigger than itself by making totality look like an object, a form, a style, a composite affect, which effectively makes the mind its own object, its own model.[69] Illusion is the artistic object's subject and predicate, its means of doing and the thing done; the model-illusion is a locked-room mystery, a manifest subjectivity, ontologically forgetful, absent the necessity of proof in the appearance of a self-justified and pleasurable aesthetically rule-bound totality. (Theater is unable to prove either [its] reality or the illusion it projects, since illusion requires no proof. At the same time, theater fetishizes causality so as to give the appearance of rule-following. However, predicating cause does not constitute proof, so much as it manifests the desire for there *to be* proof. Within the closed system of representation, desire becomes the subject of a new predicate—pleasure [and displeasure].) The model is, in and of itself, exemplary, meaning that it not only has and holds value—it is evaluative. The model is both a repository of rules and a tastemaker and lawgiver. It is a noirish hat, when hats are and are no longer in fashion. This hat floats through frames, creating a mental composite from a set of particulars that do not even need to add up to achieve a sum total, or alternatively, do not add up at all because they form a system and not a mere aggregate.[70] (A detective in *Somewhere in the Night* [dir. Joseph L. Mankiewicz, 1946] says that he never takes his hat off because "if you have to shoot a guy, you don't want to be holding a hat in your hand. Seems the movies was right.") To my amazement, as the small (model) plane becomes big (life-size), as perhaps only one in a series of noir hats or as one such hat in a series of frames, I think that I am seeing my modeling of an idea land, as it were, artfully, as the fulfillment of some previously unintelligible intuition.

Another world is not announced in this landing, but the sign of another system perhaps is. The vexed seriality of small and big connotes some new causality. That the object arrived as an artful retelling of nature is unsurprising given the mind's need for systemicity, which, Kant tells us, art imposes upon nature to help fulfill this need.[71] The world also being *a* world but a world not necessarily being *the* world, it remains for us to judge when a system and a world are commensurate in figurative size and scale. If there is a system that is perhaps *the* system, then we are always seeing the incommensurabilty of that system with our view of the world, perception being only a partial understanding congealed into a judgment shaped like a world. Is our intuition that other worlds exist within this world merely this world's various systems coming teasingly-episodically into view (sometimes onstage, often in the movies)? Does the world model the systems by which it is known in the form of other worlds? Does this manifold modeling compensate for man's inability to cognize an absolute a priori of nature's and our own purposive existence? Does such modeling represent our attempt "to actualize the world through our acts"?[72] Even or even especially the dead men serving as protagonists in films noir are moved by this intention that is, in a (fictional) sense, stronger than death. The overdubbed first-person narration of dead, soon-to-be-dead, and virtually dead men and women who populate this book requires the mechanism of the flashback (to which I will return) as a way of systematically and cynically rewinding the mechanism of time.

A Brief Epistemology of the Shadow and the Slap

In *The Creation of the World or Globalization*, Jean-Luc Nancy bemoans the loss of "the [world's] capacity to 'form a world' [*faire monde*]. It seems only to have gained that capacity of proliferating, to the extent of its means, the 'unworld' [*immonde*], which, until now, and whatever one may think of retrospective illusions, has never in history impacted the totality of the orb to such an extent. In the end, everything takes place as if the world affected and permeated itself with a death drive that soon would have nothing else to destroy than the world itself." Nancy sees the signs of this in the "dissipation of certainties, images and identities of what the world was with its parts and humanity with its characteristics." Certainly there is nothing new in what has been a recurring complaint, along with other signs Nancy cites such as "the indefinite growth of techno-science, of a correlative exponential growth of populations, of a worsening of inequalities of all sorts within these populations—economic, biological, and cultural," but it seems now more than ever that the ever-shrinking, globalized world, in no longer being able to tell us, even representationally, what "[all] the world is. . . . ," is that much closer to breaking apart as a concept.[73]

By contrast, the aphotic world that film noir depicts as being likewise permeated with a death drive is, signing in and through shadow, so conscious and citational of its own dissolution and demise as to suggest an anxiety disguised as a desire for a premature end. Film noir offers a sort of complaint that contributes to making the world small in the images, signs, representations, types, and motifs it obsessively employs to create a perverse stand-alone world at odds with the larger world it is meant to represent. Noir takes the world personally because it makes its own world, and yet in making its own world it manufactures the illusion that the individual is powerless to do anything to escape this world of his own creation. And yet in this it shares something with philosophy, which, Levinas states, "is the intrigue of cognition, the adventure of experience between clarity and obscurity." In this shadowy in-between space, people, thoughts, and things are lost or else are revealed in much the same way that darkness is made visible.[74] Philosophy is largely responsible for pushing or else framing "ontology as obsession," of calling the question of being without resolution in terms of light and dark, proof or merely theme, reifying the agony of being toward non-being.[75] Noir tropes such as the doomed man and the femme fatale represent the inevitable inability of a created world to disentangle itself from its own fatal meaning, the very meaning that Nancy suggests constitutes a world. Nancy, whose vision of the world is not particularly or specifically (post-)noirish, acknowledges that, although the world's destroying itself must be taken as an operative premise for any thinking we might do about the world as well as a fact, "we do not exactly know what 'to destroy' means, nor which world is destroying itself."[76] To this, we might offer film noir as depicting a world whose demise precedes it like an anticipatory shadow and whose characteristic omniscient (all- and already-knowing) voice-over flashbacks allow the destroyed world to be de-storied, even as its own more intimate world reconstituted by and from images asserts its spectral presence.

When Blanchot describes the image as "not the same thing [object] distanced, but that thing as distancing, the present thing in its absence, the thing graspable because ungraspable, appearing as something that has disappeared, the return of something that does not come back," he could be describing a shadow, which is, of course, the image as distancing at once incarnated and de-storied. The shadow is the dark inverse of the reflection, but likewise an image, a "presence freed from existence, form without matter," Husserl's "inauthentic cogito" (a cogito that is not "actually positing"). The shadow constitutes death revisiting place, this noirish return being a sort of recidivism, the inescapability of one's life in/as crime, the shadow of a doubt, of guilt expressed in various amnesiac scenarios in which shadows ubiquitously appear as what Blanchot might call "the prolixity of the not-true."[77] The shadow is a sign of displaced personhood in film noir. Noir shadows lead us back from mere image to (self-)consciousness and as such return us to being conscious and to the contentiously evidential in/determinacy of the body being "there" in terms of what the body, like any object, "actually" *is*. In this narrative recognition process a name hails its body like that body's shadow, enfolding future and past into the present, only not seamlessly, so that the labor of making something what it is remains stubbornly visible, like a living corpse that is no longer itself ("formerly" so inadequately perceived) at a distance.

Like the shadow (and its enabling chiaroscuro lighting), the ubiquitous slap of the face in film noir, is, despite appearance, less directional than citational, part of the lingua franca that transcends mere style, or makes of style something more than it merely is (like the aforementioned noir hat). I would relate the slap to what Deleuze and Guattari call a "monument," whose action is not memory-creation but instead "fabulation."[78] The slap confabulates sight and sensation into an event, a composite of percept (recognition by the senses of an external object, or action) and affect (demonstration, possibly even divorced from the feeling of something taking place). The slap is not only something; it *becomes* something. It "makes a being of sensation," a compound-counterpoint of relation, and in so doing it demonstrates conduct unbecoming in its overstatement of the situation at hand.[79] Hysteria and hyperbole provoke recognition to face performance, which is to say an act of mimetic remembrance. But as in a syncope, the slap in itself can contain no memory in or of the actual moment. In this regard, it may preview what it's like to experience one's own death in its Levinasian, "homicidal directness . . . traced out as the trajectory of the blow [intentionally] delivered and the arrow that kills."[80] If, as Levinas contends, the face of the other interrupts consciousness's certainty in its "ontological perseverance or its being-toward-death," whatever joy there is in this is riddled with melancholy.[81] The slap is an event that is both intimate and thwarts intimacy. The noir slap becomes a percept, much as "it is not perception of the moor in [Thomas] Hardy but the moor as percept."[82] Born of flesh and to flesh returned, like flesh (in Deleuze and Guattari's construction) the slap "is only the developer which disappears in what it develops: the compound of sensation." The slap is also a suddenness, a striking like that of a clock that in announcing time, stops it while defining it as being diachronic, as diachronic or interrupted being.[83] The slap to the face calls into being the suffering of the norm as being in some sense unpredictable, unreal. The slap is an act and form of wor(l)d-limit.

In *Criss Cross* (dir. Robert Siodmark, 1948), protagonist Steve Thompson's younger brother corners his girlfriend and when she refuses his advances, he acts like he is getting ready to slap her across the face backhanded. His "acting like" is both preparatory and citational, as if intended not for the face before him but for the face of silent witnessing ("the silent command of the face"), a backhanded slap speaking to a certain power of misdirection. The face stops the slap by showing its vulnerability in the face of violence, signaling the truth of Levinas's statement that "what distinguishes the face in its status from all known objects comes from its contradictory nature. It is all weakness and all authority."[84] It is, in a sense, the phantom face of "precariousness" that elicits the phantom backhanded slap, which in turn functions like a time stamp (21:33) on the rough cut of a film taken from a life whose reality claim makes us vulnerable to what is to come.[85]

The slap does not always mean the same thing in film noir, and people are slapped in many films that are not noir, but everywhere and only in film noir is the slap an *episteme*. In noir, characters slap and are slapped both openhandedly and backhandedly, by unseen people who are out of frame, and with coffeepots with their scalding hot contents along with other objects that take the place of human hands. (In *Raw Deal*, dir. Anthony Mann, 1948, a gangster throws a flaming pan of what looks like cherries jubilee in a woman's face.) People are slapped once or multiple times (two and three times being the most common, since a single slap of one cheek is merely decorous, a show of offense having been given or taken.) There is then an articulated language of the slap that while it begins with gender specificity (men slapping women) is turned around enough times (women slapping men, men slapping other men, women slapping other women) that it can be played for different effect. The slap is not just an effect, though; it's a signature. It encapsulates the genre's sense of humanity's animal-like entrapment and the inability to separate love from a desire that can too easily turn violent and become self-loathing. It may also speak to or even expose momentarily what Blanchot calls "the casuistry of relations," which opposes Levinas's belief in the necessary fraternity of the face-to-face, the self and the other's alterity.[86] The slap not only disarticulates thought and meaning as a violent form of inter-human disassociation. The slap is as flustered in its execution and its effect as a right hand being offered to another who removes his left glove and shakes with his gloved right hand.[87]

We do not merely see or experience the slap; we *become* the slap, its violent shaking and destabilizing of the world. Wor(l)ds fail. The slap causes the entire picture to shudder, or more precisely it is the shuddering of the picture that the slap articulates as a character and an observer's internal shuddering inside the picture. In the same way, the shadow does not just double the human figure. The physical character (which is, after all, only rumored to be physical on film) is configured by the darkness that the film brings to light, making the question "what came first, the man or his shadow?" moot or possibly rhetorical. (Film noir instructs the actor to remain in shadow; the stage instructs the actor to find his light.) With the slap, in the slap we become animal even as the slap is itself an expression of the landscape of the film and its world. We become the landscape of the film and in so doing we lose a bit and a sense of our humanity to the machine, a fact that the reflexive nature of slap and recoil, slap and counter-slap articulates without wasting words. "What is the meaning of this?"—the question posed by the recipient of the slap—is nearly always rhetorical, and the expression that is captured on his face is priceless, without value.

The stage room pays death its poor man's wage. Film exposes the limit of the frame fatale. This is reinforced by the cine-figure's patented walk to the frame's edge, here synonymous with the edge of disappearance, the point at which the figure would fall off the stage, at least the stage that I have constructed inside my mind. But at the point of disappearance, there is nearly always the call—to return, to reinvest in the picture. It is, in a sense, the call of the frame itself. The frame says "Just a moment." And in this, there is an expansion of/in every frame; there is a call that names the picture and the inside as such. The "as such" is a paradoxical double naming of what a thing is in itself and what it only appears to be. So what? No death? In discussing Leibniz, Badiou frames the notion that there can be no nothingness in the world. The world is, in fact, synonymous with *non*-nothingness. Since we are in and of the world, we cannot, as we are mentally constituted, merely cease to exist. And yet we die. Death does not then affect being so much as appearing. Being is, after all, being *something*. There is no being *nothing*, except perhaps as a form of mental aberration. The frame and the stage (the one being an imbrication of the other) cue the aporia of death, as a materialized non-presence. They allow for the self-contesting possibility that seeing is believing and also that we cannot believe what we see. Stage realism, which I consider to be an oxymoron, is always bursting at the "seems," even as the rooms it articulates as being physically manifest threaten to burst at the seams with what cannot be so directly said or seen. The stage, realism's defenders say, would show more but there are appearances to keep up and appearance to consider. The aporia of appearance is by definition inescapable, but its very impassibility is a function of the disappearance it likewise unfolds.

Someone shouts, "Action!" and the clapboard marking the scene snaps shut, making the figurative sound of a slapped face. There is in this a facial eclipse, from which you want to turn away but cannot, away from this shocking of countenance into alterity, into a dumb response to a violent demand. "Is anyone watching?" The sound alerts the actor or rather the re-actor to the audience as a possibility. The audience is less astonished to see what they have seen, since they are astonished at being in the right place at the right time to witness the posing of the spatial question that is the nominal scene. The slapping sound that announces the scene provides a shock to the system that the system not only withstands but absorbs, takes upon itself to draw to the audience's attention. The film wants to speak rhetorically, like an analysand to an analyst, about what it knows about itself at every stage. It wants to tell you that it is of two minds and that the camera eye is not monocular but compound, like a fly on the surface of an invisible fourth wall.

The slap bruises the surface so it shows—darkening and widening the surface, exposing its shadows, crooking its angles, fish-eyeing its body blows, spreading its mysteries. Ears are slapped deaf, eyes are slapped blind and mouths are slapped dumb, at least figuratively speaking (the private investigator Philip Marlowe is blindfolded in *Murder, My Sweet* and the former criminal Jeff Bailey is partnered with a deaf mute in *Out of the Past*).[88] Watching from the shadows, you know when you see someone get slapped that you are seeing *something*. But what is the something you are seeing? What are you being told? "Wake up!" Is that it? Are you dreaming—sleeping through the performance or performing your own sleepless state? You feel yourself to be trapped in a dark corner without knowing whether or not you are concealed. Just then, when you might discover whether or not you are acting . . . BLACKOUT. Then suddenly a frame of light appears and someone runs through it. Is it you or the person who slapped you? You hear what you think is a shout and run through the door. Death follows. . . .

The Ontology of the Monad

I am slapped into consciousness, newborn. Someone's hands catch me as I enter what Deleuze has called "a world of captures instead of closures.[89] It is 1948, the year of *The Big Clock* (dir. John Farrow). My clock starts then. The film's and my life's metonymic namesake ticks away and so recounts a simultaneous sense of dis/continuity, of death in life. My film surrogate wonders ontologically, "What happens if I get inside of the clock and the [night] watchman's [a noir figure's] there?" The big clock is "set so that you can tell the time anywhere on earth," so that the anytime/anywhere the watchman materializes as ubiquity (when is the watchman not "on the clock" and when is the clock not "on"—like an actor, when not being watched?). This ubiquity is what Borges called, in what could be but is not in relation to film noir, "the unanimous night."[90] Attempting to escape capture, *The Big Clock*'s time-obsessed killer (and the protagonist's boss) falls to his death down an elevator shaft. He makes it down to the bottom in no time flat, which only figuratively stands in for no time at all.

It's unanimous, then, the baroque night always waiting to end and never ending. This is the aspirational monad's mise-en-scène of spectral life-capture, the Borgesian "unbearable lucidity of insomnia."[91] The clockwork monad is not just something that exists but something that expresses a condition, that is conditional, and, in my appropriation, a simplicity that is also a totality to which human minds and bodies can and do aspire. This aspirational monad-in-the-making is not part of Leibniz's original concept but is, in fact, a reimagining of what for him was a sort of elemental aspirant to a life that only builds upon it (the monad) to reach its complexity. Like the flashback thinking that film noir and this book employ, I have figuratively switched the reels and allowed characters to actually (in the context of fictions) *be* monads from the start, as they might be dead from the start, to have realized a form to which they aspire in a narrative that features the form but conceals their and the form's aspiration.

"In Leibniz, the monad is not only the human soul; it is also the archetype of all being."[92] A monad in my coinage can (uncharacteristically) be insomniac and hypochondriacal (i.e., not clinically pathological)—whatever it is that puts its singularity to the test in the contested but symbiotic relationship between mind and body not at home in the world. Hypochondria, for example, constitutes a mind-body relationship crisis in that either it allows the body embarrassed direct address or else allows the mind to manifest an embodiedness that the body might not otherwise express. I recognize the irresponsibility of such usage but trust that performing the obverse of Wittgenstein's putting the world before the self, that is, putting the self before the world but with a counter-action of self-denial in retreat from the world, will expose different pictures and familiar pictures in different light. I have opted not only to give the monad a body but also to give it (back) its dreams. The world that some call objective is rendered conditional once necessity becomes hypothetical. The construction "if this . . . then . . . that" only sounds logical when it is applied as a proof.[93]

Absolute interiority, if it really exists, can, after all, only be known *in relation to* the self. It stands ("I" dare say) to reason. Herein lies the uninflected (with personal melancholia) self-enjoyment of which Deleuze after Leibniz speaks—a sort of self-bonding, whether or not this appears to the outside world like a semaphore, an aleph, or as an anthroposophic sign. In keeping with my overall sense of the baroque, the monad is an "is" that *does*. Still, Deleuze allows that "the presence of the world within me [as a monad], my being-for the world, is an 'anxiousness' (being on the lookout)." And even "the small solicitations of anxiety . . . are integrated in a pleasure that can be continued, prolonged, renewed, multiplied; that can proliferate, be reflexive and attractive for other accords, that give us the force to go further and further."[94] And how could it be otherwise, since to be without anxiety I could not really be myself or know anything else to be un/real?

The Considered Illusion of Flashing Back

> The fact is that consciousness is by nature the locus of an illusion. Its nature is that it registers effects, but it knows nothing of causes.
>
> —Gilles Deleuze, *Spinoza: Practical Philosophy*

The noir flashback is an attempt to locate and identify a first cause in the crisis moment of logic's breakdown. I use "first cause" here not as a basis for psychological behavior but as a philosophical indicator of how a particular world was made, what it was made from as an idea. Robert B. Ray writes: "The *noir* protagonists' relentless search for the moment where things had begun to go bad was an image of the American postwar mood—vaguely disillusioned, convinced that somewhere along the line the wrong turn had been taken, intuitively aware of the power of historical determinism for perhaps the first time in the nation's history."[95] While this statement does not rise to the level of philosophical first cause, of how the world is made, it does suggest that the noir flashback (which became decidedly more baroque in its complexity and more mannerist in its novelty and overuse) responds to the question of worldview. The philosophical question of origin on some level recapitulates the question of the origin of philosophy itself, which nets this observation of great relevance to this study: "It appears that at its origin philosophy depends on a theatrical coup de force: there is the simple minimal device which defines the theatre, the curtain, which serves as a screen, but a curtain not to be raised, not for many years—philosophy appears as the art of an actor behind the curtain."[96] The flashback is a device that throws spatiotemporal presence into question and into crisis. It may seek to illustrate first cause but as often produces a new effect, since it compels the person who experiences it to relive the experience of the first time and redoubles the sense of residue and remainder in him that went looking for a cause in the first place. The past is lived *through* the first time and lived *as* the second time. This is where performance comes in, which is only proper since the flashback is nominally a re-creation in present time of what only appears to be the past and of the past in what only appears to be (the) present. Taking effects for causes is what is called *the illusion of final causes*.[97]

With this in mind, the theatrical device of the dream is not so much shown in flashback but is nevertheless in the play of first and second times. As per Walter Benjamin, in Calderón de la Barca's Spanish baroque drama *Life Is a Dream* (1635) allegory overwhelms history, as Segismund's story and what it teaches us usurps royal power and logical plan. Segismund, the proto-noir antihero, succeeds in vanquishing his fate (the mechanics of baroque antithesis) the *second* time, because he is only conscious of his allegorical role the second time around and so performs his role according to the rules that his allegorical tale dictates that he follow. This is the reason why he is able to succeed his father to the throne rather than owing to the accident of (royal birth), because history as he knows it is baroque, discontinuous. In history, Segismund rots in a cave unknown to himself. In allegory, he emerges from the cave and makes his rightful claim to self-knowledge. He must visit the court twice not so much to learn from his mistakes or to awaken from a dream, since, as both Descartes and Pascal attested, there is no proof of being awake or in a dream. Segismund returns to court a second time to live *as* rather than live *through*, not to reenact history (otherwise he would throw a *second* man out the window) but to fulfill the symbolic value given to him in allegory.

The uncanny is rooted in the notion of "the return," which Freud describes as "that species of the frightening that goes back to what was once well known and had long been familiar." Freud was of course referring to a long reach back to the infantile rather than a story arc, a reversible, retrievable narrative in our lives. That being said, there is something profoundly uncanny in a corpse's recollection of even a part of its life as in *Sunset Boulevard* or a living corpse's retracing the steps leading up to its imminent demise in *D.O.A.* (dir. Rudolph Maté, 1950). For that matter, the flashback in general marks an impossible return that though it says in effect, "if memory serves," does not so much serve memory as exposes it in a series of pictures that belies series, that lies about series as a construction of memory which is itself a construction. The "uncanny valley," a term used by animators to describe the precipice into which too-close-to-real-life images tumble into spectatorial "revulsion," casts its shadow across flashback narrative storytelling that ventures back only so far as the point of incursion of some deadly virus that will distort and destroy the life of the subject.[98] The subject becomes host to the flashback that is itself viral in its depth-seeking sequentiality, its targeted inversion of life-norms, the animating presence of his death drive. The subject at some point invariably turns to regard himself in the figurative mirror the flashback provides and asks, "Can that really be me?" and "Am I really capable of this?" and even, "Why can't I stop myself from doing this?" The answer to this last question is, of course, because what I am doing is necessitated by the flashback itself, which once it begins cannot be halted in its inexorable movement toward a present that has in fact already been achieved. You have already flipped the doomsday switch.

Flashback offers the antithesis of the cleanskin (a new identity) or re-credentialization of one's personal identity. It affirms who you *were* rather than who you no longer wish to be. The flashback makes the present recognizable, comprehensible. The cleanskin renders one unrecognizable as oneself and one's actual past no longer recognizable because it disappears into a new version of where you were and what you did when you were someone other than who you really are. The flashback shows the rub. The cleanskin rubs everything away that no longer wants to be seen. When *Dark Passage*'s (dir. Delmer Daves, 1947) initially faceless protagonist is surgically transformed into Humphrey Bogart's iconic noir countenance, for example, the revelation of "Bogart" is uncanny in that it exposes the über-familiarity of the actor's celebrity as being not already achieved but rather arrived at, despite the advance publicity of his celebrity's appearance in the film. This is then the rub that also rubs away and is another signature of the flashback.

Flashback is a metapoetic (self-transformative) narrative device, a representation of what Blanchot calls "the death that is the impossibility of dying."[99] The dramatic protagonist narrating the flashback cannot die in the flashback, although he often dies shortly after bringing his narrative up to "the present." Blanchot observes that "the tale is not the narration of an event, but that event itself, the approach to that event, the place where that event is made to happen—an event which is yet to come and through whose power of attraction the tale can hope to come into being too."[100] Even more to the point, the protagonist does not die in the flashback owing to the shifting point of contact between his life and death: "The tale is a movement toward a point, a point which is not only unknown, obscure, foreign, but such that apart from this movement it does not seem to have any real prior existence, and yet it is so imperious that the tale derives its power of attraction only from this point, so that it cannot even 'begin' before reaching it—and yet only the tale and the unpredictable movement of the tale creates the space where the point becomes real, powerful and alluring."[101] In other words, you can't kill what you can't catch, and you can't catch "it" because it cannot be reached until the narrative that generates it and of which it is generative is complete. "It" does not exist as a recognizable entity and can only be mistaken for the human subject about whom the tale is told. And you cannot kill the tale itself, because without it there is nothing.[102]

As with the sense of there being nothing to kill, how can we really even die when we are living in fictional time? And if we cannot really die, what exactly is it that we are recalling? In this regard, the flashback is not so much a function of actual recall as it is the lived experience of its own story-making structure. We do not then dream to awaken our minds to their unconscious behaviors but rather as metapoetic commentaries on the unreality that structures and stands in for our lives. With this in mind, the insomnia to which I allude offers a "despair verging upon rapture," a way of discovering and experiencing the secret that our daily lives and nightly dreams whisper in our uncomprehending ears.[103] We cannot comprehend what we fear and what we fear most is being driven mad by the acknowledgment of an unreality that cannot be dismissed as being merely a Siren's call—a dismissal to make the Sirens themselves weep real tears.

2

✦

House

> The epistemology of the house remains entirely commensurate with its size.
>
> —Mark Z. Danielewski, *House of Leaves*

Metathesiophobia

Two of Kant's initiatory relational images in the *Critique of Pure Reason*, the body that is heavy and the tumbled-down house, run through the content of the ensuing chapters, from *Double Indemnity*'s Walter Neff to *Phaedra*'s eponymous antiheroine.[1] The person who is himself an appearance is self-undermining and fashions space and time to reflect this condition. This person's days are numbered, as are they in the Kantian sense that "*whatever is conscious of the numerical identity of itself at different times is insofar a **person**.*" I myself have reached the age where the "where" compresses no less self-evidently than the "when." The ground rises up to push the toes and scrape the heels of my shoes, the walls move in to brush against my elbows, and all objects are closer than they appear to be and to non-being. Space seems everywhere to be making room for another occupant in my place and is dropping less-than-subtle hints in falls, breaches, and breakages in the immediate, embodied environment that will not let me (just) pass.

And yet, I have a recurring dream of a house in which I live that grows and grows without ever being completed. The workmen, who started building onto the house, stopped showing up. All that remains is an infinite corridor (there are no rooms) leading to whatever the house is/was eventually supposed to be, through which an anxiety dream-within-a-dream about waiting plays upon my interior, mental scrim. In the course of thinking through building and dwelling as ways of "thinking as," Heidegger may have found a way out of the conundrum of (the) room as being a measure of some sort of failed expectancy. "A space," he said, "is something that has been made room for, something that has been freed, namely within a boundary, Greek *peras*." By translating the contained singularity of a "room [of or that]" into the general openness and potentiality of "room for," particularity is rendered relational, even somewhat ambiguous, allowing us to have our boundaries ("Space is in essence that for which room has been made, and which is let into its bounds") and to *not* have them too ("That for which room is made is always granted"). Furthermore, Heidegger writes, "a boundary is not that at which something stops but, as the Greeks recognized, the boundary is that from which something *begins its essential unfolding*."[2] The proto-Deleuzean project, specific to his discussion of the baroque, in which foldings and unfoldings drape and overlay rather than solidify and cut off, restrain, again recalls Heideggerian lexography, this time in German where "to free actually means to spare. . . . *The fundamental character of dwelling is this sparing*."[3] Having room for is to have room to spare but also to be spared, safeguarded, free—from the wait, perhaps, but for who or what to arrive? The dreaded sleepless morning . . . or the more dreaded unanimous night?

"Thinking," Hegel said (in attempting to satisfy its "highest inwardness," which he likens to spirit) "gets entangled in contradictions; that is to say, it loses itself in the fixed non-identity between thoughts, and therefore it does not reach itself" and yet "thinking will not give up, but remains faithful to itself, even in this consciousness of its being at home with itself, '*so that it may overcome*.'"[4] My oneiric house is possibly and nevertheless an exercise in thwarted self-maintaining and self-overcoming (very much obsessive-compulsively biting its own oneiric tale), an extension of the incapacity that is in-dwelling. Still, my thinking, proper to dreaming (and to writing), will not give up on what it cannot realize except as a mental representation. But because this representational idea allegedly aspires to become a materialized form imbued with real content (as evidenced by my frustration both inside and outside the form), the dream reveals itself as a masked surrogate reality as opposed to an actual unreality imbricated with waking life. There is always a better, although not easier way, or else the same way made to seem better that is harder still. *I* am not so free as Hegel imagines in *his* dreams.

Ideas that obsess us leave little room for freedom. We create imitations of imitations and of intimations as well. We draw frames inside of frames and outside of frames too. Time speeds up and space slows down. "Room for" turns back into room behind (there is no beyond) the proscenium frame that grows more arch, ironic, self-parodying, and self-revealing as it pulls the house toward it from the other side, where most of the people are. The house in which I actually live is an inexact double of another house up the road that has a river running through its basement. Kant uses a house and a body of water as stand-ins for empirical intuition (of solidity) and apprehension (of fluidity), respectively. These two states stand in relationship to time, which is defined in human terms as alteration. "It is only in time that both contradictorily opposed determinations can be met with in the same thing, that is, *one after the other*."

My mind may be following Kant's directive to "make the successive existence of ourselves in different states comprehensible by means of outer intuition."[5] Thus, the incompleteness, the arbitrariness and non-rule-following of outer actions that cannot be parsed except as absences in time reveal not a real house but rather the question of whether and to what extent I am at home in relation to an outside world here rendered as a rough transparency of my own interiority. Kant sees drawing in the shape of a house as a way of synthesizing thought and inner sense. The house of which I dream is not so much a dream as it is a question in the form of a dream that asks whether I can think something I know has shape without drawing it in my head; whether representation can constitute thought without an act; and whether I can escape the apprehension of apparent freedom in the paradoxically limiting form of space and its placement in and as the equally self-limiting fiction of time, inclusive of causality. The spontaneously expanding but unconstructed house challenges once again the intelligibility, even the possibility of there being a grounding to thought beyond the appearance of thought as representation. That said, why *can't* my mind draw a room? Do I fear that it will be as mentally airtight as a syllogism or only as airtight as a syllogism appears to be? Do I suspect that on closer inspection the lines from which the house is assembled will turn out not to be lines at all but rather strings of numbers, more code of my mind's own design that it fears to break, breaking defining a limit and not a breaking free? A room suffers completion, and so then must I.

Leibniz, whose baroque philosophy gave Deleuze the bends if not the folds, takes up the possibility of space that is only hypothetically necessary and so does not really exist. Although the context for his thinking, like that of Spinoza and Pascal in the same period, is God, what Leibniz more than the others is describing enables the appearance of dream space that does not entirely escape logic but which helps to make the mind free of ironclad necessity. Leibniz states that, "a possible thing is something with some essence or reality, that is, something that can be distinctly understood. For example, a pentagon would remain possible even if we were to imagine that no exact pentagon ever was or would be in nature." Despite his belief in the certainty of God's existence and that all other existences are contingent upon it, Leibniz gives human consciousness its due and the imagination its marching orders.[6] A mathematician by training, Leibniz thought in terms of shapes, and shapes do not always immediately reveal what they are shapes *of* in any functional sense. You don't have to dream a thing for its ambiguousness to take shape, to be shapely. And sometimes, without knowing it, you are making room for a labyrinth, the very labyrinth you are already in, a continuous line that only looks like a corridor stretching out ahead of you when it is really folding in. And sometimes it's a dark room you don't know you are in until the door opens to light. The last time I physically entered a maze, I suffered a panic attack not because I was lost and feared not being able to find my way out, but because all the bodies rushing toward me from the dead ends, the false exits they had already reached, made it seem impossible for me even to move forward. I was not myself waiting for the builders of my house extension to return. I *was* the builder who could not return, because there was no means to move ahead. I was on the edge of something, perhaps "the precipice" from which Leibniz was brought back by "the consideration of possibles, which are not, were not, and will not be."[7]

"We have all these forms in mind" may be recited as a benediction over *Dead of Night* (dirs. Alberto Cavalcanti, Robert Hamer, Basil Dearden, Charles Crichton, 1945), in which the architect Walter Craig reenters a house he built but never visited with the idea of building on to it. Discovering a nook where there is a place to hang his overcoat, Craig realizes that he has dreamed this house before.[8] On the face of it, this is what an architect does. But Craig has also *dreamed all of the people in the house* before as well. The various houseguests try to rationalize Craig's dream as having drawn upon fragments from real waking life, such as newspaper photos in which one or the other of them may have appeared. "Yes, but why should I always dream about meeting you altogether, here, in this room?" Craig counters. There is in this something of the baroque concept formulated by Leibniz in which God, the great architect, created a world in which he recognizes all of his subjects but, as with the evil that men do, the individual's actions result from his own free will. In this particular case, Craig's preoccupation with his own mortality (no wonder he first notices a place for hanging) may lead him to offer counter-evidence to God's economical and sublime geometry. Leibniz called this counter-logical performance that the individual perceives as being an intuitive vision, "the ridiculous art of geomancy," suggesting a neological fusion of geometry and necromancy, or communicating with the dead—and with yourself as if you were dead.[9] The title *Dead of Night* is an indicator not only of dreamtime but of the identities of the dreamed-of characters as being dead or, at the very least, sleepwalkers.

Hypnophobia

At the start of *Double Indemnity* (dir. Billy Wilder, 1944), the badly wounded insurance salesman Walter Neff returns to his office while the custodial night shift is at work in what suggests a virtual night-for-day inversion of a normal sleep schedule. Inside the Dietrichson home, where Neff has gone about getting his agency's client to renew his auto insurance, Neff steps into the living room to wait for Phyllis, the client's attractive wife. Neff's voice-over, extrapolated from his diegetic recitation of his story into a Dictaphone (manifesting voice-over as a narrative mechanism) that structures the film's flashback sequencing, tells his unseen office colleague, the insurance claims investigator Barton Keyes: "The living room was still stuffy from last night's cigars. The windows were closed and the sunshine coming in through the Venetian blinds showed up the dust in the air." Striated light (the kind that blinds produce/let in) and colloidal dust or smoke (as in the drug hallucination scene in *Murder, My Sweet* to which I will return) are the lingua franca of film noir, sculpting the room on the inside, with the outside serving only as a referent. Noir's metaphor-and simile-laden interiority further crowds into interior spaces such as rooms and cars. The outside of Phyllis's house (no. 4760, high enough to be a prospective insurance policy number) smells like honeysuckle to Neff but, retrospectively and in concert with the perfume she wears but (only) says she cannot recall, smells also like death.

Phyllis is descending the stairs in a mental time loop, and Neff is ogling her like a camera from foot to head after the decadent fashion that speaks to inversion and redoubling to the point of sensual ennui. He is especially taken with the anklet she wears, which, she says, bears her name (and her fragrance). He even more especially likes "the way it cut into her ankle." The pleasurably painful first impression that the anklet makes will ghost them both to their deaths before their time(s). Indeed, our first glimpse of Neff has already seen him ghost-walking into the Pacific (All Risk Insurance Company) in the dead of night, fatally chest-wounded which the coat draped over his shoulders vainly tries to hide, looking for all the world like William Holden, with a coat draped over his shoulders, will look on his way into the dead pool in *Sunset Boulevard*.

After Neff rejects Phyllis's veiled proposition to help her with her husband's murder and write an accident insurance policy on him without his knowledge, he leaves the house in a hurry, his shadow less so. So when Neff returns to his apartment, smoking in the dark, lit only by a light in his gridded window, he realizes that he never walked out on Phyllis or of that room at all. They are still very much with him, like a scent that does not so much linger in the air after you've gone but follows you home. The last thing Neff did before exiting Phyllis's house was to don his hat, so when she drops by his place to return it, we sense a frame. The non-hat is not an object but an instigation that performs a greater agency than Neff's real hat could show and he could sense. Thus far, Phyllis is defined as being married and Neff not so. So, when we spy a wedding ring on his left ring finger, we see much more sharply the labyrinth in the frame that discontinuity provides. Neff's wedding ring might respond in turn to Phyllis-Ariadne's anklet's "*I am your labyrinth*." With this, Dionysus-Neff "offers himself in turn as a maze for [Ariadne] to penetrate and retrace with her thread." In "this reciprocity . . . each is the container or labyrinth of the other," and in each labyrinth something like sleep appears to be lost.[10]

"Here, take his hat," Neff later instructs Phyllis after laying Mr. Dietrichson's corpse across the railroad tracks as part of his and Phyllis's executed plan. The hat that has been defined by its spectral dis/appearance finds its rightful owner in the dead man, a status that is accorded to both Dietrichson *and* Neff. In order to be left alone to perform Dietrichson's mock-suicidal leap off the back of a slow-moving caboose, Neff fakes having forgotten a cigar case in one of the other cars that he had not actually brought with him on to the train. The man whom Neff sends to retrieve the phantom cigar case (kindred of the non-hat), the jovial Mr. Jackson who had tried to strike up a conversation with Neff, later testifies about the spectral, faceless Mr. Dietrichson but, oddly, not about *not* finding the cigar case in question that was *not* there. Perhaps Jackson thought that (fake) Dietrichson only thought he left the cigar case in the next car when he really left it on *another* train which will be the *next* train to arrive. In a dream, Michel Leiris seems to remember an earlier dream in which something similar happened, only with a suitcase rather than with a cigar case. In another, not to say parallel dream, Georges Perec "recalls" boarding a train only to find his bags, and then his car missing. What he loses in continuity, Perec gains in correspondence, in this case between his (dream) itinerary and the metro, which is also here called the circle line.[11] These contrarian examples collectively erode logic but at the same time affirm the film's own insular counter-logic, so that when Neff is later summoned to Keyes's office he walks past Mr. Jackson smoking a cigar, the phantom cigar of the ghost-walking dead man whom Jackson still does not see before him (before him, as in foreseeing *his own death*?). This is a world in which Keyes can say that when a murder is committed by two people instead of one, "it is not twice as safe. It's ten times more dangerous." The numbers, in a sense, do not add up in logical sequence. Instead, they leap, as does the imagination. Keyes runs his numbers while smoking his ubiquitous cigar, defying the very odds ("not twice as safe" but "ten times more dangerous") that comprise the actuarial tables he knows proleptically by heart that forecast early death from smoking.

Perhaps Neff's ring is there to conspire with Phyllis's anklet to contrive (Cartesian) error through the senses and the particularity of an easier-to-consume part to the whole that reasonable thought represents. Or is this an instance of Leibnizian compossibility, which contests contradiction and error? The theory of compossibility says that a thing although clearly untrue in one world could be true in another, with the addendum that we do not always know what world we are in or looking at or how many worlds we are in or looking at simultaneously. Maybe Joe Gillis, lying face-down in Norma Desmond's swimming pool on Sunset at the beginning of his own flashback film six years later, has gotten his signals crossed in the retelling.

Neff tells Keyes via the Dictaphone that he let himself jump through Phyllis's hoop (ring) partially to see whether through his knowledge of the tricks of the insurance trade, he could "crook the house." Is beating the system anything like winning the betting pool on love, to double down on Neff's casino phrasing and Gillis's fluid demise? "Suddenly, the doorbell rings and the whole set-up is right there in the room with you," Neff now ruefully observes. The story's frame, though, is neither negative nor absent, so much as spectral, nonobjective, abstract, like Neff, who does not even allow himself to believe that he murdered a man either for his money or his wife, neither of which he now possesses in the end (which is, of course, the film's but not the story's beginning). Neff makes a point of saying this last part at the beginning of his extended recording of his live monologue, which he "supposes" the absent Keyes will call a confession when he hears it in the morning. Confess or not, it's all the same, cynical Joe Gillis would say. Either way, you're dead in the end . . . and from the beginning too.

When Neff turns down a job as Keyes's assistant, Keyes tells Neff that it turns out he is not smarter than the other men at the agency, "just taller." On the night of the murder, Neff, wearing the same color suit as Dietrichson so as to be able to double him, doubles up his taller body so it can fit unseen beneath the back seat of the car. On the same night, Phyllis tells her husband, who has one of his legs in a cast inside the death-car, "Remember what the doctor said. If you get careless, you might end up with a shorter leg." "So what," he says, "I could break the other one and match them up again." Neff, the subject who is nominally not there, whose flashback narrative is a doubling back, overhears all of this from inside his own overdub, as if cocooned inside a bad waking dream (his legs folded under him inside the small room-like magician's box). There he rehearses his performance as Dietrichson, the shorter man, whose legs do not match his own. Dietrichson and Neff unknowingly overhear each other's bodily dissociation from personal identity captured in Kierkegaard's story of the drunken barefooted peasant who because he was wearing new shoes and stockings did not recognize his legs when he awakened from sleep. He does not fear a cart running over them where he lies in the middle of the road because, he believes, the legs are not his.[12] When it comes time to don Dietrichson's clothes and plant the body, does Neff think for a moment about whether to position the body parallel to or across the railroad tracks, so that the next train that runs over does or does not sever the legs, making the dead man that much shorter and Neff that much less externally recognizable as being him(self)? This play of physical non-/correspondence bears witness to what Neff's narrative frame testimony tells us and tells him—namely, that he underestimated his ability to not lose sleep over losing himself. Narrative is for him a form not just of confession but of vigilance, a means of keeping himself awake and so alive.

Insurance companies employ actuarial tables to place table bets on whether a person will outlive his money. In the insurance game, bodies are made to be counted more than counted on to be there.[13] Does Neff think he can "crook the house" with a table that has two legs longer than the other(') s? Inside the car, Dietrichson is doing the talking for Neff, setting the stage for the unmatched legs performing the illusion of the ostensibly matched (like Phyllis and Neff) pair. This precise imprecision (and hypnophobe-speak) can likewise be heard in Neff's telling Phyllis that they can only meet at the same nondescript local market "sort of accidentally on purpose." The oral report that Neff makes to Keyes is, in apparitional fact, an explanation of how language and space alibi but also confess one another via correspondences that speak to the complex interiority of the mind that admits to doubt without contradiction. Neff is transitioning along correspondence's horizontal plane from possibility or acting according to a plan that could work to compossibility, which, in his case, translates into feeling that nothing could go wrong and that everything would go wrong at the same time, figuratively speaking. He can no longer hear his own footsteps, because even though he is alive, he feels that he is also already dead. His legs have shortened, as has his life expectancy, while Keyes's self-described "little man," his practiced intuition, is eating away at his insides because something does not make enough sense to be true. Joan Copjec calls this "little man" "a remnant of the Cartesian tradition: a somewhat hypochondriacal version of the *cogito*."[14] The compossible has no claim on Keyes, any more than it did on Descartes. It is unreasonable and so uninsurable.

Aquaphobia

"The last week in December, the rains came," Joe Gillis's voice-over intones, as he lies face down in the water. "A great big package of rain. Oversize, like everything else in California. It came right through the old roof of my room above the garage." The camera pans down from the courtyard where the rain has been depicted as falling to the room's ceiling imprinted with the shape of where the water has pooled. There is leakage. It is an impossible scenic passage in relation to the narrative—the courtyard is not, of course, located above the garage, making it impossible for the rain to flow through one location/scene to another, except of course, in the "crooked" house containing *two* garages, one belonging to the Dietrichsons and the other to Norma Desmond. The two share a trapped floor or ceiling, depending on your perspective and whether you believe that the water is flowing up or down.

The courtyard in which this rainy sequence started contains the estate's rectangular swimming pool, which was filled with water and with Joe Gillis photographed from below lying face down in the dead man's voice-over. The rectangular framing of where the voice pools allows us to see voice-over as the expression of a phantasmatic dis/continuity in relation to the body and to the corpse as the body's surplus at the start of a film that contemplates a figure's (Norma Desmond's) suspension in silent film long after the advent of the talking picture. Joe's corpse with its non-/acousmatic voice (i.e., we see the voice's source while knowing that it cannot be real) suspended inside/by the pool's rectangular frame allows us to see what we cannot know to be true, but nevertheless know via the baroque excess of the setup is being performed, has been staged. Later/earlier, the pool is empty when Joe first arrives at the estate and looks at it through a window in the house. What Joe can/not actually see at Sunset is what Gadamer might call "a reconstructed question [that] can never stand within its original horizon: for the historical horizon that circumscribed the reconstruction is not a truly comprehensive one." Neither he nor we truly know where and when we are. We do not question this indeterminacy. We question "namely to make things indeterminate," fluid, but again narrate our dreamlike fear of drowning in the very thing our minds devise.[15]

Joe had flinched and turned away from his first framed view of the pool, nominally because he saw some rats in it. Rats here represent neglect and decay, an after-ness. But it is this after-ness confused with a before-ness that Joe is also experiencing which produces in him (with the suddenness of a question) the syncope, the day-flash that is the surplus of nightmare, the flashback within which the future suddenly sparks before his eyes as if it has already arrived. Is this not what a premonition of one's own death "looks like"? He knows it in the way Polonius's voice-over from behind the arras recalls.

In the scene following the reveal of Joe's garage ceiling leakage, we see him walk across a room in Norma's house. The expensive camel hair overcoat Norma bought for Joe and that is now draped over his arm makes it appear like the leather bag he is carrying is floating in air, like it's being carried by a ghost. Joe is, after all, a ghost writer for a ghost, "Norma Desmond," as she was called back in the days when movie stars "had faces" (in the same way that ghosts do and do not).[16] The great room of Norma Desmond's mansion presents a multitude of framed photographic self-portraits, no one of which can capture the size of the pictures that she imagines she remembers. Norma and her butler Max project (only her own silent) films in her home on a screen hidden behind a larger-than-life-size framed painting of herself. (For the purposes of this study, "larger-than-life" cites a comparison that is real and particular and able to be captured in descriptive and representational terms. The "bigger-than-life" is a non-discernible and perhaps non-describable object that I argue brokers a relationship between the real to the unreal that retains a quality of abstraction.) This is their way of "crooking the house," preserving Norma's mansion and her film persona as a central feature of the back-lot reality of the old Hollywood studio system. Joe sees evidence of this while strolling through a back lot with the starstruck script reader and would-be writer Betsy Schaeffer under a perfect sky being painted above them by studio artists so that they can play her romantic version of their two-character scene. Among the guests at Norma's bridge nights is Buster Keaton (wearing his poker face for the wrong card game), whose career also was cut short by "the talkies." They had dead or neutral faces then too, Keaton's stone face acknowledges. Norma is not just a has-been of the cinema, she is what cinema is—both ghost and medium, always conjuring without ever really foreseeing anything beyond performance. Norma is no more life-sized than cinema is, but being human she is material and subject to decay despite her best efforts at (self-)preservation. Behind her dark glasses, her eyes peer into darkness, where film, fatality, and fatalism cohabit.

Norma is dead before she knows it; Joe already knows what "it" is only by being dead.

This is what happens when you get stuck inside a labyrinth and can't write your way out. When Joe finally walks out on Norma for good, he only gets as far as the swimming pool. The typewriter he is carrying doesn't make it that far. It's as if Joe is remembering how the word "prolepsis" is defined and illustrated:

> a. The assignment of something, such as an event or name, to a time that precedes it, as in *If you tell the cops, you're a dead man.*
> b. The use of a descriptive word in anticipation of the act or circumstances that would make it applicable, as *dry* in *They drained the lake dry*.[17]

The foregoing strikes particularly close to home, spectral Joe imagines. He is/was living in someone else's house, after all, when the cops discover(ed) him floating face-down in the pool, tipped to his state and location by his own flashback voice-over. Joe tells Norma he's a Sagittarius, whose symbol is a centaur—half man and half horse, a physical neologism, a compossible sign. When in this overlay of compossible worlds does it rain inside a room? When metaphor leaks into the narrative frame. However, the rain inside the room is also an event, and, as Borges asserts, "all things happen to *oneself*, and happen precisely, precisely *now*."[18] The impossibility of following a logical visual path for the water awakens our mind to the possibility of metaphorically linking and leaking language and image to and into thought-space. We have become the film's mechanism and its prisoner, within the house, the room, the pool, the floor or ceiling. Our spatiotemporal inclinations have become metaphysical reincarnations of what film in general and what these two films in particular (*Double Indemnity* and *Sunset Boulevard*) do.

Joe notices that there are no locks in the house. The doctor suggested it, Max tells Joe, given Norma's history of attempting suicide. When the lights are turned on in a room, the lock holes look like eyeholes and also like narrow-beam film projectors. When the lights go out, the lights in the eyes go out and the film goes off while Norma sleeps—the only time that it does, since Norma is dreaming her waking life as if it were the film Joe is writing aloud. It's not so much that the eyes go blind as the eyes stop looking, peering inside the next room with a paranoid conviction. When Norma throws a New Year's Eve party that turns out to be only for herself and Joe, he jokes that maybe they should blindfold the orchestra that is playing and break their champagne glasses over Max's head. Norma cites this blinding of the extras when she directs Joe not to run up the staircase, since the musicians will suspect (sense rather than see) that something is afoot. Ironically, the ornate mirrors in Norma's bedroom in which she lies in her post-suicidal state, reveal nothing but more ornateness. What we see is only the elaboration of surface, its non-depth, which is image. Joe's spec script *Dark Windows*, dug up by Betsy who wants to help him revise it, captures the impregnability of a surface that promises but does not deliver transparency. Betsy tells Joe that the only scene she likes in his screenplay is the courtroom *flashback*.

Old Hollywood studio back lots were crisscrossed by costumed actors and extras and by production staff members—carpenters, costumers, prop-makers, electricians, and the like—conveying frames and scenic illusions from one soundstage and from one film to another like inside a composite dream. A Roman gladiator or a biblical prophet might momentarily cross paths with a set for Wyatt Earp's Tombstone or George Bailey's Bedford Falls and so for a moment appear to be magically and anomalously transported there. Like-wise, an extra might be mistaken for a star and a deliveryman for an extra. At Paramount Studios, where Joe waits in the car with Max for Norma to finish her visit with the real Cecil B. DeMille, Max asks him, "Do you see those offices, Mr. Gillis?" Joe turns and looks in the direction of the exterior staircase leading up to the offices in question. What he sees, though, framed by the rectangular mock-screen window on the passenger's front-seat side (it's a British car so the driver sits on the right) is a man carrying a large jug of water on his right shoulder, which he will take up those very stairs and deliver to one of those offices. With and without knowing it (since he is the film's dead narrator *and* live protagonist), Joe is looking at his death in water, only metonymically. Joe is here transformed into a moviegoer where the frame blocks him from seeing the big picture. Max, who is staring directly at Joe, does, however. The "offices" to which Max refers speak to place but also to position. Joe cannot ascend the staircase where the paid staff writers work not for lack of talent, but because he has ascended the baroque staircase in Norma's dream mansion to reach her bedroom first. The now one-way delusional link between Norma and Paramount and Norma and Joe is made through water in a reduced capacity. Norma's introductory salvo fired at Joe, "I *am* big. It's the pictures that got small," is addressed by the screening of the jug that does not hold enough water to fill even a small corner of Norma's rectangular pool, a pool she has left empty so as to remove the possibility of reflection. She fills the pool only after Joe acquiesces to her love, which she would now reflect upon. Does the water jug being carried by a deliveryman cause Joe to see himself as being an extra in his own life? When Joe first arrived at the mansion, he was mistaken for the undertaker who had come to bury Norma's pet monkey in a child's coffin. One here recalls the child's coffin that crosses the path of the doomed lovers in Émile Zola's 1873 play *Thérèse Raquin* and notes the telephone in the Desmond mansion's hallway, the only lifeline to the outside world that is housed inside its own small sarcophagus. Norma's first line to Joe accurately and ironically captures his position vis-à-vis time as well as function: "You there," she says, "why are you so late?" Death or lateness is, like the child's coffin, an unthinkable reduction, and Joe's association with the dead monkey for whom he partially substitutes as the object of

Norma's sadly obsessive affection is likewise a downsizing of Joe as kept man and resistant houseboy. What is a voice-over narrator if not a person who is absent *in* his own life, a life that is already in a sense dead like a stagnant standing pool of water, bottled up and taken away, like a decision that has already been made in which he is complicit, along with narrative time?

Reducophobia

> Granted there is a wall, what's going on behind it?
>
> —Jean Tardieu, quoted in Georges Perec, *Species of Spaces and Other Pieces*

What does it mean to say that something is life-size? "Being the same size as an original," is the dictionary definition.[19] Life-size is, in fact, a comparative term and that comparison, is, in effect, based upon chronology. Something came first. Something else came after that which was like the first—but not so nearly as to be lifelike, in which the quality of approximation is made explicit. And yet the dictionary definition of "lifelike" is accurately representing "real life." In both definitions, of life-size and lifelike, the example given is a statue: a lifelike statue—but also, a life-size statue.[20] So, in the case of something being life-size and lifelike there is a strong implication of constructedness, of artificiality, unoriginality, and deceit. And yet both of these terms do not solely bring a constructed quality to their real-life originals, they allow us to see there is a constructed quality to life as well. If Leibniz was right to believe that God bears existence within him, then life can be no more than synonymous with His idea and yet neither man nor life is God-like. The question that is before us again cites metaphor, a term of agency that corrodes as it would appear to sharpen the original so as to allow us to widen and focus our perception, which is itself a limiting, framing mechanism. Since life is always "life as we know it," how can it ever be anything other, anything more than lifelike? Life is a limit-situation, in the perceptual as well as in the conceptual (mortal) sense that puts us in its frame. If we have no choice in this, can we still be complicit, or are we charged with complicity because we are being framed? In either case, narrative and narration will have their say within which the shapeliness of mise-en-scène draws upon the object lesson of said self-distancing.

Bigger than Life's (dir. Nicholas Ray, 1956) Ed Avery, a dedicated American schoolteacher, who is about to enter the hospital with an unidentified medical complaint, stands at the mantel in the living room of his suburban home. Hanging on the wall behind the mantel is a framed print entitled "WORLD" depicting a bifurcation of the world into its eastern and western hemispheres that the film will analogize to the brain's two globes, its two compossible worlds, once his condition is diagnosed and treated with drugs.

The framed print is framed in turn by two wall lamps comprised of two lights each, marking perfect symmetry and doubling. One light in each lamp would produce a similar but not the same impression, as the two-light-per-lamp solution indicates more than is necessary, a surplus, an exaggeration or intensification of effect and affect. The clock sitting atop the mantle reads 1:10, the time at which Ed first blacks out. When he blacks out a second time leaving the house, he grasps the doorframe to steady its crooking, his hand freezing on the doorbell, which buzzes uninterruptedly, like an audio EKG warning. To treat Ed's rare and fatal artery inflammation, his doctor prescribes the "miracle drug" cortisone. The pain subsides under treatment, but upon his hospital release Ed's doctors warn him that cortisone can be "tricky," that overmedication may lead to feelings of grandiosity, paranoia, and delusion. Death and delusion are both bigger than any life Ed could formerly imagine.

Ed tells his wife Lou that when he came down to the hospital lobby and saw her and their son Richie there, he felt ten feet tall, to which Lou responds that to her that is his true height. When Ed asks his students why Cassius described Julius Caesar as "a colossus" he is already reading himself into the plot. Mortal pain has caused Ed to fall, but pain's surcease under the influence allows him to become a dark colossus too big for the room that constellates, comprises, and collects domestic life as a form of staged realism. Ed's newly hyperbolic sense of the real and his collateral hypersensitivity are as outsized as his sudden reckless intensity. He is becoming not-himself, imperious to his wife and others. Reflecting in the mirror taking his pill, he likes what he sees, a cracked otherness revealing not merely psychosis but the manifold nature of surface and the depth of surface that neither conceals nor peels away like a mask. It is the two layers of leakage—the center spot being wetter than the older, large spot that surrounds it—that Gillis earlier saw in the garage above Sunset. I had a similar experience with a mango skin activating the gridded design to bifurcate and then pull a three-dimensional image from the surface of an oblong plate. This hyper-reality disordered perception to make new meaning as a way of beating the system by making it accountable *to me*. Surface was manifold and also in crisis, baroque.

When Ed first starts exhibiting symptoms of grandiosity, he insists upon taking Lou to an upscale women's clothier to model and purchase dresses she has no use for and they cannot afford. She models the dresses for Ed, but not in the mirror which is there for that purpose. Instead, the mirror reflects the important but momentarily displaced or overlooked presence of their son Richie, whose image occupies the space between the parents' two "live" bodies. The son's eye-line matches his father's only approximately. The chair on which Richie sits is rendered invisible and ghostlike by a sheath of gossamer white fabric that might be used to fashion a wedding dress or veil. The child is specter to the man, a fact enhanced by Richie, who is seated behind his mother but is virtually (not literally) out of the frame. The saleswoman stands in the lower-left corner of the film frame with her back toward the audience. We imagine, as in think we see, her eye-line running through Ed, who is seated opposite his standing wife, and connecting with a reddish gloved hand affixed to part of a dead black arm atop a telephone. The hand is bent toward Richie in outsized relation to his physical but not his imaginary corpus of proleptic mise-en-scène in which his efforts to stay the murderous hand of his figurative father Abraham will be cut short by the latter's severing of a phone line. Proleptic mise-en-scène allows function to double in the way that language constructs parable. Scissors, which are unseen in the scene at the women's clothier, are of course a tool for tailoring and for editing. The severed hand is also a body-edit, a self-inflicted punishment for the offense of the mind's complicity with delusion owing to the mind's inadequate knowledge of how heavily a body weighs upon us, like Walter Neff wearing a dead man's legs as if they belonged to (a) near relation or were your own legs already dead.

In a dream signaling cure, Ed Avery's punitive father Abraham morphs into healing father Lincoln whose beneficent homeliness declared that "a house divided against itself cannot stand." The "life-size" and "lifelike" which Ed previously saw as being "dull" and "trivial" and only passing for "real," like a (faux) scenic model, the life he needed to tower over his family like a plaster(ed) Caesar, has now been reframed to include a wall map of bi-hemispheric worlds being looked at by a mentally rebalanced man who looks a lot like himself. I wish my father were still alive to discuss this with him. I keep dreaming (I think) that he wielded a knife to cut through my obsession-compulsion starting at the hand.

Achondroplasiaphobia

> The problem now is to find the mailbox. One of M.'s friends explains that it's hidden in the lobby walls and sometimes even in the pipes (which are in fact false pipes); they're huge and mask the real ones; in one a miniature theater has been installed.
>
> —Georges Perec, *Le Boutique Obscure*

Lee Breuer's re-sizing of Ibsen's cornerstone of dramatic realism, *A Doll's House* (official premiere, 2003), asked its audience to reconsider what is meant by life-size and lifelike. Common critical wisdom saw Breuer's casting of little people in all of the men's roles as a redressive commentary on the social and sexual inequities of Ibsen's day and, for that matter, on gender as a theatrical construction that dramatizes power relationships. Breuer's production likewise comically undercut stage realism's claim to authenticity by foregrounding its many contrivances, the faux-infinite regress of scenic performance inside the frame of finitude. The human figure that seems outsized in relation to the room whose conventionalism is in turn outsized in relation to the reality it claims to represent (or which we claim it represents, even in the face of physical and material evidence to the contrary) is both bigger *and* smaller than life. Ibsen's "doll house" acknowledges this as metaphor and metonymy, taking its cue (as Meyerhold noted) from the letter box that contains within it the manifest truth of Nora's forged loan letter (an earnest but ill-advised attempt to save her husband's life) that Krogstad (himself an ethically compromised man fired by Nora's husband) put there. Also in the letter box is family friend Dr. Rank's announcement of his own imminent death by way of a calling card with a black cross marked upon it. And later there is a letter from Krogstad countermanding his first enclosure, not relieving Nora of her guilt but stating that he will take no legal action against her and Torvald, the husband who is now ready to forgive her a moment after she has realized that she no longer wants or needs to be forgiven. These foldings of figures and objects inside a smaller box inside of which they illogically fit leads us to Kant's bigger-on-the-inside-ness as being less a spatial condition than a condition of illogic itself—the apprehension of an intuition that cannot be fully comprehended, because (as it appears to us in the "form" of a mental representation) it is incomprehensible, that is, beyond mere appearance and so, necessarily, concealed.[21] Breuer's little-peopled production (and its letter-boxed subsets) reframes the play's doll-housing as illogical fear/fear of illogic.

The stage knows achondroplasia when it sees it. Except, that is, when it pretends to be life in another mode, as it does in *Dead of Night*. The ventriloquist Maxwell Frere loses his voice and his will to his miniature self-creation, his dummy, who in one horrific moment in the story (concerning dreams-within-dreams surrogating reality) appears to come alive minus the ventriloquist's presence and attacks another man inside a jail cell. The dummy is going for the man's voice box, which the cell represents as the nominal limit-space that cannot keep the ineffable in. In the moment of the attack, we suddenly realize that a real human body, that of a little person or more likely a small boy, is impersonating the dummy, the inanimate object. The camera pulls back from the scene in mid-action, reducing it (the scene) in scale to the metaphoric dimension(s) of the cell, now framed by a vast darkness signaling a mental confinement that has shortened limbs and contracted human presence into something horrifically real and unreal at the same time. By which, one might mean, an actor, who "must be created, right there, before our very eyes, but at an infinite distance. . . . in *that oscillation between likeness and likeness [that] defines the actor.*"[22]

This exercise in representational achondroplasia (which tweaks what Severo Sarduy calls "the vanity of representation") ventriloquizes *Dead of Night*'s baroque anachronistic wraparound structure of temporal foreshortenings, so that one person's dream elides with another's, one person is dreamed by another, the end of the story is in the beginning and the beginning of the story is in the end.[23] No one person is bigger than the dream, the symbolic order, which is retailed in and represented by a stately house. The person who claims to have dreamed all the other characters in the house "actually" (for now) designed the house but never before visited it. This "never before" is, of course, a fateful, foreboding construction, as in "He had never visited the house until that fateful night," which reads the way a voice-over sounds. A phone call to the architect, Walter Craig, who is sleeping in his own bed at "another" (for now) location, summons him as if for *a second time*, which puts in question the authenticity of his narrative voice. How can you return to a place where you have never been? Why would you not have already seen the house you designed built to completion? Are you being summoned in real time, and if so, where is real time located in the symbolic order? Who is doing the summoning? Is it someone else's voice on the other end of the line acting as your voice's *surrogate,* as is the ventriloquist's dummy? *Is* it the ventriloquist's dummy? Is Craig awake when he asks as if by rote but not rhetorically, in another man's voice, "Just how long have I been thinking, dreaming of this plane that I am on as one phantom being (or) another and will the fullness of my consciousness appear to me in time?" No. That is not his voice asking this last question. It is mine.

Nora Hellmer succeeds in wresting her voice from the letter box wherein it has been confined, the letter box manifesting the voice box as a cell inadequate to hold the ineffability of the voice, *her* voice, the full force of which breaks apart the door-in-wall realism with a dramatic slam whose figurative voice constitutes a slap in the face of manifest reduction and the de-animation of theater's own ineffability. Breuer's production ends with Nora stripped naked and wigless and grown to gigantic size that eludes while it parodies bedridden (by masturbatory Eros and dreaming) Torvald's outsized desire. Torvald is still short-arming what desire is as what it sees and what it sees as being the manifestation of a will to preserve even by expanding his own symbolic order in which he remains (in his own mind) bigger on the inside than his achondroplasia confesses or allows.

Récit/Climacophilia

There is no "sunset" on Sunset Boulevard, only Norma's "sundowning," a term that describes the confused state entered into by Alzheimer's and dementia patients. "What is the scene? Where am I?" Norma asks as she begins her final dark descent into the madness of *Salome* for which she thinks she is being filmed. "Hold it!" says the camera. And she does, the moment of unanimous night into which she falls, dreaming the monad's starry-dark canopy of self-celebrity mapped by some baroque astrologer. Certainly, *Sunset Boulevard*'s baroque aesthetic gives this away—its ubiquitous gilt mirrors, statues and cherubs, its decadent celebration featuring blindfolded musicians, the general air of romantic decay laced with ironic self-awareness—above all, the aging star who employs her own Dorian Gray to forestall her having to look in the mirror and see only herself. Joe is Norma's "beard" against the rumor of death and the prying eye of time. The finger petrified by a ring holding a cigarette (a coffin nail), its stiffness doubled by the clenched teeth of her rictus smile that betrays the reality her stalwart face pretends to keep out. The tragedy of the face that no one turns to look at anymore, this "no one" having become the camera eye, making a record of this painful rejection and turning the performance of seduction into cruel self-parody. "I didn't know you were planning a comeback," Joe, a marked man in a well-tailored chalked-suit, says to Norma early in the plot. "I hate that word," Norma says of "comeback." She prefers "return," but I think, given her employment of Joe Gillis, *récit*. "The tale [*récit*]," Blanchot asserts, "is not the event, the place where the event is made to happen—an event which is yet to come and through whose power of attraction the tale [*récit*] can hope to come into being too."[24] Blanchot, after Duras, uses *récit* as "a hole-word," a means of sleepwalking present and presence out of life, like Duras's female protagonist in *The Malady of Death* (1982) who nearly always sleeps but also is not unlike her insomniac male counterpart, "who would keep his eyes open in the grave, awaiting a wakening not promised him." Unable to lose consciousness, "Joe Gillis" (re)presents a literary as opposed to literal man. His corpse persists as a negation—"a nothing [that] demands to speak." The flashback not only keeps Joe's death-heavy body afloat, it, in the form of his death, *is* his story. It materializes consciousness *as if* the latter "falls outside the possibility of death."[25]

At the beginning of *House by the River* (dir. Fritz Lang, 1950), the writer Stephen Byrne has one of his manuscripts returned to him by a publisher and not for the first time. He compares the cycle of submissions to the tide in the river adjacent to his property going out and coming back in with whatever has fallen into the river—for example, the dead steer that we see floating on its surface, perhaps representing the pretentious symbolism of Byrne's own narrative imagery in the rejected manuscript. In the meantime, the older woman who lives next door is puttering in her garden, an alternative burial place for bodies and things that you don't want bobbing up to the surface. When the married Byrne strangles the pretty young housemaid Emily who rejected his sexual advances (another rejected submission) at the foot of a characteristically melodramatic staircase (favored in gothic noir), he unknowingly stumbles upon a story idea that draws upon his habit of rejection. What is being rejected other than the fact of what the writing does not know? Stephen's work-in-progress is called *Death on the River*. The title encodes the writer's dilemma of writing (about) what he knows without writing over his unknowing.

The first and second times that Stephen attempts to submerge Emily's corpse in the river, it bobs back up to the surface. Each time this occurs (the "each time" misrepresenting the self-same time), Stephen sees a shiny thing, a fish, flash up from the river's surface and pass like a quicksilver flashback before his eyes to mark the corpse's return as his corpus's personal rejection. The scene recurs on the staircase where Stephen mistakes his wife Marjorie for Emily, which scares her, her fright mirroring his own fear of rejection. Emily's corpse then hails Stephen's complicit brother John ("complicit" and "brother" marking a redundancy as common as the name "John"). John walks with a writer's limp, as if Stephen wanted his readers to note in his brother a manifestation of his own cramped, repressed desire for the writer's wife, for the wife only as written and her likeness to death in the posthumous person of Emily.

Unsurprisingly then, Stephen murders and throws the corpse of his surrogate self, John, into the river to stop him from speaking of their climacophiliac complicity. John's impossible reanimation while Stephen is attempting to strangle Marjorie re-marks climacophilia as unconscious desire's return. The ghosting of this self-image provokes Stephen to hallucinate a curtain blowing in the window as the corpse summoning his own death. The curtain-as-page's actual strangulation of the writer, which leads him to fall from his own story's central staircase, marks a properly asphyxiophiliac end to his climacophiliac story *Death on the River.* But this, the writer's corpse thinks, was not his intention. The writer is not supposed to die in the plot any more than we are in our dreams. Yet we can imagine a posthumous epigraph to *Death on the River* that reads: "I only became a real writer once I learned to kill." Joe Gillis's waterlogged corpse has blue-penciled through "*kill*" to read "*die.*"

Récit/Cleithrophobia

Secret Beyond the Door (dir. Fritz Lang, 1947) utilizes regression psychotherapy to save the dead writer from herself. As water circles concentrically, a female voice-over intones: "I remember. Long ago I read a book that told the meaning of dreams. It said that if a dreamer dreams of a boat or ship, she will reach a safe harbor. But if she dreams of daffodils [which now come into view], she is in great danger. But this is no time for me to think of danger. This is my wedding day." Celia the bride, one fears, will make a beautiful corpse in the story she retells of her hasty marriage to the troubled architect Mark Lamphere, who cautions her that "most people are asleep." She reads "caution," though, as a call to life and not to death. "One door closed and another opened wide . . . Everything was behind that door," she says, voicing over what is for now unvoiced as real concern.

"You know. I have a hobby. I'm collecting rooms, felicitous rooms," Mark tells Celia without apparent affect. "My main theory is the way a house is built determines what happens in it . . . Certain rooms cause violence, even murder." Mark's dream of building such an oneiric house has so far been rejected, as he feels he is by his new bride when Celia locks him out of their bedroom (while she is, as in a fable, brushing her hair two hundred times). Mark angrily leaves their house and Celia has a premonition dream in which she fears *his return*. Mark summons Celia via correspondence to join him back in the United States, but when she accedes to his request, she is met at the family home not by Mark but by his sister Caroline. On the house's second floor, Celia sees a series of alternating shadow-and light-demarcating wooden ceiling beams, in all resembling a series of tessellating frames, doorways that are decreasing in size toward a closed and, one assumes, locked door at the end of the hallway, an Alice in Wonderland-like illogical limit-that-is-not-one. Curtains draw Celia into the marital bedroom, its walls page-papered with a pictorial village setting, a sign of unconsciousness's exteriority that reads, in (pictorial) effect, "*The entrance is here.*" But where is "*here*"? The modeling of perspective in two stories or storeys (the crossword puzzler's surrogacy predicament) has revealed to us the Deleuzean monadic design in which the first floor contains "the material universe of bodies" inside a common room "pierced with [internal] windows." The upper floor, which may be likened to a private apartment, is a "dark room or chamber decorated only with a stretched canvas 'diversified by folds.' " The second stor(e)y of this "Baroque montage" is, in Mark and Celia's case, a reproduction, not of any real place but of the complicity between dream and flashback, a psychological regression as (if in) a movie (Celia's analogy) seen through tessellating frames that overlap to disguise appearance.[26]

Mark insists that although (or perhaps because) the various rooms he has collected and reassembled in his house contain all of *the original objects* from the rooms on which they are modeled, *they are not copies*. Original objects suggest fit, and fit suggests a singularity that cannot be duplicated. There is a seventh room but it is locked, like the forbidden room in which Bluebeard kept his seven murdered wives. (Mark has allegedly murdered his first wife, Eleanor.) Celia enters the seventh room via a key she had made and therein encounters an exact copy of her own marital bedroom. Did Mark re-key *the copy* of the original or the *original* of the copy? In this sense, the seventh room, be it the first or the last, is purely theatrical, and, in fact, behind another set of curtains Celia discovers a brick wall that signals backstage. "It's my room," Celia melodramatically realizes. "It's waiting for me." Which is to say that this is not properly Celia's room but a room that makes *room for* her performance by appearing to await or time her arrival.

"I forgot something at home," Mark, who is fleeing his impulse (literally his dream) to act upon Celia's fears, tells the conductor, rejecting the train so as (unconsciously) to allow Celia to conduct him back to the originary moment in his past where "I forgot something at home" achieves its real and symbolic, its unreal, pathological meaning. Celia dresses the second bedroom, where the death scene is nominally to be (re)played, with fresh-cut lilacs (rather than with the daffodils of her dreams) and awaits the scene of return. In Greek mythology, the nymph Syringa escaped Pan's ardor by turning herself into a lilac bush. In a sense, the nymph's forethought defeated the desire of the god of the forests and the fields by re-coining object recognition as a symbolic value.[27] Celia prompts Mark's memory of his mother who loved lilacs (lilacs also symbolizing love), but who also (he misremembers) locked him (the double-dealing lilac's concealment motive) inside his room at bedtime and departed the house with another man. In this perverse co-opting of the Proustian memory story-prompt, the son has written for himself the part of "the something that was forgotten at home."

Mark's cleithrophobia is arrested before it (again?) turns murderous by Celia's making him see (with the lilacs' help) that the Proustian moment is both factually and ontologically unreal. It was actually Mark's sister Caroline who locked him in his room as a childish joke. Nemesis serves delusion in the compensatory role of making sub/conscious counter-agency seem real that must otherwise remain locked up like a secret beyond a door. By robbing Mark of his maternal Nemesis, Celia effectively saves not only both of their lives but their life together as well, "their life" here eliding the "both of" of the original and the copy, the first and the second, the first and the last.

Celia diagnoses strangulation (the false reporting of Mark's having strangled his wife and her lover) as being an autoerotic (asphyxiophiliac), self-sustaining fiction. A room, even a locked room, does not, as Mark claims, necessarily engender a person's actions. It performs the function of showing what the aggregate of such actions looks like, resembles—like the "furtive shadows pass[ing]" on staircases between stories "of all of those who were there one day." By recasting Mark's fictional "one day," Celia not only survives his design for restaging it inside the murder room, she proves to her husband that they fit, she as his proper analyst and he as her only analysand, as I think in psychotherapy I do.

Récit/Thaasophobia

> He could hear not the slightest murmur of the halted world.
>
> —Jorge Luis Borges, "The Secret Miracle"

Billy Wilder's *The Private Life of Sherlock Holmes* (1970) was severely cut by studio mandate and the footage that was shot was either lost or destroyed, so that it must now be augmented with still photographic images and an audio track to give a sense of what Wilder and his cowriter I. A. L. Diamond originally had in mind. Ironically, the case in question works better this way. The disembodied voices become a voice-over of our own thought process as we study images that appear to be suspended in the mind. It is as if we are Joe Gillis, a posthumous man, facing away from logic and into a depthless surface, with all the clues being on the outside, a fact that flashback voice-over acknowledges even when it affects a performative narrative of intervention (surprise and discovery, realization without self-acknowledgment). The setup is that a blind piano tuner rented a room to a man with an English accent, whom he never "saw" again. Sometime later, after the man has gone missing (missing without "being seen," much like the "Curious Case" itself) and his room door has been opened, the corpse of an Asian man is discovered lying on the floor where the room furniture should be. The furniture is not missing but has been nailed to the ceiling.

In Conan Doyle's original Sherlock Holmes story, "The Adventure of the Speckled Band" (1892), an intended murder victim's bed is nailed to the floor so that she will remain in place for a poisonous snake (the metaphoric "speckled band") to bite into her skin after it makes its way down a rope pull that has been installed for this express purpose. In that the person in the bed could conceivably leave the bed prior to the snake biting her, it makes more "sense" for the legs of the bed to have been nailed to the floor to keep the person in the bed from falling out (enabling her to escape on foot, my baroque mind says) *should the room be turned upside down*. The basis for this seemingly irrational argument can be found in the philosophical "Case of the Speckled Hen," whereby Elijah Chudnoff argues the difference between two cases of visual awareness inculcating belief. Whereas you can base a belief that a hen has three speckles solely upon what your eyes tell you, you lack the "recognitional capacity" to take at face value that a hen has *forty-eight* speckles. This does not mean that it is impossible to determine the truth claim of the forty-eight speckles. The two cases Chudnoff cites distinguish between "being in an epistemic position—such as having justification, or being in a position to know—and being able to take advantage of that epistemic position—that is, forming a justified belief or gaining knowledge." Intuition is the charge that leaps the apparent break in the psycho-visual wire. Holmes demonstrates this in his determination of how the bell pull that is detached from the bell mechanism in "Speckled Band" was meant to work, through the agency of some alternatively logical (and not an oxymoronically illogical) process of deduction. (The crux of the matter being not so much where belief comes from but what makes this belief "justified.") Like the bell pull that does not work (i.e., does not summon help) but at the same time in an opposing way does its directed work (by summoning death), the bed that is nailed to the floor (or to the ceiling) calls forth a belief that justifies and is justified by counter-epistemic assumption.

Holmes, who has been called in to investigate the alleged crime in the upside-down room, immediately surmises that the corpse was dressed *after* death. He knows this because the corpse's suit jacket buttons have been buttoned from left to right rather than from right to left—that is, from an outside or spectatorial perspective (house right and left vs. stage right and left) rather than from a first person's. So, who dressed the corpse and why? Not the blind man, since he is not an agent but a referent, his blindness the something that has entrée to the locked room to make it a paradoxical and "nontotalizable space," that is, a space that namely cannot be key-locked, only clue-locked.[28] The overstaged eccentrism of the room's upside-downness is a play upon dream symbolism as a kind of overt self-exposure of the so-called "real. Unsurprisingly, Holmes knows a crooked house when he sees one—in the affect of its effects, in what has been strategically made to *not* go missing in the absence of a murder/er.[29]

In *Philosophical Investigations*, Wittgenstein remarked that "a signpost does after all leave room for doubt," attaching to this an additional measure of doubt by saying "it sometimes leaves room for doubt and sometimes not."[30] In other words, we must even doubt the possibility of there being "room for doubt." I take this proposition to belong to a philosophy of mental space in whatever is its seemingly impossible physical manifestation. What does a room for doubt look like? Is it like the first dark room cited in this book that we did not even know we had entered until we saw the light? Is it a room not fully written, one with an unfinished manuscript inside it? But can an "inside" be not fully written or merely not fully described? Does a room for doubt gesture toward the idea but not the actual situation of context or actual practice? Still, as Wittgenstein did philosophy, we or rather our minds do doubt, and so, by citing Sherlock Holmes as the foremost exemplar of reasonable deduction, the upside-down room shows us that this doubt does and does not look *like something*, like a room-darkening insularity, which deposits Holmes back in his self-consuming baroque consciousness of living death.

Early in his career, the theater director Robert Wilson did what looks to be a charcoal sketch of a room. He scribbled over this roughly sketched room with three walls and a floor and titled it not "Room for Doubt" but "Entrance."[31] There is a white profile that may or may not represent a human figure projected against the room's upstage wall. It is unclear whether someone is actually inside the room or how someone could have entered it. The problem worth considering here is not so much the drawing as the title "Entrance," since it leads us to a "doubtful" solution based in grammar and not on the kind of logic that undergirds representation. Wittgenstein's brief was for grammar as the philosopher's stone of the ordinary-cum-extraordinary. Grammar is not merely syntactical; it is situational but also conditional. It contains the capacity of names and naming, of entitling and entitlement, of possession and self-possession, of taking in the vista and constraints of the mind's doubt as regards itself and the world. I think, therefore I am (in doubt) and doubtful of the world, the reality that is and that is contained within any and all said constraints.[32] Here, I am threading Wittgenstein through Descartes with a pin that pierces the plenum of what philosophy and art hold so dear, the agency and default acceptance of a reality, even if it is truly only available to us as signs. In the compossible world that enables not just the positing of a room for doubt but also its representation, what is an entrance, what is the title "Entrance" if not a doubtful sign of an action that may be called hypothetical? “Entrance” is “in fact” a double sign of the hypothetical extending to both the action and the space it engenders or vice versa, the grammatical sign that there is something to be said for saying what cannot and need not be realistically seen.

Now, consider this in terms of the upside-down room that Doctor Watson in fact prepared for Sherlock Holmes. By nailing the furniture to the ceiling, Watson has created (with the in/voluntary support of a blind man serving here as a signpost/doubtful witness) a hypothetical room, one that exists without any realistic context or function. The room is, as it is intended to be, a space for doubt into which Holmes is expected to enter. It is immediately clear to Holmes, however, that there is no entrance to be made where there is no genuine doubt, only the appearance of doubt in the form of an implausible reality (furniture nailed to the ceiling of a room). (Here, of course, Holmes overlooks or rather goes beyond the “reality” of the dream in which one can enter through the ceiling.)[33] “Entrance” in the Wilson drawing and the Watson installation is an invitation to think toward or against the comforts of reasonable, realistic thought or mental space constraints, which include directionality—interiority and exteriority, being upside-down and right-side-up. This is a grammatical and specifically a nominal problem, in the double sense of naming and the hypothetical, that is, the (mere) naming of (mere) appearance as such. Once the logical leap is made to mise-en-scène, it becomes merely a logical choice and not some irrational act to nail the furniture to the ceiling of the room, to suspend the world as fiction and image. The dead body in this case was never doing more than “phantasy sitting” on the furniture, and not even as Husserl suggests an actor would, because as far as this furniture in this particular room is concerned, the body is a morgue cadaver delivered to the scene by Dr. (Doctor/Director) Watson.[34] The scene as scene is announced via the overdetermination of its strategies, by the presence of too many clues for the “room” to remain locked.

In this regard, Watson’s scene recalls Borges’s story of overdetermination, “Death and the Compass,” in which what appears to be a series of murders created after a symmetrical kabbalistic design in search of the four letters said to constitute the Name of God is in fact a labyrinth constructed to resemble the foregoing design that has been created to entrap the detective investigating the crime so that he can be murdered. The detective becomes a victim of his own interest in solving the larger puzzle of God’s name. Given this premise, each clue is one too many, in that they are not clues at all but rather components of a simulacrum of ostensible meaning. It is not coincidental that there are namely four letters in the secret name, the Tetragrammaton “‘YHWH” for “Yahweh” (in a story populated by an excess of numbers), since they suggest the pattern of a square or a rectangle, which are the normal shapes of a room. Actually, though, only three points are mapped in Borges’s story, forming an equilateral triangle, suggestive of a perfect symmetry. The fourth point is undrawn (concealed and heteroclite) as it is synonymous with the detective/

seeker's entrance into the space which immediately becomes the dead man's room, death ultimately being a virtual design that only masquerades as a symmetrical one, as a visible spatial logic. The dead man tells his murderer that the next time he tracks him down, he wants the labyrinth to consist of "a single straight line that is invisible and endless."[35] This labyrinth, which the detective claims exists in Greece, is in fact the schema of a Borges story, and, as such, would see the author of the labyrinth trapped by his own devices but also saved from an ending which does not exist except as a fiction in reality. Death is a function of apocryphal series, symmetry, and unity, an ultimate plot point from Corneille's *The Cid* (1636), in which the Rule of Law—the Palace and the Unities—says, "Often, what seemed at first to be a crime / Has come to be acceptable in time."[36] The rule of Law, of Reason in the baroque is the reasonable suspension of disbelief, but not necessarily as Leibniz demanded of all possible worlds, of "sufficient reason."[37] It is this "sufficiency" that is staged reality's real issue in two senses of the word ("issue").

One of the clues to the problem of the detective's labyrinth in "Death and the Compass" is the name of the signee of the letter that predicted the apocryphal fourth letter figure—"Baruch Spinoza." Benedict de Spinoza ("Baruch" is his Jewish name) professed a geometric method for formally constructing philosophical arguments, consisting of "definitions, axioms, propositions, demonstrations, proofs, scholia, and so on" that begins with ultimate conclusions.[38] At the heart of Spinoza's philosophical inquiry was our knowledge of the nature of God. So, in Borges's story, one name figuratively searches for another, which is akin to searching for *The* Name in order to discover the truth of one's own Being that may be better named "being."

The blind man's surname in the posthumous Holmes story is "Plimsoll." A "Plimsoll mark" is the depth line "to which a merchant ship can be legally loaded under specific conditions."[39] His name, then, is a sort of acknowledgment in plain sight—albeit in the plain sight *of a blind man*—that the room is in fact a scene that by usage if not definition bears too much weight. That a plimsol is also a British rubber-souled athletic shoe or sneaker names costuming as a subcategory grounding the scene's overall identity as non sequitur. If the singularly suit-jacket-less blind man did not dress the corpse, is the corpse nonetheless wearing the blind man's jacket buttoned stage right or left? Plimsol's pocket watch fob hangs from a buttonhole in his jacket-less suit-vest, creating a reversible time signature for the upside-down wall clock's pendulum which is rigidly suspended above the clock-face, holding time, like this movie picture still scene. It is a rare glimpse in time of the metaphysical unreality of life experienced as image.

This redoubled unnaturalness cites/sights the (already) artificial constructs (clocks, watches) we mistake for time. In his story "The Secret Miracle," Borges describes how God grants the fictional fiction writer Jaroslav Kubin the year he requests to complete his baroque verse play, *The Enemies* (which observes the unities of time, place and action), by suspending time, literally stopping the bullet intended for the fiction's fictional author in midair. The play is set inside a library in which the author dreams of a conversation he has, while hiding in the library, with a librarian who has gone blind searching for God "*in one of the letters on one of the pages of one of the four hundred thousand volumes in the Clementine* [the library's name]." Awakening from his dream, "Kubin" in the person of his character "Hladik" acknowledges that "reality was not so rich" as we imagine it.[40] It lacks mazes, stages, stage-wings, and the suspension of seriality (a library-inflected designation suggestive of "surreality"). What reality does have is a blind librarian named "Borges," whose dead eyes produce from memory (he went blind at age fifty-five) retinal inversion while re-rehearsing this inversion as a form of reality suspension. Plimsoll wears blind man's glasses that lend symbolic if not actual agency to how the room looks and what the room is (for). His dark spectacles speak to a visual incapacity that we and the fictional room share. For a scene whose dialogue is all unintentionally spoken as voice-over, the blind man's acute hearing (he identifies the "victim" solely from his voice as being an Englishman and not even, as Holmes suggests, an Asian man educated in England) is intentionally no help in authenticating the scene's "reality." The blind man's foolproof hearing is, in fact, complicit in signing the scene's unreality, a sentence that itself appears to turn logic upside-down.

We are told that Erik Lonnrot, the detective in Borges's "Death and the Compass," "thought of himself as a reasoning machine, an Auguste Dupin (Poe's famous detective and a literary prototype for Sherlock Holmes), "but there was something of the adventurer in him, even something of the gambler." Lonnrot is willing to gamble with his life but not with wasting his life on possibly imaginary chance. When someone suggests to him that the murder of *an insomniac rabbi* (another baroque night watchman) may be the result of a jewel robbery gone wrong thanks to someone entering the wrong room, Lonnrot responds:

> Possible, but uninteresting. You will reply that reality has not the slightest obligation to be interesting. I will reply in turn that reality may get along without that obligation, but hypothesis may not . . . I would prefer a purely rabbinical explanation, not the imaginary bunglings of an imaginary burglar.

By mislabeling the obvious (that this really was a murder by misidentification) as being imaginary, Lonnrot becomes ensnared in a larger labyrinthine pattern of crimes that recycles objects from the first scene as props in additional scenes that tell the detective the story he *wants* to see—a mystery whose complexity is commensurate with his solution in the baroque night.[41]

Holmes, on the other hand, recognizes from the first that the upside-down murder scene is Watson's because it is overwritten, like the stories the doctor has spun from his "real-life" adventures with the famous detective. The scene is clue-descriptive but clueless. Watson (Holmes quickly understands) has been content with creating an effect and in so doing underestimates his friend's need to involve his mind with the greater understanding of cause. Spinoza, Deleuze attests, argues that "it is not enough to show how effects depend on causes, one must show how true knowledge of an effect itself depends on knowing the cause."[42] In order to alleviate Holmes's real nemesis, boredom (living death), Watson has unknowingly created a boring problem in the sense that it does not require an ascent to a higher order of knowing for it to be solved. Watson's sanguinity in being equal to the task he set himself is manifest in the way the puzzle is built, with the particular jumble of objects inside a frame merely constituting a universal manifestation of what a puzzle (and for that matter, a conventional mise-en-scène) looks like. And if the puzzle as puzzle is manifest, then there is no mystery to solve, no cause of the effect for Holmes to ponder. Holmes pronounces gravely and conclusively upon what he knows with certainty happened. Watson, who as a doctor has been trained to deal only with symptoms (i.e., clues) that "present," is ill-served (thinks Holmes) by his writer's desire to treat only that which *represents*. Holmes would agree with Gertrude Stein that "resemblance is a pleasurable sensation, but it is also a human weakness."[43]

Is the blind man who returns to the upside-down room to attest to its alteration (furniture on the ceiling, corpse on the floor) able to perceive difference and so also resemblance? Can he distinguish the original from the copy, and which if not either or both of these is likewise a "scene"? Anecdotal evidence, even if fictional, says "yes" to both questions, but in ways that are similar and different than those that are available to the sighted man. Stop me if you've heard this:

> A blindfolded clairvoyant walks into a room and immediately knows how it is arranged. You walk in and immediately see how it is arranged. Though both of you represent the room as being arranged in the same way, you have different experiences. Your experience doesn't just represent that the room is arranged a certain way; it also visually presents the very items in the room that make that representation true.

Citing this passage as a premise, Chudnoff asserts that "in addition to perceptual experiences, presentational phenomenology can be found in intuitive, introspective, imaginative, and recollective experiences [what we might otherwise call 'scenes']. I also argue that presentational phenomenology is epistemologically significant: it plays a central role in explaining why the experiences that have it justify beliefs and give us knowledge."[44] Here we return to the blind man's watch fob, inverted by the wall clock's pendulum hanging upside down like a picture wire grown stiff with suspension. The blind man cannot see any of this, cannot see the picture, the semblance, the representation, and yet intuits that it is so, much as he intuits time's passage being suspended in a representational mode by the pocket watch attached to his fob, whether or not the watch is presently there telling time. Intuition, like clairvoyance, is not locked into an either/or relationship with common knowing as seeing. These heteroclite nonvisual ways of seeing (phenomenologically) present as symptoms of an intelligible unreality that is an inseparable, *nonfictional* part of what we give the universalizing, totalizing name of "reality." Unreality is not thought, so much as sensed as being concealed inside of reality, this un-rendering reality bigger on the inside than it can say, even if it could bring itself to say "unreality." The upside-down-ness of the room can do no more than model what is otherwise left unsaid, as mute as death and no more or less corporeal.

Récit/Scopophilia

> I stood out in the darkness and looked *in*.
>
> —James Ellroy, *My Dark Places*

The Prowler (dir. Joseph Losey, 1951) opens on a rectangular bathroom window, with scalloped curtains in the upper left and right corners. This is, of course, meant to represent a film screen or even a stage's proscenium arch. We see a woman in shower cap and towel in a medium shot that scales her relative to the inside of the frame. The camera moves in and the woman, now shot in profile while regarding herself in an unseen/invisible mirror, grows larger. She engages in a private moment of what certainly looks like, as in resembles, vain self-regard, momentarily unaware that her body and her image are simultaneously being regarded by some other eye outside the metonymic and metaphoric frame. Her now profiled body is bisected by the unseen shade's drawstring with a circular pull at the end. The unseen shade is thrown by the gobo effect that shadow leaves upon the walls and by the (camera) eye that is shadowing her form as image and her image as form. The light inside the frame interrupts the darkness, without managing to invert the darkness that remains in the story's theme of inversion.

At this point, an interesting thing happens. The noir-troped woman in the window, Susan Gilvray, gasps upon reentering the frame *having already sighted the voyeur* intruding upon her mental frame. She gasps only once, enough to register surprised umbrage (as if single-slapped) at the impropriety of watching and of performing "real" fear. The gasp detached from the window shade's pull cord that if used would draw down upon the obligatory scene of gasping, recalls the silenced bell disengaged from its pull in Holmes's "Speckled Band," where it signified some sort of regressive agency, the overwrought speckled band binding its woman-in-peril to her stepfather. When Susan does draw down the shade, she creates a dark background upon which appear, without apparent irony, the words "HORIZON PICTURES presents" and an "Eagle Production."[45] Has "the Prowler" himself vaingloriously composed these *opening credits*? Are the police then called not to catch the voyeur (which they do not, and cannot for reasons that will become evident), but to restore law and order to the mechanism that threatens to invert both story and frame? Who is "the prowler"?

A police "prowler" (the automotive variety) arrives and shines its spotlight on the Gilvray home's address: *1918 Orchid*. 1918 is the publication year of Freud's *Totem and Taboo*, subtitled "Resemblances between the Psychic Lives of Savages and Neurotics."[46] In this collection, Freud addresses, among other things, the terror of incest (also in "The Speckled Band") and the overdetermination of thought, image, and action drawn from childhood relating to developmental sexuality. The L.A. neo-noir novelist James Ellroy, whose favorite film noir is *The Prowler*, credits his life and career to his personal experience as a voyeur, which was a by-product of his mother's murder when he was a child.[47] In his memoir, *My Dark Places* (1996), Ellroy relates how in his mind his murdered mother transformed into the aspiring actress Elizabeth Short (Susan Gilvray was also once an aspiring actress), whose severed body was discovered in 1947. Smart was dubbed "the Black Dahlia" given her propensity for wearing black clothing and given the release of the film noir *The Blue Dahlia* (dir. George Marshall, 1946) the year before her demise. The Orchid (Ellroy's mother as the "Dahlia's" one-off) refers to the Greek youth Orchis, who was torn apart for attempting to rape a priestess of Dionysus at the god's theater festival but later turned into a flower. Despite their difference, the Dahlia and the Orchid correspond to one another via the real-life behavior of severance. Caught between the Orchid and the Dahlia and perhaps conflating the two, double-"l" Ellroy "looked into a bright bedroom window. I saw a woman putting on a robe. She looked in my direction. She turned the light off and screamed. The scream didn't sound like the scream I thought I heard . . . I figured out that the first scream wasn't a scream. It was a woman making love."[48]

The circular spotlight attached to the police prowler floats abstractly in space like a false moon to bait us with the lure of somehow performatively complicit female sexuality that the plot's mechanism will continue to manufacture. The logo on the prowler's front passenger-side door that reads "POLICE DEPT." inside a black circle that is shaded in gray on the inside is a lunar sign here advertising an externally monitored watchfulness that recasts "voyeur" as "prowler." What if any of this is *lawful* viewing? Leibniz maintained that the artist makes use of imperfections, such as shadows and dissonances, in a way that parallels God's use of sin, to serve some greater good.[49] The totemic camera bonds and breaches the self-community relationship and likewise troubles usefulness with aesthetic value.

"Quite a . . . hacienda," says Charles "Bud" Crocker (recalling Phyllis Dietrichson's place), the policeman (the lawful viewer) whose spotlight exposed the house number as a mode of address, exoticizing the stylish form of Susan Gilvray's abode. Crocker instructs junior partner Webb Garwood to check the empty lot that borders the house for footprints, which Webb, who has already picked up and is studying a framed photograph of a younger Susan Gilvray, does. We don't get a good look at Webb's face, but Susan does, and she appears to be confused by who or what she sees, or whether she has already seen it. Is her insomniac mind ("I don't sleep much at night," she says) eliding Webb's face with the prowler's, and if so with which or what "prowler"? What is the prowler there to see or be—the baroque, insomniac night itself?

We see Webb walk around the house, shining his flashlight first in the direction of the empty lot (the unseen audience, the drop site of the Black Dahlia's body, Ellroy's quasi-mother) and then turning to gaze at Susan and his partner talking inside the illuminated house. Webb bends in close to the window just as Crocker says to Susan, "And that's where you saw the face, huh?" Susan appears to see Webb's face through the window's gauze curtains, but makes no indication that she sees it, instead ushering the older cop into the room through whose window she saw the prowler's (real) face. When she and Crocker reach the bathroom, Susan draws the shade up so as to expose the window and possibly herself, while Crocker peers at her over his eyeglasses with arms folded in an attitude bordering on the judgmental. "Well if I was you, from now on I would keep the curtain closed," he pointedly remarks. (Although we know that closed curtains signal a mode of performance no less than open curtains do.) "You ever notice," he continues, "in a bank they always keep the countin' room out of sight so the customers won't get tempted." In other words, a woman's body must be kept under wraps, hidden away because it cannot help but be a desired object whose agency of being seen makes it complicit in male desire. In this way, the woman's body is regularly discounted, which, Walter Neff would argue, is not how numbers trend in the insurance racket. The voyeurs in this unsubtle analogy have had their identity sanitized into "customers" and their aberrant behavior naturalized by displacing desiring agency (tempting) onto the object of their gaze. "I suppose you're right. I just didn't think," Susan answers, reflexively and erroneously equating Law with Truth and so inverting any claim of Logic or Reason.

And then it happens again. Susan, who has turned toward the window, only now from the inside, emits a short gasp a moment before Webb appears in the window frame on the outside. It's almost as if her gasp causes him to re/appear. His body is cut off at the badge on his shirt where his heart should be by the window frame, approximating his partner's body image in the passenger-side seat of the squad car when he first shined his light on the number "1918." This severance elides as well with the analogy that the older cop just drew between Susan's body and monetary currency kept inside a "counting room," severance from the public eye of desiring and desirable private space. For insomniac Susan, the framed Webb must look like he is something she saw or is seeing on a late-night faux-Mexican noir where the sets counterfeit the interiors of real haciendas. The two characters are already related via their nominal parts—Gilv-ray referring to light and "Webb" being "web" with a ticcing "b" for "be"-ing. It comes as no surprise that they will later marry and she will take his last name, thus becoming more entangled with him. "Dreams are spiderlike," wrote Michel Leiris, "given their instability on the one hand and their veil-like quality on the other."[50] When Webb suggests to his partner that perhaps "the lady" was just imagining things, Susan assures Crocker that "he was just as plain as your friend's face just now," abruptly drawing down the window shade, eclipsing Webb's visage.

Later that night, Susan's front doorbell chimes as if introducing a radio program and with it Webb, who's just checking up "to see if everything's still alright." "Why yes. At least I think so," she says. "Do prowlers generally come twice in the same night?" Webb, who makes himself at home, responds, "No, but *we* do. It's part of the job." His every statement confesses to un/reality's pathological self-concealment. "I looked around me to assure myself that the scene was real," he might have said, and then speaking of himself in and as the third person, "he seemed deterred by some degree of uncertainty as to the true nature of the scene."[51] Susan's husband, John Gilvray, is an on-air radio personality, whose tagline "I'll be seein' you, Susan," is known to Webb. It's a prowler's job (or at least hobby) to know where the voice comes from when his is not the film's voice-over (*The Prowler* doesn't have one.)[52] Susan tells Webb that she must listen to every one of her husband's radio broadcasts "because he always asks me how he was." Radio captures the husband's tenuous sense of self that leads him into a (justifiable) state of paranoia over what part of who he is, what he is in possession of (his wife, his house, his voice), is securely his. "I thought I heard talking. I thought I heard voices," Gilvray later tells his wife, who is trying to keep those voices (Webb's and her own in the midst of their affair) hidden. "You must have imagined it [the voices]," Susan tells him, hailing Webb as now the double imaginary, the double prowler, who is at once real and unreal.

Allowing Susan to catch up with his narrative reimagining of a past that included her, Webb acts surprised when Susan (she thinks) "independently" recalls him as having breached her own past. "We might have met there in Terre Haute," specifically at the school dance, Webb prompts Susan, like he is prospecting for memory and allowing her to discover fool's gold that he planted in her mind as being the real thing. In the process of filling in the imaginary "gaps" in Susan's memory, Webb's recitation of the "bad breaks" that life has handed him since those halcyon days reveals a Kierkegaardian self-despair that defines in what real sense he is a prowler. He resembles the lost souls who roam through *The Sickness Unto Death* (1849) like shadows, not even of their former but rather of their missing selves. Webb is obviously a sick man—a prowler, a stalker, finally a murderer—but it is really only his abiding, angry belief that his life's course has been determined by bad luck over which he had no control that lends itself to a Kierkegaardian diagnosis of basic and utter despair. The world has unfairly turned him into a number—a badge, a civil servant, a nobody—and so he is no longer himself, if in fact he ever was. "When the world is taken away from the self and one despairs, the despair *seems to come from the outside* [my italics], even though it always comes from the self."[53] Webb believes that the only (albeit objectively irrational) play is to recalibrate the possibility the world has taken from him and renamed necessity, but in so doing he has reimagined possibility where it does not exist—using the other (Susan) to reestablish himself, to reclaim the self on his and not the world's sense of disengagement. Fantasy invests in self-disengagement with the so-called necessary real. The unrecognized hero self "is [essentially missing] the power to obey, to submit to the necessity in one's life [symbolized by Webb's rejection of his career in law enforcement], to what may be called one's limitations." Kierkegaard concludes, "the tragedy is not that such a self did not amount to something in the world . . . [but] that it did not become . . . aware that the self is a very definite something and thus the necessary. Instead, he lost himself, because the self fantastically reflected itself in possibility."

Kierkegaard believed that of the many ways one can get lost in possibility, there are primarily two: "The one takes the form of desiring, craving; the other takes the form of the melancholy-imaginary hope/fear or anxiety." Following this script, Webb first tries to fast-forward his relationship with Susan, then suddenly breaks it off over the phone, as if he were saying "I'll be seein' you, Susan" just to see how he might answer the question he asked her when first hearing her husband on the radio: "What does a guy like that look like, anyway?" The answer, he now knows, is an anxious, "He looks like me": "melancholically enamored, the individual pursues one of anxiety's possibilities, which finally leads him away from himself so that he is a victim of anxiety or a victim of that about which he was anxious lest he be overcome."[54] Unable to separate the necessary and the possible within his own fantasy, Webb manifests a Kierkegaardian "boldness of despair" by breaking up with Susan (over the phone). Here, Webb's unnerving smile (and consumption of body-building magazines) resembles the consumptive, who, "when the illness is most critical, he feels well, considers himself to be in excellent health, and perhaps seems to others to radiate health." Perhaps body-builders do not have to "make weight" because they are not real fighters and so they are free to let their houses fall under the phobic weight of their own incompleteness.

But Webb and Susan reengage, resulting in the shadow of Webb, the double-named prowler (cop and voyeur), hailing Gilvray three times ("Halt! Halt! Halt!") and shooting twice—one bullet for the victim and one for the self. "Accidental homicide," the court decides. Pack the gun in a suitcase and honeymoon in Vegas with the ghost's ex-Mrs. The gun has one more in the chamber, as Susan is four months pregnant. "Then comes a moment in their lives—alas this is their best time—when they begin to turn inward. Then, when they encounter their first difficulties, they turn away; it seems to them that this path leads to a dismal desert . . ."[55] Webb drives the wife of the spectrally voiced man he made a ghost off the grid to a ghost town in the desert. Webb's defensive strategy is to gain keyless entry into a grid-less paperless life that can no longer ID you or your untimely child, conceived prior to the ghost's murder.

In *Where Danger Lives* (dir. John Farrow, 1950), Jeff Cameron and Margo Lannington likewise set off for a grid-less life, like noir-others before and after them, in Mexico. In this case, she killed her much older husband and allowed an amnesiac Jeff to believe that *he* was responsible, a fact that the radio broadcast we hear spectrally voicing Jeff's concussed brain and proleptically Gilvroy's death has not yet discerned. En route to Mexico, Jeff and Margo stop at the town of Postville, California, which is celebrating its "Wild West Whiskers Week Frontier Days"—a performative nod to history that cannot offset the fact that ghost towns are at their haunted root amnesiac. (Perhaps Jeff has summoned up this place as Joe Gillis has Norma Desmond's house on Sunset Boulevard—two proto-amnesiac death scenes crooked by nostalgia.) Upon arriving in town, Jeff is "arrested" and taken to the real local sheriff, who is here playing himself, to face charges of "no beard, no costume and driving through the streets of Postville without due respect to or observance of the customs of said city." The charges recall the premium that Wittgenstein placed on parsing the rules of the games that govern our lives. Jeff must answer not to a false, as in untruthful charge, so much as to an unreal or theatrical one. While negotiating their fine (benefiting the local cowboy hospital) with the sheriff who offers them either jail time or a marriage ceremony in Postville (Margo had told the sheriff they couldn't pay the fine, because they needed the money to get married in Mexico), a photo of Margot comes across the police wire. One of the local "cowboys" immediately takes the photo and draws a beard on it, because the rule of play is at least the equal of the rule of law. ("Hey, no beard. Everybody's gotta have a beard.") In the process he disguises Margot's picture, so that it and she are unrecognizable.[56] Maybe he inadvertently senses who or what she really is—a murderess passing as her own beard. The doctoring of the photo (aside from being a verbal-visual pun on Jeff's professional status as a doctor, which is now in question) dramatizes how little it takes for the truth to be obscured or *drawn over* (whose double meaning speaks of being stopped/arrested by the police). The action of the cowboy eraser/enforcer is parenthetically saying, "Just a moment" to the picture outside the frame, the picture that is ontologically not true to itself by being unframed.

Playing house in a desert structure lacking a literal fourth wall, the ghost listens in as Webb and Susan listen to his no longer quasi-valedictory recording of "I'll be seein' you, Susan." The couple's inadvertent but inevitable fetishizing of the dead (no less, the absent voice) via replay returns us to Freud's *Totem and Taboo,* and we now allow for the possibility that the "1918" affixed to and spotlit on the Gilvrays' four-walled Orchard Street house concealed the bond and breach of a colon to make it "19:18," which is a time-stamp and a timetable for Susan's difficult labor.

Compelled by circumstance to fetch a doctor, Webb muddies his car's license plate number so that it cannot be read, while the doctor's house number is 119, a preemptive inversion of the emergency number 911 where incoming calls for help are recorded, but which only became operative in the United States in 1968. The doctor escapes with the newborn so as to remain a step ahead of Webb, who, Susan warned, would kill him so as to erase the birth from public record (and with it, chronology and all it contains and all it makes both necessary and possible). Webb confesses to Susan that he murdered her husband for the $62,000 he read about in the Last Will and Testament he found inside the cigarette drawer in the house in which Gilvray forbade her to smoke (akin to the letter box inside the doll house). The police arrive to hail bullets upon Webb after hailing him with the "Halt! Halt! Halt!" with which he had earlier hailed the ghost. "Webb tumbles down a hill as if it were a staircase," I write as if this were a stage direction seeking to delimit "the entropic slope of language."[57]

So, who or what is the prowler? Susan's initiatory gasp marks the already thought as the suddenly seen, or even the already thought as the *already* seen. She gasps not in helpless surprise that something unfamiliar has appeared, but rather in amazement that what has been there can now be not so much seen as pronounced (or pronounced upon like the body's death). Her mind has already drawn something unspeakable directly on the magic window, something she cannot speak of, but whose outline is filled in by Webb Garwood's anxiously desiring body matching her own on the visually metaphoric pretense that two lonely souls would appear to be separated only by (a) glass (pane/pain). The appearance of the hypothetical prowler is insignificant in the end. It is the prowler's return (a sex-and-death-inflected Freudian shadow or shade) in the person of Webb Garwood that counts, and to paraphrase slightly Crocker's advice to Susan following the initial reappearance, the counting room is kept out of sight so as not to tempt the consumers of the image to contemplate *what the image costs them* to see or re-see, even as difference. "And remember folks, the cost of living is going down," the ghostly Gilvray voice forewarned on his radio program in a film that was originally called *The Cost of Living*. But what do you think he meant by "living," the ghost of Walter Neff asks, caught as he was between the policy and the claim?

Spinoza writes, "The human mind does not perceive any external body as actually existing, except through the idea of the affections of its own body."[58] The fact that the prowler appeared only to Susan and does not reappear in the body of the film once she becomes involved with Webb means one of two things. Either Webb *is* the prowler, which makes this a story about a woman who falls in love with her stalker, or else the prowler is her mind's projection of its own darkly romantic idea (as James Ellroy might reimagine in his writing) of how her body is affected by other bodies. Spinoza, says Deleuze, offered philosophers the body as a new model, but owing to the body's neglect, its being made to stand in the shadow of the mind, "we do not even know what a body can do."[59] The prowler's non-/appearance reveals what the (magic) window shows—"that the body surpasses the knowledge that we have of it, and that thought likewise surpasses the consciousness that we have of it."[60] Susan's private moment in the window (frame) speaks to the limited knowledge that one mind has of its own and of another's body. Beyond this, Spinoza argues, "we can have only an entirely inadequate knowledge of the duration of the singular things which are outside us."[61]

Thus, the prowler does not recur because his singularity is absorbed, at least in the viewer's mind, into Webb, much as Susan is progressively absorbed into this same figure. To conflate these thoughts, the scene of the lonely and unsatisfied married woman in the towel concerns body image both in the singular and the plural sense of visualizing an idea of which we have inadequate, that is, limited knowledge (visually formalized as/by a frame). This theory does not rule out the idea of Susan falling for her stalker and realizing too late that she has been ensnared in his plot to possess her and all she possesses (including her fears). It is the true nature of this possession that is in question. The irony in all of this is that in the end it is another body, the couple's child, that comes between them, that produces a nonnegotiable alienation of affections, a confession and a physical reimagining of what the mind makes of the external body—it is a miniature, a model with its own story to tell.

Récit/Scopophobia

> One evening upon entering my room, I see myself sitting on my bed.
>
> —Leiris, *Nights as Days, Days as Nights*

The overhead shot says we are viewing a "ground plan," foregrounding the derivative, self-aware formal quality of the film *Pushover* (dir. Richard Quine, 1954). The police hope to catch a bank robber named Wheeler not just with but in this ground plan, which is later tacked to the wall of the room from which an apartment is being staked out. The person being watched is Wheeler's alleged girlfriend, Lona McLane, who the watcher, police detective Paul Sheridan, picked up earlier outside a movie theater running the double feature *It Should Happen to You* (dir. George Cukor, 1954) about a woman who wants to see herself in the movies and *The Nebraskan* (dir. Fred F. Sears, 1953), a western starring Philip Carey, who plays one of Sheridan's colleagues, detective Rick McAllister. The viewer succumbs to the illogical but not unreasonable possibility that the film is watching *him* with its peripheral vision.

"Paul Sheridan" represents the compossible reality of "Walter Neff," likewise played by Fred MacMurray never having died. "Never" is a long time, but it is an abstract "long time" that ignores the materiality of film characters' and film stock's demise. Hadn't the studio jettisoned Neff's big-house execution scene in *Double Indemnity* for a more viewer-friendly and vague bleeding-out, dying in ellipses, a death made unreal by not seeing it through to the end? Lona (her name conspires to have us call her "lonely") repeatedly phones for the time, indicating to watcher Paul that she has nothing with which to occupy it. Is Lona, who Wheeler has expensively attired, guilty as advertised or just as guilty as advertising (watching, staking her out) says she is? Is she only being framed? Lona's body, like Susan Gilvray's, has an inadequate knowledge of itself and what it attracts. It attracts first Wheeler, then Paul, without knowing what either of them does for a living and what their real interest is in her. If they just want to watch her or watch her being watched, she would at least like to know what film she's in.

Paul's fellow watcher, Detective Rick McAllister, late of *The Nebraskan*, knows what film he's in but is too focused on the "good" body of the industrious young nurse who lives next door to care. Does the nurse's "goodness" legitimize her body's being looked at, the implication that staking out goodness signifies good intentions, such as future courtship and marriage—a preview of coming attractions? (Who's to say this is not another prowler's rationale? Webb married Susan, didn't he?) Later, Rick will put a name, "Ann Stewart," to this good body without acknowledging to her who he is, as his illegitimate watching of her creates a Cartesian mind/body conflict of interest on his part. Paul later admits to Lona that he is watching her but not that he is still wearing Walter Neff's wedding ring from *Double Indemnity*. "So, you are a *(pause)* married man," she asks, but in the "*(pause)*" she might have been thinking "celebrity," since it's Fred MacMurray's ring (which he refused to remove) that Paul is again wearing, in the same way that Jean Gabin wears a monogrammed dress shirt with the initials "JG" on the breast pocket as *Pépé le Moko* (dir. Julien Duvivier, 1937).

"What TV show are you watching?" and "I'm not watching TV" are the call signs through which Wheeler and Lona conspire to disable the monitoring of denotative language over the tapped phone she otherwise uses just to check the time. "The coast is [not] clear"? these figurative sentences say, but isn't "the coast" a strange way to walk back meaning from a perimeter to its center on a ground plan or a map? It's like Pépé le Moko living inside the Algerian casbah's protective labyrinth on Inadequacy Street (which he does). Paul and fellow detective Paddy Dolan wait outside Lona's apartment building "322" for Wheeler, whom Paul and Lona have secretly conspired to murder and rob. The detectives see Wheeler enter her apartment, "423," this "423" conspiring with "322" to the clandestine additive value of being watchful. Extruding this watchfulness from number combinations creates new neologic value. When Paul and Lona meet on the roof of her apartment to plot Wheeler's death, a multitude of TV antennas bear witness to what others can neither hear nor see. When Rick and Ann arrange to go out on a date when the case is over, his exit line, "Then you'll be hearing from me sooner than I thought," doubles back and doubles down on the ghostly tagline, "I'll be seein' you, Susan" in *The Prowler*. Inherently neological time recalls a "date" as a number that is recorded, already self-monitoring, listening in on what the present has promised, and watchful.

Paul has been pretending to watch over his alcoholic partner Paddy, who missed intercepting Wheeler when he entered Lona's apartment building, because he was off drinking in a bar. Paul offers to alibi his absence, but only if Paddy, who saw Paul kill Wheeler, will cover for him. Paddy balks at this, a physical struggle ensues, and Paddy is shot dead with his own gun, but not before he moved Paul's car. Paul and Lona go back on the roof for an overhead view of the neighboring streets, but fail to locate the car prior to police and ambulance vehicles arriving at the scene. The film's opening ground plan has inexactly recurred, ticking like a stopped clock but not at either of the two times, day and night, when the time it tells would be right.

The brick wall behind which Paul and Lona hide on the rooftop is inexactly doubled by Ann's leaning against a brick architectural support near the building's entrance, waiting for Rick to appear. It is Ann who earlier ran into Paul at the entrance to Lona's apartment, giving Rick the indirect evidence he needed to put Paul not just at but *in* the scene, that is, *in*volved. At the time, Paul covered his absence from the stakeout by lighting and burning down a number of unsmoked cigarettes, allowing cigarette logic to testify to the fact that he could be in two places, in two *scenes*, at the same time. But chronological time is a straight line bent in many different places. It is a labyrinth unsuccessfully covered up by logic in order to save us from the dizzying, sickening effects of the mental bends of self-monitoring. No matter how inattentive we are in tracking narrative's formal devices and the mental fatigue it causes, we are affected, made ill and fearful of what this illness portends.

Paul stakes out Rick and Lieutenant Eckstrom's interrogation of Lona in her apartment but is nevertheless caught in the sights of his own scopophobia (e.g., he watches Rick pick up the phone in Lona's apartment and call him at the stakeout.) Paul experiences the mental bends, with the apartment building answering his illness's call by becoming a labyrinth of doors opening and closing on rooms and corridors, with Paul barely able to keep from running into Ann *who has seen him*.[62] Paul abducts Ann so that she cannot identify him to the police, but the film space and structure having conformed to Paul's phobia have already called for the police. The police prowler parks directly behind the dead man's (the aptly named "Wheeler's") vehicle with the stolen money inside its trunk. Paul makes a run at the prowler and is shot by another policeman, the illness of time having achieved a manufactured fullness in a reel but unreal mortal end. "I think I have found a large room in my [house], but it turns out it's not mine, and, in fact, it's the street." The prowler has ushered me in. It's not a house, but there is a door. I strain to see myself in the rearview mirror, but it says: "[ ] does not look like himself."[63] I realize that it's not a mirror but a set of anxiety brackets that does not see me so much as show me being seen not for who but what I am. This is a phobia, not a complaint. The prowler drives away, without ever really leaving.

3

✦

Train

> "People are always seeing things on trains."
> —*Union Station*, dir. Rudolph Maté, 1950

In Hitchcock's *The Lady Vanishes* (1938), Miss Froy, an English spy passing as a governess, is sitting up the night in the club car of a train that might be traveling to Munich in Carol Reed's *Night Train to Munich* two years later. The same two English cross-talk comedians, Caldicott and Charters, chatter like train wheels tracking across the two films. They are speaking of the Indian rope trick that "never comes out in photographs." "I've never heard about anyone who's seen it," a very English retired general chimes in, "unless he was going to see it first," to which a matronly woman who is doubling Froy says that she doesn't understand. "You hear about the thing," explains the general, "you hope to see it, and then you'll see it."[1] What's this got to do with me, Froy wonders before vanishing, one magic act apparently vouching for another. Like me, Froy is awake inside her sleep body.

"A million Mexicans" drink Froy's special Harriman's Herbal Tea, she tells winsome young Iris Henderson, whose surname betrays a syllabically encoded but unconscious familiarity with Froy via Harriman, the "-son" being only a generation removed from the "-man." Iris and Froy bonded over a falling window box that was meant to kill the old woman but instead landed on Iris's head prior to boarding the train. The accident has made Iris woozy, disoriented, and the always sympathetic Froy appears to have taken some of this befuddlement into her own head, along with some fictional scenes that are set in Mexico. Or is the befuddled Froy merely *Iris's* mental projection? After returning from the dining car where she finger-traced her surname FROY on the window, Froy tells the recovered (but now with an inclination toward disorientation) Iris, "There's a most intriguing acrostic in *The Needlewoman*. I'm going to try to unravel it before you wake up." There is a most intriguing *cross-stitch*, she might have said, and effectively did say by crossing an acrostic with an unraveling. The return/unveiling of Froy will ultimately appear to hang upon Iris and her ethnomusicologist fellow traveler Gilbert staying awake after being drugged by the noted Prague brain specialist Dr. Hartz, who, along with others on the train, is working for the enemy. I say "appears," because the fake nun who was hired to drug the young couple performed a substitution of her own, so that Iris and Gilbert have, in fact, been acting out a placebo effect, the affect of what being asleep only *looks* like.

The Lady Vanishes climaxes when the villainous Hartz uncouples the part of the train bearing the protagonists so that "there is nothing left of the train beyond the sleeping car" (metaphorically rendering the brain inoperative). The steam emitted by the train for a moment looks like Hartz's colleague, magician Signor Doppo's prop birds frantically flapping their wings in the air after Gilbert inadvertently released them from a prop trunk in the train's higgledy-piggledy baggage compartment presenting as a word jumble.[2] Not just the image but the thought *behind* the image has migrated, along with any truth of originality the image purported to contain. Gilbert seizes on the moment of Iris's feinting at Hartz's mere mention of the drug he has given them, that is, of the drug *in name only*, to pretend to lose consciousness (of) himself. By consciously doubling Iris's unconscious action, Gilbert sells Hartz on an act of misdirection that effaces the nominal act with an act that is only apparently real. In so doing, Gilbert does a convincing imitation of Doppo, minus the music hall Italian's impersonation that the latter unsuccessfully attempts to pass off as being real.

That a newspaper called *The Needlewoman* contains an acrostic rather than cross-stitching instructions for needlework is as compelling as the fact that Froy will succumb to needle-work (she is drugged via an injection) and become the proverbial needle in the haystack, the unconscious body on board the limit-space of the train that cannot be found. Froy brings up the acrostic (a message-constructing puzzle form) in *The Needlewoman* while a boy sitting next to her is overjoyed (an extension of "Froy-rhymes-with-joy," as the governess said after writing her surname on the train window) by Doppo's transparently obvious object-disappearing act, the function less of sleight of hand than of open concealment of the object and the hand by handkerchief. Doppo's unsympathetic magic is designed not only (as magic is) to ostensibly break the bond between cause and effect, to disappear the cause of the effect (of disappearance), but beyond this to deny the very existence that there *is* an effect (that it is *you* who are claiming truth in illusion). Spinoza reminds us that "*any thing can be the accidental cause of joy, sadness, or desire*." By "accidental," Spinoza means that the mind can be affected by a former affect rather than by the former affect's "true [or 'efficient'] cause."[3] This sounds like a case of indirection, if not of misdirection (as well as of a placebo effect). The name and its namesake, "Froy," will disappear shortly thereafter when the train, or at least Iris's disordered mind, enters a dark tunnel of sleep and possible dream (since no one else on the brain-train will admit to the woman ever having been on board). Logic dictates that the old lady is still on the train, that there is no room for disappearance, no room in which anyone could disappear, because that room does not exist. The no-room motif of the train as a self-contained limit makes the room as a theatrical space appear in which people and things do disappear.

The idea of there being *no room* as a constraint of physical space seems clear enough, logically speaking. But the "no room" of which we speak is a product of disorientation, befuddlement as regards not physical space so much as personal identity—or alternatively, the "no room" of physical space standing in for the "no room" of personal identity that is rendered insubstantial in both its forgetting and remembering. Thomas Nagel asks whether the "I" completes a "centerless [perspectival-less] world," and whether the *mereness* of a particular person is "an accidental and arbitrary" thing. He affirms that "sameness of self cannot be adequately defined in terms of memory, continuity."[4] The accident meant for Froy that befalls Iris creates a discontinuity of self-sameness that enables the disappearance of FROY and Iris "seeing herself running toward *the seer's point of view.*"[5] This occurs when *Eye*-ris returns Froy's eyeglasses to her, thus initiating a change in perception. *I/ Eye* is not an identity, but "a subject-predicate proposition" that our train of thought intuits without being able to fully express. The haunted insomniac hears the amplified, impossible sound of the Cartesian's phantom train of "intuitive presence . . . without distance and closeness, without inside and outside, and without here and there," from which the philosopher said, "*I* am displaced, one more mental image.[6]

As Guy Maddin demonstrates in *My Winnipeg* (2007), in which he reenacts his childhood using real actors to play his family members in his old family home but within a context of sleep and dreaming (the past as mental apparatus), we have no real "memory of the thing itself . . . but a memory of an image."[7] His "mother" is Ann Savage, who played the femme fatale accidentally strangled by a telephone cord run under a bedroom door in *Detour* (dir. Edgar G. Ulmer, 1945), her death-noir aura being redolent of cruelty and injustice's (the past's) exhumation. Savage allegedly starred for fifty years (dream time) in the Canadian television show *Ledge Man* as the mother of Madden's suicided brother Cameron, who spent each episode standing on a building ledge threatening to leap to his death. Maddin is death-haunted, but more so by himself as a ghost medium, as evidenced in his *The Forbidden Room* (2015), shot and assembled on board a train from a history of previously discarded and derealized film scenes and effects. (*My Winnipeg*, "however," was presented by Manitoba's "*Documentary* Channel," newsreel footage being a kind of neologism of the un/real.) "What if I had already left decades ago?" is an insomniac's question posed by the I's baroque train of thought, whether (Maddin's) sitting up the night or (Froy's) imagining being mummified and disappeared in Doppo's magic box of sleepless, dyslexic dreams. It is namely in these dreams euphemistically called "the past" that we play a part.[8] "We are allowed by civic law to carry the keys of these old dreamy domiciles, these old dreamy addresses," Maddin's voice-over intones, guiding the probably false memory of silhouetted men, seers in noir fedoras and overcoats carrying keys to ghostly homes and underground passages dangling from sticks that they hold before them like divining rods. "What if I *film* [shoot] my way out of here?" the insomniac voice-over noir-rhetorically ponders.

Becoming a third-person seer is the start of a life of mythomania. Parfit argues that our minds connect quasi-memories, braiding them together with actual experiences "like the strands of a rope." This "strong connectedness" surreptitiously forges a new "continuity" that like fiction writing erodes actuality while legitimizing an unreality that both literally and figuratively leaves the past behind.[9] Iris's budding mythomania conceals the reality of Froy's disappearance inside it. Froy's disappearance is, then, as much Iris's doing as her rival spies' undoing. However, Froy has not survived this long without knowing how best to be remembered. Froy's disappearance into (a) thin (musical) air is its own clue to her retrieval, as if she both vanished into and appeared as a clue in a crossword puzzle of her own design (as a spy must often feel). As Iris and her partner in abstract salvage and recovery, the musicologist Gilbert, sit outside London's Foreign Office, Froy begins piano-playing the musical passage her saviors have already forgotten. Likewise, Froy has used a quasi-Mexican noir to recall and affirm her own imaginary Mexican writing inside the discarded but self-identifying Harriman's tea packet as an intelligible ontology of reality's fictional passage through and as continuous quasi-memory of diachronic time.

The silver-haired and predatory-visaged actor Lee Marvin plays "the Killer" in a noir shot in Mexico City called *A Life in the Balance* (dir. Harry Horner, 1955). The Killer goes on the run with a boy named Paco Gomez who witnessed his (the Killer's) murder of a young woman who was his father Antonio's friend. The Killer entered his victim's apartment by imitating the remembered rhythmic knocking that would-be musician Antonio had used while visiting her several moments before, and so Antonio is wrongly suspected of having murdered the young woman. Much as the two men's entrances are proximate, so too, says Police Captain Saldana in so many words, are the character of the artist and the criminal: "Let the facts judge the man. He's irresponsible, disorganized, emotional—all characteristics of a murderer." Later Police Lieutenant Fernando reinforces this connection: "He was like you, Antonio, a dreamer and a wanderer. He was lonely, full of piteous righteousness." Indeed, the Killer's penultimate moment is a Levinasian realization that he cannot live without the other (in this case, without having Paco as a friend). That being alone only works if you are already dead.

Paco has used a slingshot and white marbles to shoot out police call boxes so that the police can track him and the Killer serially. These calls interrupt the police operator's game of chess, spelling out in Levinasian fashion the diachrony of time, that is, time as interruption. In time, the intuitive (i.e., creatively thinking) Lieutenant Fernando realizes that there is a pattern to these calls, plotting them out on a wall map of Mexico City, where they appear as a series of lights, like moments of inspiration. Phone calls are placed to restaurants in the vicinity of where the pattern and Paco's morning hunger (a behavior conditioned by always eating breakfast with his father at the same time each day) can be satisfied. When the Killer intercepts a call to one of the restaurant owners, Paco plays a musical air his father taught him on harmonica so, for the first time, the boy's voice is actually heard over the phone, albeit in the form of (a) deferral. Froy has been recalling this to herself, but only inside Gilbert's vanished memory of the coded melody she asked him to remember. "Mexico," for its part, is an irrational interruption in the sequence of causal, logical perceptions and so-called objects of resemblance from which, says Hume (who did not, of course, reference Mexico), we draw conclusions about specific and continuous identity. Mexico effaces identity, undoes, un-invents it. Mexico is the place where, in film noir, persons and reasons go to die.

Hume's notion is that identity, the self, is in fact synonymous with the error that a succession of perceptions (call boxes) can constitute an actual continuity, and it is from this imagined continuity that we, the idea of the self, is made up.[10] *The Lady Vanishes* offers numerous examples of perception as the product of coincidence and contiguity that affect continuity, that is, a fake perception of what perception really is. Aside from the actual conspirators, passengers on the train lie about not having seen Froy out of self-interest conspiring to manufacture disbelief. Gilbert and Iris are seated at the same table where Iris dined earlier with the old lady, enabling the window memory trace "FROY" to reappear to Iris (only to disappear again upon the train entering a dark tunnel where it elides with "Freud"). Froy's body disappears prior to her name, and with it the memory of her having been there at all. The consequence of this is that her *being* there and her being *there*, that is, her identity and her proximity to her name, are played off against one another like a magician's illusion. Froy's identity is transformed into, reduced to a contentious memory. Memory, then, coalesces identity's error in a sort of fictional time during which all things—mind, body, and name—were truly related in a single subject, a self or person. "FROY," though, signifies beyond memory, escapes memory, as if it, the name "FROY," the identity was itself traveling to Mexico in a car that has been unhooked from the rest of the train.

"Because the I exists recollected," says Levinas, "it takes refuge empirically in the home. Only from this recollection does the building take on the signification of being a dwelling."[11] What then of the homeless "I," and can there be a homeless "I"? Froy exists in a more or less fluid state of unhoused being that opens out as in a long shot inside a de facto compressed fictional frame. She is, in this sense, my neighbor or kindred spirit or perhaps even the mental architect of my ever-expanding dream house. She cannot inhabit anything other than fictional recollection. Our inchoate "I's'" mental data is far too random to be cataloged and performed by Mr. Memory, the music hall performer in Hitchcock's *The 39 Steps* (1935), whose prodigious recall enables him to regurgitate facts, numbers, formulas, and finally his own death on demand. Memory has nothing to do on board the train but to sit up all night and all day talking to himself as if *he* were the *only* fiction, the "I" and the "not-I." It is an obsessive thought we share, even though he cannot know this since he is *my* intelligible representation, but I am not his. He suffers from what psychiatrists call "obsessive-compulsion *without insight*," meaning he does not acknowledge that he has it ("Memory" is a rote learner), ascribing his strange preoccupation with acted-out repetition rituals as being merely a gift or talent, maybe even a trick, or simply how his mind works.

"My theory was a perfectly good one. It's the facts that were misleading," says Dr. Hartz, who chalks up Iris's memory of Froy to hallucination—hallucination and, in fact, "chalking up," concretizing the spectral, fitting a corpse's outline for a funeral suit. Hartz ascribes the Freudian-inflected "Froy" to "some past association, an advertisement [akin to a Harriman's tea wrapper?], or a character in a novel, subconsciously remembered." "Miss Froy" is an image, not a person, and so "never was" in any substantive way. She becomes for a time in the minds of Iris and Gilbert "the vanishing lady" on the poster advertising Doppo's stage magic act. To my obsessive mind, this and other magical illusions necessitate checking and rechecking the *possibility* of disappearance (Am I still here?). That is, it is not so much magic but rather disappearance that is suspect. Magic does not precipitate disappearance as it alleges. Instead, magic covers (up, for) disappearance. Once the mind embraces its own capacity for making or at least observing or even considering the fact that objects can and do disappear, the mind battles its inability to keep disappearance from becoming an obsession. Now you see it, now you are misled into thinking you don't, or else now you see error. The optical illusion (of which Kant does not speak) is an extension and representation of logic being eroded by the possibility of error.[12] This is the entire premise of *The Lady Vanishes* and of all the "wrongness" we see so anxiously depicted in Hitchcock's films.

In the storage car among Doppo's scenic illusions, the young couple gets to try on various modes of physical disappearance as "acts" themselves. Gilbert's chance sighting of a HARRIMAN'S HERBAL TEA packet wrapper adhered to a train window, looking for all the world like a giant theater ticket, freed his thinking to magically enter into Iris's un/reality of FROY. Their lives will undoubtedly return to normal once the train ride ends (they are getting married), since it is the train itself that performs the role of code-making mechanism, blurring the line between corporeal and incorporeal materialism, that is, between material and immaterial realism. Brian Massumi notes that the sixteenth-century Italian philosopher Giordano Bruno "had a word for something like an incorporeal materialism that is even more troubling [than Deleuze's term 'transcendental empiricism']: *magic* . . . [whereby the] body comports an incorporeal dimension." Massumi adapts Leibniz's "small perception" to mean an *infraempirical* sensation that is "'too small' to enter perception." But "whereas the feeling of the relation may be 'too small' to enter perception," Massumi writes, "the relation it registers, for its part, is 'too large' to fit into a perception since it envelops a multiplicity of potential variations (it is *superempirical*)."[13] In this, I again catch sight of my un/real (air)plane and offer the noir citation, "A [dead] body has to have two tickets on a train or a plane. There's a regulation about it somewhere."[14]

The matrix of illusionism and psychopathology confirms the contours of the vanishing room that the magician's disappearing boxes with their false walls and false bottoms materialize. In Terry Gilliam's *The Imaginarium of Dr. Parnassus* (2009), a space much bigger on the inside than on the outside is peopled by various incarnations of the same character in the same white suit but in different behavioral guises and played by different actors to cover for the real-life death of the actor, Heath Ledger, who originated the role. "Now you see him, now you don't" is transformed into "Now you see him, now you see him via the oxymoronic repetition of different bodies bearing the same name differently-but-the-same, as if there were several-bodies-in-one." He(ath) as someone else/one-of-several-someone-else's as "He(ath)" renders intelligible the unreality of the stage as an internally expandable room that plays (at) the limit of what is real in/as representation. Appropriately, the one piece of physical evidence that Gilbert and Iris discover to prove Froy's existence on the train is Froy's eyeglasses—which the Magician falsely claims are his. What does a magician need eyeglasses for—as a prop to put us in mind of optical trickery, of the trompe l'oeil, the scene(ry) that is painted to look real, as in three-dimensional, like a room where there is not one, like a train that conceals the possibility of concealment, that possibility itself constituting a room (for)?

Why do films noir set on trains so often rely upon body substitutions to move their plots along? Perhaps the reason can be found in Leibniz's notion of parallelism, which Spinoza, according to Deleuze, applied without naming to characterize the non-/correspondence(s) of the body and the mind. This parallelism can be seen in Deleuze's consideration of mental and physical modes in Spinoza's philosophy: "There is an automatism of thinking (*Treatise on the Intellect*, 85), just as there is a mechanism of the body capable of astonishing us (*Ethics*, III, 2, schol.). Each thing is at once body and mind, thing and idea: it is in this sense that all individuals are *automata* (II, 13, schol.). The representative power of the idea simply follows from this correspondence."[15] The superficial fact that trains run on parallel tracks both individually and collectively and that the parallel tracking of one train cannot intersect the same point at the same time as another train without producing a collision and possibly death should not be overlooked. The original body and its substitute cannot and do not appear in the same scene/frame at the same time. In fact, great pains are taken, as in Richard Fleischer's noir *The Narrow Margin* (1952), to keep the original body and its impersonator apart, with the latter largely locked away in a room inside a room on a train where death nevertheless finds her because the body insists on speaking out, voicing itself.

A train is a narrow passage with in/visible choke points at which the overlay that constitutes identity and relation(ship) intersect. The self-identified "fat man" who clogs the narrow corridors in *The Narrow Margin* turns out to be a railroad detective whose overly demonstrative (self-referential and Hitchcock-allusive) girth creates an obstacle that helps him function as an incognito. He is a visible blind spot in a film in which two leading characters have secretly switched identities and so, in effect, play one another's scenes. The railroad detective's broad back to the film screen blocking prying eyes from seeing what would otherwise be demonstrably before them recalls Hitchcock's use of characters' foregrounded backs to cover edits in *Rope* (1948). This action, call it a back-edit, in that it seals off news photographers and reporters from the escaping Chicago police detective and the gangster's widow he is hiding in order to protect in *The Narrow Margin*, encroaches upon and renders impossible seeing the big picture and the whole story. This picture/story is that the Chicago detective is unknowingly protecting not the late gangster's wife but an undercover police woman who is acting the role of gangster's "moll" to the hilt, overacting it in fact, even as the late gangster's wife is playing the dutiful, innocent mother role to perfection, underplaying it in fact as she travels with a nanny who handles the bulk of caring for her obstreperous young son who is his father's likeness. One woman takes the slaps and later the bullets that are meant for the other. Someone has to get her ticket punched, even if the detective does not himself know which one it is and insists upon taking what a woman tells him at face value, even though he has no facial recognition of the woman in question. The mind of the broad-shouldered Chicago detective (narrow-marginally different than the broad-backed, overweight railroad detective) who has been entrusted with picking up the gangster's wife and with safely transporting her on the Los Angeles-to-Chicago train to testify in court plays to the fake negative stereotype of the gangster's moll. It is a performance fueled with anger and resentment over his partner's losing his life in the scene of the moll's initial pickup. At the same time, the detective falls into an on-board romance with the real gangster's wife, who left her husband upon learning of his crime. These two parallel *and* intersecting developments answer the lead detective's earlier question posed to his late partner, who originally thought it to be rhetorical: "What kind of woman marries a gangster?" His soon-to-be late partner surprised him with a prescient answer whose truth the lead detective could not foresee: "Anyone." Anyone is, of course, both "Everyone" and the incognito, which is distinctly different from the "No one" (as in no morally upstanding, law-abiding man in his right mind) that the hero had in mind at the time the question was asked and throughout the bulk of the film.

Error often constitutes a narrow margin, and in this case the trial of the passage predicated upon error leads directly to the confession of testimony and trial. It is possible to assert, though, that two women with swapped identities do not board a train; only one identity does and it is rendered binary and unstable, wobbly by the inescapability of the room that the train has become. What we see are the dark and light sides (as we do in Hitchcock's *Strangers on a Train*, 1951), the complexity of character along with the conventions of role-playing and how the two—character and actor—never fully merge but rather reveal a surplus in the overlay, all of which may be derived from a commonplace misperception or illusion of what a self or person is. How else to account for Froy's "*1,000,000 Mexicans*," who, she says, drink Harriman's tea and whose number and provenance appear to be equally dubious?

Tucked into death in the semblance of sleep, awake to the "what" but not the "how" of it—Froy, though mummified, remains. "Abracadabra," says Gilbert to Iris, when he produces Froy from the next room where she has been bandaged to keep up appearances as being incognito (appearing to be incognito being a variation on the room of disappearance that the last train car housing the magic acts affects as a dramatic scene of propped-up reality).[16] Another woman, "Madame Kummer," was earlier introduced wearing Froy's clothing to reinforce the idea that "Froy" is no more or less than a sign of correspondence, of associative logic, of illogical association. She is a suspect-montage, a solution that denies a mystery. "Kummer" is herself a visual allusion to the magical illusion of a woman (Froy) who has been sawed in half, the by-product of which is a trunk show, a private viewing afforded the only two people who are not buying the staid-respectfully named "*Madame* Kummer's" performance.[17] (Where there is a "Madame," there is or at least was a "Monsieur," whose title vouches for her own in relation to commitment and stability regarding marriage as an institution, i.e., to the Law.)

That Iris and Gilbert are seated at the same club car table where Froy wrote her name on the train window enables the ghost-written scene, which like the rope trick referred to by Caldicott and Charters "never comes out in photographs," to create a scene. That is, it leads Iris to create a scene when she stops the train. ("I hope she doesn't make another scene," one of them later says when Iris brings up Froy again.) After Hartz discovers that Kummer, the substitute Froy, has herself been substituted for the real Froy as the bandaged or vanished lady, Iris, Gilbert, Froy, and the other more and less innocent travelers are left on the detached sleeper car and diverted onto a branch track (a mechanical sleight of hand), like a story that has gone off course in order to reach another, more original, but no less real destination than the nominal one. The fat man that Froy saw getting on the train at the beginning of the trip (and who, being the film's director, Alfred Hitchcock, not so mysteriously vanished for the rest of the film) was carrying a cello case in the shape of a woman. Who is to say that even though the bandages appear to have been removed from her eyes, Froy is not still trapped inside another form-fitting enclosure? No one would think of looking for an old lady inside the cello-like shape of a young woman's body. Not even Gilbert, and he's an ethnomusicologist.

The disappearance/reappearance of Froy's name-tracing on the inside of the train window renders it eventful, theatrical. It also recalls Freud's brief note on the then new-contrivance of writing and erasure dubbed the Mystic Writing Pad.[18] Freud analogized this way of making writing disappear with a trace by lifting a double-layer transparent sheet away from the wax slab to which it is attached to the discontinuous twofold perceptual system in our brains that, he theorized, produces our sense of time. The situation of writing either on paper or a chalkboard is transformed into a both/and. This opens for us the possibility of there being a dual reality in operation on board Hitchcock's train in which, like her name, "Froy" is both there and not there, which is, in fact, the case. Now you see me—now you don't see "me" but "I" am still here. And if I am still here, I am still me, although you don't see me that way, because I am under wraps and the focus goes to your neurotic blindness. (And here we note Hume's observation that the self/the "I" comprised from perceptions is a fragile if not entirely untruthful notion, so that seeing someone as being one thing or the other is not really the point.) When he was young, my son was temporarily "blinded" by a piece of paper that was thrown in the general vicinity of his eye without ever touching it. Convinced by his panicked mind that he could not see, *he could not see* until his mind allowed him to see that he could. Recalling here in my childhood drawing directly on the television screen with "magic" crayons minus the "magic" plastic screen bound transparency (with which I was also provided to interact with a TV show) in such a way that it could no longer be seen through. This too describes a neurotic function. Froy traces her name on a window and it leaves a permanent trace on celluloid, whose mystery is why it can be only intermittently seen until it is universally seen through by means of plot resolution. The film narrative enacts a neurosis that, to borrow John T. Irwin's term for Borges's work, is "the Mystery to a Solution."[19] If perception is the solution to the general problem of knowing what it is we see, the mystery is how it is that we can see without knowing (or, as Wittgenstein would say, without recognizing) that frumpy-kind Froy who turns out to be a spy is not only a purposeful misrepresentation of who she is but of what she is. It is a misperception of what it is we think we know just by looking at her. When she is identified as the mummified incognito being smuggled off the train, the mystery of her undercover status is solved not once but twice.

This doubling is another sign of the theatrical. What makes it baroque in my definition is that it is enabled by a radical intervention or breaching, in this case the b(l)inding of the body from head to toe, so that perception suffers a whiteout that instigates an intuitive surface reading of name and figure, of nominal figure and figural name. Derrida writes under the sign of Freud, "Life is already threatened by the origin of the memory which constitutes it, and by the breaching which it resists, the effraction which it can contain only by repeating it." That "effraction," which may be equated with breaking into a house, redoubles the theatrical sign of repetition in terms of this book's general argument for the baroquely insomniac and the oneiric. That Froy's body must be so tightly wrapped might be connected to Derrida's belief (after Freud) that "in a certain sense, there is no breaching without a beginning of pain." One may see in "Froy" a (painful) breach with or in "Freud," and what Derrida calls "the insistence of his [Freud's] metaphoric investment [through which] he makes what we believe we know under the name of writing enigmatic." It as if in and through "Froy" Freud is made strange, is estranged from himself by an error in naming an incognito. This jibes with the fact that the figure of the physician in this story is its main villain. Who better than a fictional character, neurotic by virtue of its (non-)nature and its (non-)name, to disrupt and redefine the relationship between perception and memory? "Memory," writes Derrida, "escapes the grasp of 'naturalism' as well as of 'phenomenology.'" Derrida calls for a form of writing that mirrors Freud's respect for "the Being-in-the-world of the psyche, its Being-situated, and the originality of its typology, which is irreducible to any intraworldliness." Derrida proposes a change in how we perceive writing as a medium for "erasing the transcendental distinction between the origin of the world and Being-in-the-world . . . while producing it." Froy's wor(l)d-saving spy message must be committed to memory in the form of a musical phrase. It must not be written down. It is "nontranscriptive writing."[20] It must remain, in a sense, an abstract trace. In this sense, the "FROY" that Iris Henderson sees on the window is an illusion (literally, of the first time), but also an allusion (to other times, like language—"a limit that is always already transgressed"). It is not, however, a delusion, except in so far as we equate image and function under the rubric of "memory" and perception with identity.

It is then necessary to again crook the house, the system of thought-image-function that we generally call "perception." The written name "FROY" must disappear from the window that renders it transparent, because the bearer of the name, who is a spy, is not and must not be transparent as it would be if the writing remained permanent (which is what an un-disappeared trace is).[21] Her identity cannot be perceived, cannot be spied, seen (through). Such writing fools the eye not because it disappears but because it makes you believe that you have seen as in known the bearer of the name that has been written. If the name "FROY" remained as a window tracing, it would stop the plot in and on its tracks. There would be no mystery to solve because there would be only a solution. But identity, as always, gives us the Froy-dian slip.

When One Has Grasped That the "Subject" Is Not Something That Creates Effects, but Only a Fiction, Much Follows

Hitchcock often said that "the McGuffin" was the thing that everyone in the story is after that in the process of telling the story pursuing its lead becomes an afterthought. From another perspective, though, the McGuffin is the long sought after and rumored to be true "thing-in-itself" that underwrites life but that, to all appearances, can never logically appear. Specifically, the McGuffin is Nietzsche's "nonsensical" thing-in-itself, some/thing the human mind invented to serve the very logic it affects to transcendentally disregard.[22] As such, the McGuffin is only real in an imaginary world, whose sole subject is its meta-creator (i.e., Hitchcock). It is not so much that Hitchcock's characters discard the McGuffin; they lose sight of it as a concept for which they, lacking authorship, have no name. The essential thing being ontologically beyond them becomes for them merely an object of pursuit. The film's thought-to-be-delusional protagonist, truth's dogged pursuer, buys into the im/material reality of the object as unitary subject at some risk. "The true world" that he or she posits might only be what Nietzsche calls "the formless unformulable world of the chaos of sensations—*another kind* of phenomenal world, a kind 'unknowable' for us." If *The Lady Vanishes* did not demand closure, it might be only in this imaginary world in which the unreal name and body of "Froy" appear and so can reappear. If there is no getting beyond thought, the search for "Froy" as the McGuffin represents the mind in its obsessional mode of self-creation.[23] Does the name FROY dis/appearing like breath upon the train window, like the airplane I saw change size, represent an error in seeing or the error *of* seeing? The scene (as my mind has so framed it) might also be the seeing of error, a psychotic break with reality or reality undergoing a psychotic break, which, of course, only I can conceive, even if and even though this "I" (subjectivity, being self-created) is fictional. "The senses deceive," writes Nietzsche, "reason corrects the errors."[24] But what happens when reason does not?

And so, while Hitchcock points to the unidentified government secrets on microfilm and to the fictional spy "George Kaplan" in *North by Northwest* and to the coded message contained in a piece of music memorized by "Froy" in *The Lady Vanishes*, it is the physical manifestation of what the name has left behind or what has been left behind in the form of a nominal form that is most philosophically arresting. Under this category-that-does-not-want-to-be-one, I would match the fictional spy "George Kaplan's" pencil impressions left on a Chicago hotel notepad to "Froy's" mystic (window) writing pad. Being a government spy dictates that "Froy" is not her real name, nor, says her abductor, a doctor tainted (as Nietzsche would argue) by his association with psychiatry, does the unseen name's alleged signaling an actual body's disappearance constitute a real subject. Metaphysics, the doctor would argue (while, of course, concealing a Schopenhauerian "evil, blind will" that is itself, in Nietzsche's estimation, a "metaphysical ground" that appears), speaks only of itself, ultimately, making it one-and-the-same with the phantasmagorical "thing-in-itself"—a thing that cannot ever be an object nor especially a subject synonymous with personal identity. "We have," says Nietzsche, "no categories at all that permit us to distinguish a 'world in itself' from a 'world of appearance.' All our categories of reason are of sensual origin: derived from the empirical world." Furthermore, "if there is nothing material, there is also nothing immaterial. The concept no longer contains anything." A plot that is transported in equal measure by a train and by a musical air that is forgotten by the so-called material subject, Gilbert—a musicologist, no less—but remembered by the so-called immaterial subject, "Froy," inscribes the "antilogical 'x' " of some metaphysical beyond where dis/appearance is and the attributive subject is and is not. It is not for nothing that the film's title transforms "The Vanishing Lady," a magic act based upon illusion and misdirection, into an activity that the act's object can only nominally perform.[25]

Levinas suggests that thinking may be "as intention is, a project, which though not cut out from the mental fabric of thought, is 'unreally' inherent in it, and presents itself in thought as in-itself. It shows itself within—manifests itself in the in-itself or is in-itself in manifestation."[26] Froy is not a real character in a real world and perhaps not even in an unreal world, but "F-R-O-Y" are real characters written in an unreal world in which thought is similarly manifest but unreal, a train of perceptions and misperceptions, the two being one and the same, one *in* the same, inherently so. "Froy" is not what Levinas calls "the psychological phenomenon-individual" ceded us by "late nineteenth-century naturalistic empiricism," but its haunting, which is why her name is not so much a steadfast symbol as a spectral sign of dis/appearance, the unreal basis of personhood. Alternatively, "Froy" may be said to constitute "a 'reality' existing independently of its own subjectivity," meaning that it does not need to be a self in order to be.[27]

Is "Froy" not so much a personal as a universal signifier, universal not in the sense of standing for anyone (anonymity) or for everyone (ubiquity) as for a uniqueness that is not localized in the subjective but in the unchanging nature of the "I" that exists outside of justification and subjectivity in the usual sense? This marks the return of the monad, "the wonder of which," Levinas maintains, "should astonish us more than it does." In this scenario, written as a vaporous text, "FROY" is uniquely what it is (not necessarily what *she* is), which is not the literal "residue of an abstraction" that it appears to be. It is not, for all reappearances, simply or precisely a return at all.[28] In a real sense, and in an unreal sense as well, "F-R-O-Y" is neither a personalized "Miss" nor even a comparative miss (a failed perception of dis/appearance), but the train of thought's C-O-N-D-U-C-T-O-R. As to what or where "F-R-O-Y" is conducting us, we might again turn to Levinas, who twists and turns to and from "the positing of the transcendental I in its absolute uniqueness" as being locatable within the realm of appearance. "Is it [the transcendental I] not ordered, in its uniqueness, in a different light than the one illuminating the structures of the phenomenon?" There is no solution to be discovered in the subject that cleaves to reality but nor is there any loss suffered, he maintains, in "awakening to the indescribable 'pure I' of transcendental constitution, recovered by the phenomenological reduction."[29] It is, I would add, what keeps us watching for the scene.

At the 23:50 mark of *Human Desire* (dir. Fritz Lang, 1954), Carl Buckley, a jealous husband who learns of his wife Vicki's infidelity with a longtime lover, John Owens, slaps her across the face. We have seen this before, or if not precisely before then certainly again and again. The husband then compels his wife to write a note to her rich lover to tell him that she will meet him in his train compartment (the train is bound for Chicago) that night. The husband enters the compartment behind his wife and stabs the man to death. He removes the letter from the dead body so that the police cannot connect him to the murder via motive. Jeff Warren, who knows Carl on sight because they both work for the same railroad, happens to be on this same train waiting for a free room compartment to open up. Jeff is, in fact, smoking in the vestibule, the non-room in which non-waiting in the sense of not inhabiting the structure of waiting takes place. (Simone Weil maintains that waiting must be relearned as a form of attention.)[30] Place is, in effect, taken out of the vestibule, when Vicki clears Carl's escape route by drawing Jeff to the club car for a drink. Ironically, Carl has sent Vicki to another man to cover his tracks after having killed the man whom he had sent Vicki to in order to get him his job back. This particular train's engineer is a friend of Jeff's, but Jeff has no idea where or that he is being taken.

A train naturally gives off steam, smokes; a man may smoke in order to let off steam. Someone who gets railroaded is being set up. Is railroad man Jeff, smoking in the train's vestibule like brainwashed Bennett Marco in John Frankenheimer's *The Manchurian Candidate* (1962), being railroaded into taking the fall for a crime he did not commit, or at the very least into not telling the authorities that he saw Vicki exiting the compartment in which the dead body was found? This was prior to Jeff and Vicki momentarily finding one another's bodies in another compartment that was momentarily free but not taken by Jeff, who had been waiting for just such a compartment to become available. Was he, then, in some sense waiting in the vestibule not only for a free compartment but for Vicki, who had been too free with her body with the murdered man and who sought to be free from her murderous husband who held her to the letter of the law, that is, the incriminating letter that he forced her to write to the soon-to-be dead man? It soon becomes clear that Vicki is railroading Jeff into murdering her husband Carl, which will buy Vicki her freedom but lose Jeff his. Or is she just going to make him complicit in the murder by telling Jeff the story of the murder? I recently discovered an unproduced noir script penned by a pseudonymous "Norma Helmer" involving another such incriminating letter and tyrannical husband. It must have been put into turnaround and then dropped after the release of *Human Desire*. One particular scene put the kibosh on poor "Norma." After Carl leaves their apartment, which borders the railroad, Vicki opens the hot air vent (where steam is let off) in their bedroom wall where Carl is concealing the evidence of his crime (Owens's cash and his pocket watch). She is looking for the letter that incriminates her in Owens's murder. This letter-currency-vent montage compares with Nora Helmer's letter-money-letter box scene, in which the letter-in-the-letter box performs a theatrical spatial waiting theme, a metonymic vestibule that awaits the waiting it will soon acknowledge performing as a part of the spatial plot. It's too bad that "Norma Helmer" did not think to include a train in her script. "Froy" could have done something with that.

No matter how abstractedly distracted her thinking becomes, Froy's mind remains active and strangely on course, if only on a *strange* course. The disposed-of Mexican tea wrapper that served as unintentional proof of life for Froy's vanished corpse was like "the musicality of a poem, which has nothing to do with objects and perhaps varies solely in function of what thought sets aside, what it liberates itself from."[31] Froy is up against not only reality, however false, but magic in which she is the unwilling participant. Her mental travels to and through Harriman's "Mexico" are for her like whistling a melody that is defamiliarized by the darkness that the melody seeks to render known. This melody lives and dies on its own terms. Of this, on some level, there is no doubt; there is only the presence of "there is," the *il y a*, of which "the night is the very experience" of "my consciousness without me."[32] And this is what "FROY," vaporously finger-traced on the window of a train car, and Froy portended (to be)—"*my consciousness without me*."

Froy heard the sound of 1,000,000 Mexicans shifting their weight and pounding their fists on the roofs of the train cars as they hurtled through middle Europe. At one point one of these Mexicans eased his body down along her passenger seat window. When he made contact with the glass, dark makeup slid off of his face to reveal the white skin and now transformed features of a person of some middle European ancestry. "Freelancer," Froy sniffed, not yet having observed a Frenchman made up to resemble a Moor whose facial mask rubs off in the moment before his death in Hitchcock's remake of his own *The Man Who Knew Too Much* (1955). Froy's attention shifts to Gilbert, whom she now thinks she once saw play Hamlet on the London stage, or at least the actor playing "Gilbert" (Michael Redgrave) did. "Surprised I didn't see this before," she tells herself. "That boy [she means 'Hamlet']—All voice-over, but no train." No train, no Hitchcock. Stuck playing madness, north by northwest, in any case.

The Lady Vanishes offers a brief on the limits of experience in the making of meaning and coextensively on the role of the a priori in relation to experience as a form of evidence. Kant's "Argument from Necessity" ("Necessity is a criterion of the a priori") involving mathematical propositions states: "One cannot know a necessary proposition on the basis of experience." This is later adapted into philosophy's expanded "generality argument," which says:

(1) Experience is limited to *particular* objects.
(2) No experience can directly justify a belief whose content goes beyond that of the experience.

(3) Principles of inference are general.
(4) Therefore, experience cannot directly justify principles of inference.

Albert Casullo offers that the

> premise (2) of the argument appears to be a consequence of a more general epistemic principle:
> (2*) No cognitive state can directly justify a belief whose content goes beyond that of the state.[33]

As the cognitive subject/object is extracted from its original and later contexts, the question of scope of experience as posited by the notion of the a priori returns us to the question of the "bigger than life." This question has been smuggled on board a train amidst a particular sociopolitical (wartime) context that prizes a particular object (a coded message) and digressively pursues a body that has disappeared with the desired object inside her brain, making the entity known as "Froy" appear to be the desired object itself. However, the embodied Froy here serves merely as a philosophical McGuffin that sets us and her pursuers on a journey whose big picture (world war) is really only a stand-in for the picture that is bigger than life, the thing that not even *world* war can destroy because war is ideologically directed but not more broadly philosophically engaged. As such, Froy is the befuddled object of philosophical inattention. "Why," she wonders, "in all their frenzy to conceal and recover me, am I so misperceived, so overlooked? Does my lack of a voice-over text to narrate make me impossible to find? But even if I had such a text at my disposal, would they have the capacity to understand beyond their experiential inclinations?" "No," says Joe Gillis. "They would not. I passed among them more dead than alive and no one noticed. A faded actress's big-picture persona (she once worked with DeMille) synced frame and content, leaving me to peddle my beyond in a voice-over that none of them could hear. I tried to point out leakage and overflow inside the frame but found no takers. Their translation of desire into an overriding complaint drowned out my presence as being only a *formal* complaint and robbed them of their hearing. Otherwise, they would have *heard* my voice-over." But having, as I've said, been given no voice-over of her own, Froy was not of a mind to listen.

4

✦

D(r)ead

> Dread only accepts what increases it.
>
> —Maurice Blanchot, "From Dread to Language"

We insomniacs wait out the night, dreading the arrival of morning's ministry of fear. The morning says "Oh, *there* you are," finding us in a trance, it sounding self-possessed like it means to take apart our sleeplessness. "*There* you are," a being (an existent) in Being (existence), which a room no more or less materializes than a clock does time. The self walks through a room and there it sees nothing but experiential reflections coming in and out of focus while remaining in consciousness. Mirroring makes time appear to run in reverse. The implicit "now" in "there you are" may be an infinitely repeatable but non-identical "now moment" in the indeterminably long, noncausal evolution of perception through time.[1]

Stephen Neale, whose psychiatrist hails him with "Oh, *there* you are" in Fritz Lang's 1944 *Ministry of Fear*, falls asleep at a séance (he's making up for the "previous" night's sleeplessness) and awakens to the sight of a body on the floor he is accused of having murdered. Strange and fatal things transpire in the realm of sleep/lessness—accusations levied without a body (of evidence) are self-activated, even if ventriloquized in the person of other characters drawn from life fictions. Neale recalls the events of the previous day, or so he thinks about it as being "previous." He was released from an asylum (a nightmare scenario), where he had been incarcerated for murdering his wife, and he proceeded past a contiguous hedge maze to a local fair where the woman selling tickets at the gate told him that "if you wait five minutes, you can go in at the reduced price," as if time, like number, is being marked down in the counting, or as if, more paranoid-catastrophically, time is pronounced as being down for the count—as in he is out of the asylum but also out of time. Is he ticking off the hours until the dawn or trying to hold it back? Neale enters another dark room, a fairground tent housing a fortune-teller, whose sign reads (as if it could): YOU KNOW YOUR PAST/I KNOW YOUR FUTURE. Beyond the curtains, a woman in a gypsy costume (not necessarily a gypsy woman) is facing him like the depthless cheating clock face of time, claiming to be able to read the past but disallowed by unwritten law from reading the future. Her only nominal clairvoyance comes with a temporal disclaimer that subverts even its apparent authenticity. The fortune-teller tells Neale the poundage of a non-pound cake he must guess in order to win it or its cash (British pound) value—the true value here being in the small fair's (fare's) and its modest guesses' and predictions' manageability in relation to an otherwise turbulent world (it's wartime) and unmanageable life (his previous criminal confinement).[2] Neale wins the cake, which is stolen from him by a stranger on a train, a fake blind man who tries but fails to kill him for the canister of microfilm that, unbeknownst to Neale, is hidden inside the comestible. Dream is code concealed, insomnia this awareness in blinding light.

In pursuit of an answer to the contingency that has dogged him since becoming "free," Neale enters the office of MOTHERS OF THE FREE NATIONS (the fair's sponsor) through a door bearing the pallindromic number 202. The palindrome time-stamps compossibility, even as the organization's street address, "FETTER LANE," suggests that asylum (as in freedom) inside a labyrinth is an illusion. Neale is only experiencing *the limit of his release*, the localized heres and nows that the "outside world" models as so many Potemkin villages, imaginary stops inside the labyrinth that is Aporia Station. Another closed and curtained room awaits, wherein a clairvoyant (not to be confused with a fortune-teller) conducts a séance at a round table, a circle inside a square in which only apparent ir/rationalism conjoin. Squaring the circle is an alchemical symbol of female/male conjunction, of insomniac soul-body awareness and revelation of the secret of transformation of base matter into gold, or precious knowledge. A man who belatedly sought to win the cake from Neale at the fair is again a late arrival, "again" and "arrival" enabling a "scene" that again befits a dream.[3] Within this dream state, in the shadow-light of séance a man falls dead, articulating the proposition of "death" as "a late arrival" as well. This plays well with fortune-telling's predictive and clairvoyance's reiterative claims to addressing the late on the scene.

If space and time are within us, as Kant suggests, is clairvoyance merely the release of our inherent potential in tandem with our own anterior experience? Is this our intuition making sense of sensation prior to making sense of itself? If, as Kant allows, "*nothing is in space except what is represented in it*" and that "*the things with which we have to deal are not things in themselves, but only appearances, that is, representations*," might we not find a place for him at the séance table?[4] For all its plot mechanics, the séance phenomenologically renders what the world of things presents, "*only a presumptive actuality*."[5] Kant's assertion that "*what is real in outer appearances, is real only in perception, and cannot be real in any other way*," could be posted as a disclaimer at the entrance to the séance chamber to justify a no-refund policy on the way out. What does the clairvoyant do but attempt to enable what Kant says "reason demands—the absolute completion of the conditions of [appearances'] possibility"?

Kant's argument for spatiotemporal outer/inner intuition makes possible the clairvoyant drawing room expanding into the oneiric house, which becomes not a place but *a way*. "Now, we have no concept of bodies except as appearances, but as appearances they necessarily presuppose space as the condition of the possibility of all outer appearances."[6] The appearance of the dead visitor is no more unreal than that of the body which summons him. The clairvoyant Myra's (thought-rhymes with illusion-spinning Maya's) theft of a little girl's body so as to actualize her predictive gift of said body's return in *Séance on a Wet Afternoon* (dir. Bryan Forbes, 1964) is in keeping with the breakdown of truth and falsehood in the wake of unreality's reveal—the unreality not only of clairvoyance but of subjective perception's materialization of the body *as* space and time. Kant's refrain, "the body is heavy," makes sense insofar as the body weighs upon whatever foundation (or scale) one sets down to explain why something or someone is or is not what it materially *appears* to be.

"Stephen, you sat there watching the clock. I know, you waited for me to die . . . the clock stood still . . . the clock stood still," says the disembodied voice of Neale's late wife at the séance, bringing with it the D.O.A.-ness of the man lying on the cosmologically signed floor, presumably killed with a bullet from the gun Neale took from the stranger on the train, whose blind man's role foresaw his not seeing his own imminent death. And so another circle closes, or so it appears. Where there should only have been one bullet remaining in the chamber, there is, in fact, only one bullet *missing*. Its absence points to the (missing) instant in which the gunman (perhaps an amnesiac Neale) fired his *round* (a semantically circular gesture). And yet, the late man did not arrive at the séance in time for his untimely death to be ascribable to the missing bullet or even to be "late." Together, the would-be gunman and his would-be victim constitute a picture of the terror of *failure in time* to be continuous and so to make sense.[7] The "murder victim" has not really passed, the reality of his passage having been rendered impossible by death's performance at a séance. His "murder" is merely the enactment of *the missing round*, issued not from a gun but from a table whose roundness enabled the release of the "inherent apprehensions" of which Freud wrote on his mystical writing pad.[8] Recalling that the séance constitutes the body's *semblance* to someone who is dead, the séance's obligation is not to reality but to *performance*.

On the train, an exploding bomb had saved Neale from the fake blind man modeling the blackout dysmorphia of wartime London. In Graham Greene's novel on which the film is based, a case of books blows up in Neale's face, causing the protagonist to suffer from *amnesia*, the predominant form of temporal dysmorphia, presenting his condition as a figuration of a noir-ruined mind(set). The apparent sequentiality of these two events, separated by the séance scene and the missing "round," allows for the possibility that a mental condition renders event and eventfulness conditional. (Can you be amnesiac *before* the fact?) Neale pursues the spy he was alleged to have killed at the séance (he of the code-filled cake). The spy is masquerading as the tailor Travers, his surname modeling the Derridean "nonpassage, which can in fact be something else . . . which no longer has the form of the movement that consists in passing, *traversing*, or transiting" (my italics). Travers, who calls as if still in séance's non-passage mode, uses his large tailor scissors to turn the phone's rotary dial as Neale silently recites the number back to himself like a code he is committing to memory so that he can fall asleep. The fortune-teller had not predicted that ten years in the future Ray Milland—the actor playing Neale—would call his screen wife and listen over the phone while she, rather than being murdered by his proxy, killed the latter with the scissors with which Hitchcock figuratively edited *Dial "M" for Murder* (1954). He *intended* to kill her, for which Milland as Neale had already done his time in *The Ministry of Fear* but at the same time was still waiting for that time to begin, as if in a round.

At the séance, I imagine Neale's wife calling him by another name. "*Surely, surely Wieland, thou dost not mean it. Am I not your wife? And wouldst thou kill me?*"[9] Charles Brockden Brown's novel *Wieland; or the Transformation: An American Tale* (1798) discovers its dread not in seeing but in a voice-over narration that is mistaken in what and who it hears. In Clara Wieland's narrative, Carwin, a mysterious wanderer and secret ventriloquist, inflamed and disordered her brother Theodore's mind, already genetically prone to madness through their late father. The latter died a victim of spontaneous combustion in his "temple," a building that serves as *a real physical metaphor* for what is otherwise mentally unseen (in the head). Carwin produces familiar but disembodied voices in bedroom closets, secret interior passageways, and bucolic abysses. Like Webb in *The Prowler*, Carwin is not so much the self-nominated victim of curiosity as its dark genius. Carwin is drawn into his own tale by an open letter sitting on a pedestal that constitutes an objective correlative to Clara's story structure and the sensate immateriality it otherwise contains. Carwin's ventriloquism (rhetorically invoking the danger of Descartes's isolationist individualism as well as Gilvray's radio voice) likewise discovers its visual analogue in Mark Lamphere's counterfeiting of other people's rooms in *Secret Beyond the Door*, narrated by his imperiled wife. Brother Theodore in turn performs what he sees (hears) as being another's agency, killing his wife and their children at God's command.

That the super-agent of human agency not only sanctions but demands such bloody resolve suggests not the God of Abraham (or Ed Avery) who finally stayed the hand with which he commanded his servant to slay his son Isaac but a daemon, a sort of collateral god, the god of corpses as the mad Schreber named him in his *Memoirs of My Nervous Illness* (1903).[10] This daemon, whose illusion-making confuses the real, is called "the great deceiver" by Brown, a near-relation of Cartesian radical skepticism's figuration but also of Socrates's philosophical figure of a "guardian daemon" as personal "genius" and "omen" (clairvoyance).[11] Had Theodore Wieland managed to survive his madness, he might well have written of his own "peculiar relations with God" and the supernatural effects of his wholesale delusion.[12] *Wieland*, like *Secret Beyond the Door*, relates the delusional nature of sensory experience with the insincerity of representation, of not speaking in one's own voice.[13] Clara's obsessive sketching of Carwin into the dominant figure in an imaginary criminal lineup shares the one-off reality of character likeness that Hitchcock later physically represented in his docudrama *The Wrong Man*. And like the accusers of "the wrong man," "Wieland's" so-called protectors get (the) evidence wrong. "Evidence," Husserl asserts, "is in fact not some sort of marker of consciousness that is attached to a judgment (and one usually speaks of evidence only in the case of judgments) as though it were a mystical voice calling us from a better world: 'Here is the truth!'—as if such a voice would have something to say to us free spirits and would not have to demonstrate its title of legitimacy." Then again, in practice, unlike in philosophy, evidence is not always incontrovertible, in which case it is no more real than the reality it manages like some communal trust.[14]

In Kenneth Branagh's 1991 neo-noir *Dead Again*, the convicted wife murderer and death row inmate Roman Strauss is prisoner number 25101415, a study in the contrived redundancy of the symbolic (here numbers) taken to be real that is emblazoned on his brain as it is on his prison uniform. As if to prove this, if mere representation can be called "proof" of anything, Strauss, the so-called "scissor killer" (Ray Milland's undead wife's surrogacy role in *Dial "M" for Murder*) is first seen getting a prison haircut with a facsimile of the alleged murder weapon ("alleged" because Strauss refused to testify in his own defense, but also given the object's symbolic value) with which he stabbed his now late wife Margaret *in the throat* (in the voice, we would say). An amnesiac Margaret returns as a reincarnated Grace and is followed by a P.I. named Church (a reincarnated and rechristened "Roman") whom she at first cannot see. Dread follows us as easily as it awaits our arrival in our foreseeing. This being said, the clairvoyance that the regression-therapeutic hypnotist hired to treat Margaret/Grace's aura-memory speaks to is the Lacanian Real that transcends the symbolic order. Then too, this retro-clairvoyant is (again) a fake. "Madson," as he is called, is an antiques dealer who can only reclaim what memory looks like reproduced. As such, he opportunistically manipulates Grace's and then Church's memories (their names say that they are forever linked) to return them to the scene of the crime ("Go through the door and tell me what you see") in which Church-as-Roman was Grace-as-Margaret's murderer. But the mirror tells another tale in which the "mad son" (i.e., Mad-son) of the Strausses' housekeeper is seen murdering Margaret and is later as the pseudonymous Madson impaled upon the facsimile scissors, their second appearance recalling the otherness context-riving form. It is namely form, specifically of first-person reenactment, that the hypnotist wants recalled by his patient in a noir-ventriloquistic flashback to a guilt-shifting scene that never was. Madson's own mother reveals his murderous secret to Church, who interrupts her television viewing. In this telecast, a husband's telephonic voice arrives too late to prevent his wife's murder by a surrogacy he set in motion but now recalls (takes back, as if remembering too late). The film being broadcast, Church later recalls (remembers as in summoning), is *Sorry, Wrong Number*.

In *Sorry, Wrong Number* (dir. Anatole Litvak, 1948), bedridden, insomniac Leona Stevenson gets her (phone) lines (and mental wires?) crossed and experiences the seeming impossibility of hearing a voice-over plotting her own death. In response, Leona does three irrational things: (1) She continues to shout "Hello, hello!" into the receiver, a cry that if received by the two men speaking on the phone would compromise her by making her heard if not seen; (2) She shakes the phone as if to wake it up, to make it uncross itself, get its mind sorted out, as if the phone was itself a sentient thing; and (3) She redials the operator and asks her to call the wrong number with which she was erroneously connected. Leona's father dismissively posits that what she overheard as voice-over was "maybe just a gag. A couple of actors, maybe." Meanwhile Leona thinks she overhears the "actors" say (using Wieland's script), "I will grasp her throat; I will do her business in an instant; she shall not have time so much as to groan."[15] "To groan," she thinks. What do they know of my condition? Their ventriloquism (they threaten to "grasp her by *the throat*") perhaps reflects the insincerity of her real condition (as seen from an intelligible but invisible outside), which is mere hyperbole, a certain figure of hypchondriacal stagecraft. Perhaps, Leona thinks, it is her own thanatophobia that she is hearing, although she refuses to accept that a phobia, much like paranoia, is anything but real.[16] But by "anything but real" does she mean anything other than real, or something unreal? And if "something unreal," does that necessarily make it untrue? Not if you are a clairvoyant, like even those who won't admit to being hypochondriacs believe themselves to be. You *are* dying after all, and sooner rather than later, so one cannot help but look for and notice the signs. "Suppose," though, Gass suggests, "it had been Cassandra who saw but also disbelieved. That would have been more interesting."[17] This would be akin to being a hypochondriac *in your dreams*, in which insight *is* the complaint. It is the insomniac's nightmare of over-familiarity, knowing too much to enter into the forgetful state that sleep demands. The foreknowledge of entrapment, of being in the middle of something, aligns with the common figure of the labyrinth, which underscores the moment in which this entrapment is acknowledged along with the unreadiness for this moment where interpellation reconfigures the acknowledgment that had previously been (thought to be) forgotten. It's why, when the phone rings in *The Brothers Rico* (dir. Phil Karlson, 1957), we know that Eddie Rico couldn't sleep, despite the appearance of his having been asleep. The eye deceives, where hearing, in this case, does not. There is no mistaking that the call is for him. Insomniac interpellation bestows upon its receiver the unwanted celebrity of still being awake, shipwrecked in and by the night whose corpus you are.

"But how was I to regard this midnight conversation? Hoarse and man-like voices conferring on the means of death, so near my bed and at such an hour!"[18] The voice belongs to Clara Wieland, who like Leona, erroneously believes in the impenetrability of a locked (even though theatrically curtained) room and the senses being true until she hears madness's voiced individuation redoubled as a mysteriously self-indicting ventriloquism. Do they have the wrong woman or just the wrong scene? Perhaps, Leona thinks that she is not meant to die at all. There is in this "perhaps" the very stuff of the life-lie in relation to death. Leona listens closely to Carwin telling Clara, "I was to counterfeit a murderous dialogue; but this was to be so conducted that another, and not yourself, should appear to be the object. I was not aware of the possibility that you should appropriate these menaces to yourself."[19] The telephone had not yet been invented, let alone the party line. The anonymous "He" voiced in ventriloquistic practice underestimated Clara's and indirectly Leona's propensity to cast themselves in the scenes that impart motive to real life, fear to motive and dread to an immateriality that transcends even fear. In both cases, a bed anchors the scene of the crime (see "The Speckled Band"), as in "a glance thrown upon the bed acquainted me with a spectacle to which my conceptions of horror had not reached."[20] The mind here pays philosophical obeisance to the absence and abstraction that settles in the voice and unsettles habeas corpus, as in the showing of the body and what the hypochondriacal body actually presents. As Leona talks to the phone operator about the murder plot she overheard, we hear the sound of the night train passing by outside her bedroom window lending ground cover for the plot to kill her. *Sleep, My Love*'s (dir. Douglas Sirk, 1948) Alison Courtland is riding the night train, put there while unconscious by her husband, who likewise wants her dead. Her dream train rushes toward us in the first frame while what may only appear to be a second rather than *the same train* rushes toward her, the illusion of a *second* time purposely eliding acting and hallucination as the same hypochondriacal condition.

Did the phone actually ring or did Leona merely imagine it, and if it rang was the call really for her, or did she read herself in to the murder scenario as a hypochondriac will? The train noise becomes the rising hysteria in her voice, the phone "a prosthetic device that fulfills the dream of her telepathy," accrediting her thanatophobia with its call.[21] Leona may not be the subject of the call but *the subject produced by the call*. Her thanatophobia is a telepathic assertion of her addressive subjecthood in this space of doubt. There is nothing in a life that proceeds in due time to register our complaint of being interrupted by the call that fulfills the depressive prediction of our clairvoyant calling. Levinas reminds us that "every death is a murder" in the sense that it is "premature."[22] Derrida speaks of the "anxiety of interruption" he sensed in Levinas, who, "when on the telephone, for example, . . . seemed at each moment to fear being cut off, to fear the silence of disappearance, the 'without-response,' of the other to whom he called out and held on with an 'allo, allo' between each sentence, sometimes even in mid-sentence."[23] Like Leona, Levinas was trying to tell Derrida that he (Levinas) was going to die. But does anxiety over the "without-response" signal a true thanatophobia or a surrogate telephobia? Must death hail mineness with every call as if revealing said mineness's "ontological structure"?[24] Nothing says that you must take the call, but you do. It is the burden of clairvoyance as a form of neurotic self-detection.

Descartes describes how his mind's reversal of initial certainty led him to discover what he really thought—namely, that he could not deny the reality of his mind that had seemingly a moment before sought to "pretend" to truth in illusion ("*Cogito, ergo sum*"). As it turned out, Descartes was (and is) a confidence man, in two senses—his believing in himself by creating the illusion that this is of all things most possible to believe in because it requires no external proof. It is not held to any objective criterion, any argument he offers to the contrary notwithstanding. Leibniz, who largely wrote contra Descartes, refutes the latter's idea of the body as the mind's extension: "for nothing ever enters into our mind naturally from the outside; and we have a bad habit of thinking of our soul as if it received certain species as messengers and as if it has doors and windows. We have all these forms in our mind." In freeing the mind from external sources, Leibniz maintains that "*the mind always expresses all its future thoughts and already thinks confusedly about everything it will ever think about distinctly*" (my italics).[25]

In John Boorman's 1967 neo-noir *Point Blank*, sleepwalking Walker has been in the big house. "In fact," he died there. He is what Strawson would call "an index of appearance . . . criteria for re-identifying persons [not necessarily being the same as] the criteria for identifying material bodies."[26] There is no accounting for Walker "in terms of memory, similarity of character, or physical continuity" because all of these are only unfillable conceptual traces of something that never really was.[27] Walker was double-crossed, shot point-blank, and left for dead by his onetime friend Mal Reese, who also stole his wife Lynne following a payroll robbery and double homicide at Alcatraz, site of the former maximum security prison. Sometime later (Walker's hair has since turned steel gray), Walker returns to collect on the debt owed him, which includes Reese's life. "Walker," now says Lynne, "I'm glad you're not dead. It's true, I really am." There is some cause to wonder whether she is really saying, "I am glad you're not dead, Walker," or rather "it's true that you're not dead, Walker, *and that I really am*." The latter possibility is and is not reinforced (the "is" and "is not" of Levinas's "ambivalent apparition") by what she says next: "You ought to kill me. I can't sleep. [Walker's thought-to-be dead body still at Alcatraz has earlier questioned whether he is experiencing death in or as a dream.] I haven't slept. [The first thing Walker did when he entered the apartment shared by Lynne and Reese was to shoot the mattress in the bedroom repeatedly, but Reese left three months ago and Lynne's restless mind and unrested body had already gotten out of bed.] I keep taking pills and dream about you. How good it must be, being dead." Is she speaking hypothetically for herself or to Walker as *her* intelligibly unreal representation of what being dead looks like, breaking down the front door and shooting up the place as he did hers without so much as a word of introduction or explanation. The multiple bullet holes Walker left in her mattress articulate the place of non-sleeping, the space that no longer accommodates sleep. These sleep-holes articulate Lynne's chronic insomnia (a condition shared by her sister Chris), insomniac time's collapse from exhaustion from all the retrospective thinking and feeling that not even multiple flashbacks can contain and from which Lynne finally escapes by overdosing on sleeping pills, a closed bottle of which Chris also keeps on her bedside table in a film whose characters cannot sleep, except when they're dead. Aren't all ghosts insomniacs? Isn't this why they keep walking? Walker is not an insomniac ghost but an insomnia ghost. (I may have glimpsed him sitting on the edge of my bed as a hallucination.) Walker is not so much a man apart but apartness minimally given a name not as an identity but as ipseity, which Levinas defined as "separation."[28]

Walker is staking out the high-rise building in which Mal Reese lives. The street address is obsessive-compulsive disorder's magic number "1111." That is, the building's name, "Huntley House," encodes the number as 1–1untley 1–1ouse. "Thus is my desire structured," I imagine Walker mutters under his breath while peering through the wrong end of a yellow telescope (yellow being my visual anxiety as I apperceive Walker looking) stamped on the barrel with the surplus word "SIGHT," which should be but is not pointed at the Pacific (pacific = "peaceful, calm, non-violent").[29] Walker is intuitively following the dreamer's "special rules" for guilt-free surveillance, "confining one's observations to spatiotemporal sequences."[30] But Walker is not properly a dreamer; he is more of the stuff others think they encounter only in nightmare, the dark genius of sleep.

In *Life A User's Manual*, Perec describes a hotel chain, which he calls "Marvel Houses." The plan was to construct 24 hotels on 24 sites in 24 countries, owing to the fact that there were 24 letters in the registered names of each of the two companies whose merger created Marvel Houses Incorporated and International Hostellerie. The hotel chain operated on the premise that "a good hotel . . . was one where a client can go out if he wants, and *not go out if going out is a burden for him.*" With this in mind, the folks at Marvel designed hotels that offer total small-world experiences, bringing distant locales and ancient ruins, whole towns and villages, ski slopes, battlefields and beaches, surf waves and art galleries to clients who lack the desire and possibly the capacity to imagine beyond representations and beyond representation itself as a trope. The project parallels Bartlebooth's bid to negate space, and by negating travel, time.[31] This makes staying in or going out an illusion. Flann O'Brien's mad philosopher-inventor de Selby in his novel *The Third Policeman* (2002) tests his theory that the passage of time is a hallucination and motion an illusion that the human mind puts in place because it lacks the capacity to see itself inhabiting a series of discrete resting-places by traveling from point A to point B. This happens not on a train requiring an actual ticket but by de Selby "shut[ing] himself up in a room in his lodgings with a supply of picture postcards of the areas which would be traversed on such a journey. To this he adds an elaborate arrangement of clocks and barometric instruments and a device for regulating the gaslight in conformity with the changing light of the outside day." De Selby emerged from his room seven hours following his "departure" convinced that he had arrived at his destination. When outside physical evidence suggested the contrary, de Selby claimed to have journeyed to his intended destination *and* back home again.[32] "*Wake up Mal. Don't go to sleep,*" Walker, who has penetrated Reese's seemingly impenetrable bedroom, urgently whispers to Mal, who must still think he's sleeping. Maybe he is only dreaming that Walker unwinds him from his bedsheet and drops him from the top of the edifice erected on the site of his thanatophobia.

In the distance, the towers from last night's dream.[33] The final shot, in which Walker does not appear, is of Alcatraz Island seen from the shore on *the other side* of San Francisco Bay, as if through the telescope that Walker had pointed the wrong way in Los Angeles adjacent to the Pacific Ocean. ("But does not 'the side of things' offered as an element refer implicitly to the other side?")[34] It is an impossible perspective, an undoing of ground in relation to figure, an exposure of a mechanism that is in fact the higher power, appropriately represented here by a telescope, elsewhere in league with high-powered rifles with telescopic sight attachments, which, after all, have you in "their sights" (sites). Perspective has, unsurprisingly, manufactured all appearance, including that of "Walker," whom we are now being "told" died on Alcatraz Island in the beginning, the end in the beginning being the story's central narrative device. We have been tipped to this by the film's title. We "begin" with a shot delivered "point blank," as close as you can get, and end with a "shot" not fired but framed from a distance, shot and framed *as* distance. This instantiates the film's nominal and overarching theme, the Aristotelian notion of *epiphora* or metaphor whereby distance is "shifted from far to near" to imaginative effect. In this most extra/ordinary feat, "descriptive and novel reference are held in tension by the metaphor's way of looking at the world."[35] As we move further away, we move closer to the truth of the "reality" the film is willing to impart. First, the film has not actually been about seeing from a particular set of distances (e.g., from point-blank range) or point of view (perspective) but about seeing the site, the *lieu* that the temporalizing of *milieu* obscures, appearing to consume and to render time and place neologic. In this sense, "point blank" is less to the "point" as it is about the "blank," the space of non-occupancy, the blank in which we compose, draw the scene and the story as in the Thematic Apperception Test ("intended to evaluate a person's patterns of thought, attitudes, observational capacity, and emotional responses to ambiguous test materials"), only with one significant difference.[36] The trauma but not the source is given, the ipseity not the identity of the "person" taking the test, the Walker. It is perhaps for this reason that in all the scenes set at Alcatraz, the prison is empty. Walker's "murder," which precipitates the film narrative, is, like its agent, created in the future conditional tense that states: "if we realize that death is not an unimaginable condition of the persisting person, but a mere blank, we will see that it can have no value whatever, positive or negative."[37] There is, then, no death scene, and it is this that opens up the possibility for others to dream (up) "Walker." The apparent continuity of the last semicircular panning shot from one side of the bay to the other makes it clear that the real Alcatraz has not been the site of any final confrontation but that "Alcatraz" is itself the final confrontation, with our processing of story-space as a more concentrated articulation of unreality's (only nominally organizational) intelligibility. ("The model," writes Ricoeur, "belongs not to the logic of justification or proof, but to the logic of discovery.")[38] "Walker" and his "Alcatraz" together recall the nighttime journey of Umberto Eco's self-appointed protagonist whose insomnia casts him as being "the only man in human memory to have been shipwrecked and cast upon a deserted ship" in the night where he imagines an already lived-through future.[39] As in the real-life-after-the-fact experience that Alcatraz prison provides its visitors, we have been on the night tour. And I am due back at the Sleep Disorder Center to determine why I continually stop breathing in my sleep without knowing (which is not to say without realizing) it.

A dead man is quick-stumbling down a long hallway framed overhead by tessellating arches and bordered on both sides by series of doors, one of which is named HOMICIDE DIVISION and numbered "44." The dead man enters this space in which homicide undergoes the long and short division of before-and-after causality. The number "44" or any doubled number, for that matter, already looks to be divided and reconstituted, an unstable compound with its own story to tell. It conceals recursion in simple reversal, in flashback, which is the dead man's MO. From the start, as nominally promised, *D.O.A.* (dir. Rudolph Maté, 1950) makes Frank Bigelow's death imminent and immanent—he has been poisoned twelve hours "earlier" as befits a baroque retelling of life in a day. The poison in Bigelow's system locates his hybridic dramatic and hypochondriacal character of presently suffering the future, as a reimagining of Racine's and Molière's baroque themes.[40] Bigelow's mind tells his story in a Borgesian reverse chronological manner that ends with his death *having been* foretold. There is, philosophically speaking, something illogical about this on the order of what Spinoza (as parsed by Deleuze) ascribes to Descartes's putting effect before cause in his construction "*Cogito, ergo sum*": "I know for example that I exist as a thinking being before knowing the cause of my existence." This is not the same as Leibniz's notion that we have the future already in mind, "think[ing] confusedly about everything it [the mind] will ever think about distinctly."[41] Neither Spinoza nor Leibniz insists upon the clarity that Descartes equated with certainty. Their more variegated and more realistic, as in individuated (and in Spinoza's case more detailed) brief was for the possible (Leibniz) and the necessary (Spinoza) determined in large part by relation to a world that Descartes posited as being the mind's embodied extension. What all three philosophers could agree upon on a basic level was, as Spinoza said, that "the more things a thinking being can think, the more reality, *or* perfection, we conceive it to contain."[42] To paraphrase Thoreau thinking of Bigelow, the unexamined death is not worth living.

This calls for a time adjustment. What if Lady Macbeth struggles to erase the bloodstain *before* rather than after the murder of King Duncan by her husband in *Macbeth*? But, one could argue, she hasn't a ghost or seer's pre-vision to inform such temporal intuition. She has not visited the three weird sisters like Macbeth, a visit that introduces him to the woof and weave of predictive, spectral temporalities of the otherwise unforeseen. But what if Lady Macbeth is *the reason why* Macbeth has seen the weird sisters? What if they enact his sublimated but welcomed fear of what her irrational power enables in him? What if Macbeth's seeing the floating dagger is in league with the bloodstain on his wife's hand, an action of symbiotic figurative discourse? What if Lady Macbeth's before-ness is, like Hamlet's, an attempt not so much to prefigure but to distract time and action from "running their course," so as to enter into the play of unreality that characterizes all of us madmen? In my speculative scenario, Macbeth "sees" the dagger that has already dragged itself across Lady Macbeth's hand creating the bloody virtuality that allows Duncan's real blood to be spilled, but only offstage. The floating dagger is not the product of Macbeth's distracted and conflicted mind alone but rather of its dialogic relationship with the virtual knife in Lady Macbeth's dream that manifested her own mind's sleepwalked distractedness so as to forestall the moment which Macbeth in his scene sees as being *about to arrive*. Duncan dies because, as in *Hamlet* (IV, iv) (Hamlet's mind struggling with the before-ness and after-ness of death's nominal ghosting), all occasions inform against *him*.

Death makes manifest the extraordinary atemporality of time, freeing it from its workmanlike representation of the daily grind. Commitment phobia notwithstanding, *D.O.A.*'s Frank Bigelow does not frankly know why he insists on *not* taking his would-be fiancée Paula (who is receiving an anticipatory, however atemporal, "permanent" at the local hair salon) on what will turn out to be his San Francisco death trip. As with Lady Macbeth's bloody hand and her husband's floating knife, there is a kind of transference of prelogical knowledge at work here. Like Lady Macbeth, Bigelow becomes the sleepwalker he already is, as Hegel says, someone who "endures death and maintains itself in it."[43] *D.O.A.*, like *Macbeth*, like *Hamlet*, is an insomniac text, a story not so much about a man who must act before it's too late, but about a man for whom it is too late to act in the customary sense of manifesting action in real time. The poison that has already killed Bigelow is luminous, luminosity manifesting what Deleuze calls "the signs of [his] disease," an embedded sign of the flashback, which is itself embedded as time-within-time which can only be seen in the bounce-back of a figurative light.[44] Even the film's title, *D.O.A.*, the very sign of manifestation, is re-signed by the notary stamp that dooms Bigelow, a small-town tax accountant, before the narrative begins and closes the book on his murder at film's end. Bigelow's journey toward this backdated manifest sign renders time as a luminous poison that is already in our systems, a consequence whose truth is concealed by what we think without knowing to be an anticipatory real.

The flashback both rewards and interrogates anticipation, along with Derrida's Senecan notion that "to put off until later, to defer [*diferre*], and above all to defer wisdom, wise resolutions, is to deny one's condition as mortal."[45] Bigelow absentmindedly checks into his San Francisco hotel *twice*, a woman's alluring, retreating figure intervening between and precipitating the check-ins which in turn prefigure in their doubling his literal and figurative checking out. The desk clerk rings twice for the bellhop, who does not appear until the next scene when he opens the door to Bigelow's room. The bellhop's arrival, then, transpires only after the scene that embodies the indexical present. The bellhop arrives in narrative time, which is not in itself indexical, which does not carry the verdicality of Bigelow's pre- and post-condition. Bigelow checks into room 618, although the "6" is slightly out of focus (owing in part, "no doubt," to the flow of alcohol up and down the main hallway onto which the string of room doors open) and easily becomes an "8," creating a palindrome (i.e., 818), a before-and-after, back-and-forwardness of the upended (un)real infinite at the room's point of entry/exit (check-in/check-out). A disembodied hand summons Bigelow through a door to find its drink. Bigelow drops into the bar at the Fisherman's Club, where in the moment that the bartender turns his back to the bar to converse with Bigelow (who has himself left his drink unattended to chat up a blonde), a man conspicuously dressed for winter in springtime with his back to the camera's luminosity detector switches Bigelow's unfinished drink for another that will finish him. When Bigelow reaches back for his drink, his hand is reunited with something else, something different, although the bartender argues otherwise: "You saw me pour it." Eager to continue his conversation with the blonde, Bigelow does not engage with the limit-logic of the fatally inattentive bartender's suggestion, which overlooks causality's absent middle(man). Two men walk into a bar, the one is named "Bigelow," the other "Death."

Feeling not himself the next morning, Bigelow visits a doctor for whom he waits with a nurse who stares strangely at him, his distraction returned as her attention's arrest. Perhaps she instinctively sees his body's temporal dysmorphia. Perhaps, she cannot really see *him* at all. Time and again (the ghosting of the future, the future as the ghost of an unreal present), Bigelow cannot see what is going on, what is being presented, with presenting itself like a comment upon his condition, transpiring behind his back, so to speak. So, when Bigelow races out of a second medical consultation confirming the results of the first (after first looking at his hands, belonging to the body of both a dead man and a self-murderer, a sleepwalker, a two-fisted drinker, a self-conscious performer diverting attention from his feet so that he can affect walking naturally, i.e., as himself), he pauses to catch his breath. His back against the side of a kiosk where a number of *LIFE* magazines are on prominent display *behind him*, he now recognizes without the visual prompt that he is and has always been only life-like.

Pascal wrote, "there is never a pure present [in which one can find complete repose in the selfsame thought]. In the instant it exists, it already has abandoned itself; it calls, it anticipates the moment that follows it."[46] As Bigelow lives with the active regret (which is his present-tense condition) of having traveled to San Francisco to affect the role of a weekend Don Juan, he enters into the manifold nature of lateness. His after-the-factness modeled by a behind-the-back-ness confesses a lack of self-recognition in the face of an apparitional self-realization, a fulfillment of a phantom desire that is Death's calling. Bigelow did not return another man's call, and the latter, falsely indicted over a bill of sale for the rare and illegal metal iradium (distractedly notarized by Bigelow, who was *at the time* already preoccupied with his San Francisco adventure), killed himself, leaving Bigelow as an unwanted rem(a)inder for the real criminal to irradiate/eradicate. Bigelow dies to close a double thought loop involving guilt by death's dis/association. Death never stops calling until it reaches us. Why else would it call? If "a mortal can only start from here, from his mortality," as Derrida notes, as if describing the flashback's agency, then we are all dying with our memory of "how short life has been" in mind.[47] The fact that "the moment of death no longer belongs to its time," as Derrida attests, points to anachronism as a hallmark of the baroque, a form and function that deals in dreams and delusions, in distended, compressed, and recycled times.[48]

"My death" is imprecisely a temporal claim whose "mine-ness" offers us minimal insurance against the inevitable shock at how little we will realize we knew *at the time*. Bigelow tells Paula how much he *now realizes* he loves her when she unexpectedly arrives in the flashback without foreknowledge of his death, but hoping to foresee their union "in sickness and in health," a health he only now knows, as Kierkegaard observed, once we encounter the crisis of sickness. Bigelow impatiently (can you be impatient if you are actually out of time?) awaits "a oneself that one is but does not know," "the impossibility of the existence whose name is 'death.'"[49] Derrida maintains that "the death of the other, this death of the other in 'me,' is fundamentally the only death that is named in the syntagm 'my death,' with all the consequences that one can draw from this."[50] This is the significance of Bigelow's reporting a murder to the police as being "mine" and then entering into the flashback in which he is murdered but does not die. The untold, hidden motive of Bigelow's flashback is to buy him time not to solve *his murder* but to understand *his death*. In their final scene together, Paula tells Bigelow, "Frank, you don't even act like yourself" (a tacit indictment of a man named "Frank" and an aporetic sign of death's not/becoming you). The "you" of the past can only ever be *inside* the flashback, whose presentness can only be figuratively captured in order to make sense out of what has already happened, out of who you *were*.

Alan Parker's 1955-set voodoo noir *Angel Heart* (1987) suggests that being dead is a realization reached only once you catch up to your own flashback, as if shadow were your only true reflection. It is a moment that reconciles you with the guilt that lies buried beneath false memory. We can no more know this than we can know what if anything is in a dead man's mind, unless our cryptomnesiac mortality is such that we mistake a dead man's memory for the dead man's memory of *our* dreams. In the course of investigating a missing persons case for his mysterious employer Louis Cyphre (i.e., Lucifer), *Angel Heart*'s P.I. Harry Angel discovers to his horror that he *is* that missing person, a popular forties crooner named "Johnny Favorite." "Favorite" took the celebrity the devil offered him and then skipped out on his soul-debt by assuming another man's, that is, *his present* identity. The signs, of course, are everywhere. NO LIFEGUARD ON DUTY reads the sign on the beach at Coney Island. The "NO" has been added in red. The neon sign "YANKEE DINER" appears reflected in a pool of water as EEKNAY in red and as RENID—which has the word RED already IN it. There is also ID and even the hint of REWIND, missing only a Perecian "W." Perec's proto-puzzle painter Bartlebooth will die with a W-shaped puzzle piece in hand that is unable to fill a space in "the almost perfect shape of an X," for the mystery that the puzzle only in this last approximation appears to represent.[51] A car passes and the reflection disappears, while Angel-Johnny is inside the DINER making (and unknowingly taking, as in answering) a call. We briefly glimpsed the dark profile of a man in the passing car's driver's seat, but perhaps it is only a shadow, a cipher (an "X" that a "W" is only pretending to be). Who (or what) could or would erase a name, let alone a name in reverse? Harry Angel, of course, but he cannot do this alone, although his bad memory for names is symptomatic of his desire for in-lieu-of-death self-erasure, for mental simulation. "However cleverly you sneak up on a mirror, your reflection always looks you straight in the eye," Cyphre reminds Johnny in the midst of Angel's self-denial of passing for someone else. "That's some leak you got there," a cop in Angel's New Orleans hotel room remarks while looking at the ceiling and seeing double Joe Gillis's Sunset digs.

There is another way through this, which has more to do with evidence materializing intuition rather than outcome. "How might intuitions being evidence relate to them being justifiers?" Chudnoff asks. It is not for nothing that Cyphre asks Angel if he would believe that he really is the devil if he had a spiked tail and a cloven hoof. Anxiety's demand for evidence is both great in its need and small in its desire, since anxiety is, said Lacan, structured like fantasy in and by the aforementioned "unreal reality that is called the psyche."[52] Anxiety demands no proof beyond its own reality, and that reality can never be disproved to the patient's satisfaction. Such neurotic expectation wears the dreadful face your passport now reveals. Harry Angel lacks what Chudnoff calls a "propositional justifier," by which he means, "whatever makes it the case that you have justification for believing something." Angel is an atheist who fears not God but chickens (given his unacknowledged voodoo ritualistic rebirth with a dead man's heart). "If an intuition is a doxastic justifier," says Chudnoff, "then it plus the fact that you base a belief on it make it the case that your belief is justified."[53] Dread, though, is its own doxa, the acceptance of what appears to be true according to what one fears. In this regard, Angel is a true believer, despite his apparent indifference to the signs admonishing his disbelief in the self-denial of *NO*. Angel insists he k*no*ws who he is in the mirrored face of his daemon dread, which being a Cypher provides no material evidence of who he (Angel or Cyphre) really is. We cannot see the big-picture daemon in our small lives, because to do so would mean that we are bigger than the big picture created to keep us in thrall to illusion. We would have moved beyond mere representation, which would obviate the need for ciphers inclusive of daemons, and would not be made anxious by Cyphre's admonition that "*the future is not what it used to be*," because time as we know it would cease to exist if it were and we would be not dead or else only "dead again."

In Guy Maddin's retro-neo-noir *Keyhole* (2012), the armed leader of a gang who has shot its way into a house tells his hostages (there are already casualties lying on the floor), "Okay, alright, those of you who have been killed stand facing the wall. Everybody who is alive face me. I don't wanna count twice." Here nearly anagrammatic casualty/causality is purposely flipped in mentally lexical proximity to reproduce a "dead again" scenario that confounds what physics (and biology) believe to be logical: "Bodies in motion stay in motion; bodies at rest stay at rest." In much the same way, the absent leader of the gang, Ulysses (the belated homecoming king), has instructed his men to break into a house that he knew was already surrounded (much as was his Penelope by her suitors). Logic matters no more than does/did/will chronology when it comes to the (already) dead, as the devil already knows regarding such details. The house once belonged to Ulysses Pick (door locks open at the mere mention of his name), his wife Hyacinth (whose name speaks of birth and *re*birth), and their four children. No one has lived in this house stuffed with time (represented by the taxidermied animal heads on the walls) since—except, that is, for the ghosts, one of whom may well be the story's narrator.

"Are you really here?" the narrator asks of Ulysses, although indirectly through images that overlay locales or else a single locale that overlays images. "Are you really here *now*?" the voice means/meant to say. "I can't hear my own thoughts," the girl named Denny, whom Ulysses has brought to the house after having saved from drowning, tells him, as if responding to some spectral narration. She is ill, or "Ill," like the three vertical marks scratched upon a wall in the room where the dead and the living now gather. In the hallway, a female ghost from Blanchot's haunted-house novel *Aminadab* is wiping the rainwater that pools on the floors of the labyrinthine house whose lease (on life and death) was cosigned by the ghosts of Joe Gillis and Norma Desmond.

"How come you can see other rooms, and I can only see this one?" asks Hyacinth, who is locked inside a room which if Ulysses could breach he would (allegedly) kill her, like so many other noir husbands of fabulist provenance. In response to this thought, which may or may not be her own (it's so difficult to say with house ghosts as house guests), she asks rhetorically: "Is he alive enough to do that?" "Alive enough" and "dead enough" involve figuring out which states or conditions can and should have qualifiers attached to them, degrees of aliveness or of deadness. A mirror, like the one asymmetrically framing Hyacinth's face when she asks her "alive enough" question, is also a keyhole of sorts. Through it we spy the active agency of death and transformation in Greek mythology, the gender reversals of the male Hyacinth and the female Calypso, along with the Greek-into-Roman transformation of Odysseus into key-lit-through-a-keyhole Ulysses, who we learn cannot be killed twice, made dead again when he is already dead enough by a ghost's determination. As Ulysses's memory returns without the benefit of any except maybe self-hypnosis, the ghost of Ulysses's dead daughter disappears into a drowning pool.[54] And Ulysses, who sees this, says, "I'm only a ghost, but a ghost isn't nothing," in a way that only partially echoes Roman Strauss saying of himself in the third-person "past" of flashcard (flashback/flash-forward memory), "he became a nobody."

In the baroquely slow-to-unfold neo-noir *Road to Nowhere* (dir. Monte Hellman, 2010), the blogger and poster Nathalie Post is seen inserting a disk labeled ROAD TO NOWHERE into her laptop computer, along with the film (within-the-film)'s director, Mitchell Haven. Haven says by way of overdubbed commentary on the film they are watching, "Velma was always my way into the story" (and later to Nathalie who first reported the real-life events, as if echoing Strauss in *Dead Again*'s "Your story was always mine"). We see (we assume, our assumption being suspended with experience as re/play) Velma Duran painting and drying her nails on what is for Post and Haven onscreen (on the computer screen now expanded to fill our own, to become the film *and* the film-within-the-film). We watch Velma (namesake of Philip Marlowe's missing damsel in *Farewell, My Lovely,* 1940/*Murder, My Sweet,* 1944) for some time, in the facsimile real time of the screen. We are meant to be aware but also to disregard the generational loss, not of picture quality but of history and causality.

Rafe Taschen, who leaves the same house from which we think we saw Velma exit, crashes his private plane into Lake Fontana where Velma has parked her car as if awaiting the replay of the disaster. In the "actual" criminal case about which Nathalie blogged and upon which the film-within-the-film (marking film as having a vexed in/authentic interiority) is based, the "real" Velma drove her car into Fontana Lake (perhaps before, not after Taschen's death). This "Action!" (the film director's command) effectively produced the original "Road to Nowhere" (left uncompleted owing to the intervention of World War II), which was intended to provide physical access to a number of cemeteries that were displaced when the man-made lake was built. The lake (in) effect threatened to wash away the dead. Like the dead, the dead man's plane has nowhere to land but in the story space in which Joe Gillis and so many others have landed that I have seen on the wing. The "actor" playing Rafe Taschen is after all named "Cary Stewart," an amalgam of the names of Hitchcock's two most frequently used and popular leading men—Cary Grant and Jimmy Stewart, the one pursued by an airplane *from* nowhere and the other by a "man who knew too much" whose stage makeup was removed by death, like one of Froy's "1,000,000 Mexicans."

The "non-actor" Laurel Graham, who Haven hired to play Velma, visits the latter's gravesite, perhaps one of those displaced by Lake Fontana. But if Laurel (a mythically honorable name) is indeed a non-actor even in name, she may as well be or not be Velma in real life as she is and is not Velma under the camera's watchful, unforgiving and "truthful" eye. "Velma" is what is called a hypotyposis, "the iconic element in a representation that makes present to the senses something which is not within their reach, not just because it does not happen to be there but because it consists, in whole or in part, of elements too abstract for sensory representation." So although Laurel, the actress playing Velma, is decidedly sensual, as is the actress playing Laurel playing Velma, the real "Velma" is the one who escapes into a cine-space whose tessellation metastasizes unreality, the face only of analogical function (as the tie-in to Marlowe's missing-but-*not-really* missing so much as duplicitous "Velma" suggests).[55]

"Well, sometimes I think that Velma's not dead. She's only changed bodies," Nestor Duran says about the actress playing his daughter Velma in the film. An insurance investigator named Bruno who is working on the film hails Laurel-as-Velma as *the real* Velma and not (just) her character('s) name. (Bruno and Laurel/Velma and/or the actors playing them have visible but unreadable tattoos that may/not say who they "really" are.) Bruno knows that (she as) the real Velma has defrauded the state of North Carolina out of $100,000,000 (a purposely hyperbolic, mythic sum). Velma confesses as much but only to someone who already knows, not Bruno but to the actor playing Cary and Taschen in a third unnamed role, while she is on the toilet, so we (are meant to) believe that she is speaking the truth, that what we are seeing performed is (somehow, in some sense) real.

In the next scene, Taschen bails out of his plane *prior to* it crashing, and really, says the vanished image of Mr. Arkadin, why not? The trope of the character who appears to come back to a life that no longer seems real or in which he or she no longer seems real (and so feels dead, again) speaks to the movement of "figurality" that inhabits and drives the figure. Paul de Man writes: "For not only are tropes, as their name implies [from *tropos* in Greek or 'turn, way'], always on the move—more like quicksilver than like flowers or butterflies, which one can at least hope to pin down and insert in a neat taxonomy—but they can disappear altogether, or at least appear or disappear."[56] A trope in motion stays in motion. Is the return-of-the-dead an encoding of a trope-like instability—passage without progress—that the crashing plane and the cine-experiencing of reality make manifest? There being no trope without recollection, there is nevertheless always something that the trope (and a film) cannot recollect. In this regard, the trope is much like the frame (with one also exemplifying the other), or more specifically like a *puzzle* frame that puts itself together in order for it to be once again taken apart/taking a part. And so the trope of the plane crash-lands the idea of the film-within-the-film as a trope, a figural disambiguation of something else, perhaps even in error or by accident. A trope vacates authenticity at its point of origin. The real never gets on board the passage the trope manifests/of the trope manifest. Like Doc Daneeka, whose name appeared on the flight manifest of a plane that went down but which he never actually boarded in the Joseph Heller novel *Catch-22* (1961), (his) physical appearance offers insufficient proof of (a) life that has been captured and imprisoned inside a trope of death from which, paradoxically, there is (no) return.

"It's fraud, it's grand theft, it's falsifying police documents, stealing goddamn bodies, Bruno later tells Haven in reference to the prior actions of the now re-embodied Velma Duran. "We've got all of that or almost all of that" in the movie, Haven assures him as if he really knows who they are. Haven is after all, filming his dream, living in his head as he readily acknowledges. As if in a bad dream, Bruno shoots and kills Velma at close range and Haven does the same to Bruno, only point-blank. "You shouldn't have brought a gun into the scene," Haven says, pursuant to shooting the (as if) dead bodies with his camera that the police mistake for a gun that shoots all of them in turn. The police put Haven in jail for "the shooting," which is where we first discovered him at the start of the film but only now "really" discover (him) watching *Road to Nowhere* on Nathalie's laptop computer. She has apparently visited him in prison to show him the completed film and then to interview him for the DVD commentary that is lacking from the DVD of the actual film, "the actual film" being in terms of its story only a fiction—an outside with no inside, or maybe even an inside with no outside.

A closing, close-up photo of "Velma" dead and/or asleep and dreaming with her teeth peering through open, lipstick-smeared lips graces the "cell" wall nearest the mirror above the sink, reinforcing her as the hypotyposis made purely visible at representation's end. As a song on the soundtrack instructs the credits to roll, they do to the end where the standard disclaimer appears: "The characters and incidents and the names used herein are fiction, and any similarity to the name, character, or history of any person or entity is entirely coincidental and unintentional." The end of the closing credits, however, reads: "THIS IS A TRUE STORY." This is, to paraphrase Magritte, a pipe dream, as filmmaking is in the filmmaker's own description and un/reality is in our own anxious terms. There are few more difficult words to parse in any form of language than "THIS IS A TRUE STORY," a baroque construction, an insomniac tic.

Here, then, is an *untrue* story that paradoxically ends with the words, "that's the way things are." In *The Strange Affair of Uncle Harry* (dir. Robert Siodmak, 1945), Harry Melville Quincey's sister Lettie, like Leona in *Sorry, Wrong Number*, is an imaginary invalid. Both women have a heart condition that is an affect of relational anxiety, Leona with her husband, Lettie with her brother. The longtime bachelor Harry's decision to marry outside the family (irony intended) means that his spinster sisters, the combative Hester and Lettie, must find another house in which to live. Lettie rejects house after house for (her) "health" reasons, in one case saying that the house in question "smells." Smell, like feeling, is something that is not just difficult but impossible to dis/prove. The hypochondriacal obsessive-compulsive knows there is no way to invalidate the condition's invalidity. Unless, of course, the "patient" trips herself up. Bereft at having sacrificed his fiancée Deborah to his gothic family psychodrama, Harry poisons Lettie's cocoa, which she almost drops when she trips going up the stairs to poison sister Hester "by mistake." When only one of two identical cups is poisoned, death still finds its proper addressee. Harry may have meant to poison Lettie, but Lettie surely (even though accidentally-unconsciously) meant to poison the sister who competed for their brother's affections. Here the "almost" stair-drop (staircases being the location of uncommon household "accidents" in noirs such as *The House by the River* and *Leave Her to Heaven*) performs truth's reluctant show. Similarly, when Hester dies, Lettie, like a fortune-teller reading poisoned cocoa residue rather than tea leaves, recognizes that Harry's intention was to kill *her*. How does she know? Because Harry's betting on two cups to do the job of one enabled the "almost-ness" that Lettie's tripping on the stairs physically expressed. Death is again, retrospectively foreseen as the sign among signs, the name of the "dead" so overtly un/hidden inside of his/her "dread." I know I will die, but are *you* my murderer?

Harry tells Lettie that the jury won't believe that she didn't murder Hester—"that's the way things are," and Lettie is indeed movie-swiftly tried, convicted, and sentenced to hang, having lost her last appeal. Overwhelmed by (again unprovable, and perhaps imaginary) feelings of guilt, Harry decides to confess to the murder, but the judge says he will not believe him, unless Lettie herself confirms the facts of his confession (a highly tenuous standard for proof—except in dream logic—since the guilty so often protest their innocence). But hypochondriacal Lettie, who has been playing with death's affections for her entire life, now accepts her role as death's bride, allowing too that this is her gift to Harry, a desire nurtured since childhood to give him something of herself, "something worthy of your talent and your imagination." It is, she acknowledges, a "peculiar present," as might also be said about a dream wrapped up in such a theatrical act.

As Lettie is led back to her cell the scene fades into one of Harry, with his head buried in hand in what we imagine to be a state of despair. He pours out what we believe is the amount of poison that remains in the bottle following the murder, the last bit of physical evidence of his crime. However, appearance being hypochondriacal by virtue of its mere-ness, it is significantly unreal, material but non-evidentiary. And so, when his ex-fiancée Deborah suddenly enters the room announcing her desire to return to wed Harry, followed by the appearance of a very much alive Hester, we realize that Lettie's condition has not so much precipitated a real murder plot as authored Harry's wish-fulfillment murder fantasy. "I wanted to do something for you, to give you something, *something worthy of your talent and your imagination,*" she said, "*a peculiar present.*" On the verge of death, which is the hypochondriac's oft-told tale, Lettie told Harry the truth from inside a fiction, offered him the gift of a second chance not precisely by sparing him his life by offering her own in its stead (martyrdom only becomes the hypochondriac in the retelling), but rather by setting up for him the return of reality from the mere-ness of its representational *appearance*. "You see, *that's* the way things are."

But are they, really? The shadows of the passing cars pass overhead on the room's ceiling, as if being movie-screened for me in my bed, so I don't have to look anywhere but up. The ceiling gaze signals mental work of some kind, be it distracted, anxious, or even the mad place from which voices speak so as not to be heard so much as overheard giving evidence of some supernatural proof.[57] Am I waiting for something to happen or merely modeling waiting in a picture, a scene? There's a map veined into the ceiling above the bed where countless noir hit men and hide-outs are lying, like the one in O'Brien's *Third Policeman,* in which a young murderer is taken into custody by the police who are able to transform the shape and size of time within a secret, eternal world of manifestly unexplained numbers, inexplicable events and incommunicable meanings, magnified invisibility, limit-inducing hyperbole, and over-articulated expression (e.g., "his explaining face" that intends to "kill the life out of you" if you do not access "your internal imagination"). Above all, there is *room for* self-reinvention for the nameless protagonist who is sentenced to be hung the very next day if he does not widen his mind, which will balance his weight in such a way that his hanged body will be arrested in mid-fall. The mind commands the body to stop answering to gravity at the point that it has one foot in the grave. And the mind recalls awakening to thinking it "had been in the next world yesterday" or possibly in this world tomorrow, when we are already dead.[58] Dread suits a body, dresses it with a death that is not yet your own, or so it tells and occasionally shows me where the spectral bodies murmur as if in *their* sleep.

Recursion

> For just about everyone, the day after tomorrow is abstract and the day before yesterday incomprehensible.
>
> —Alain Badiou, *The Century*

The title of the film *The Night of the Following Day* (dir. Hubert Cornfield, 1968) refers to the fact that the narrative wraps back upon itself, a structural device that its director says he borrowed from *Dead of Night.* The structural transfer from one *Night* to another again calls "Death" into question as (a) dream, a reworking of a priori and a posteriori categorization—that is, we dream our deaths so that they can be realized. ["A film I am (a) watching as it's being filmed, (b) seeing in the theater, or (c) acting in," Perec says in a dream.][59] *The Night of the Following Day* is ghost-written by a consciousness that cannot frame any principle of individuation outside of a scene.[60]

A young woman, generically called "the Girl," deplanes and is abducted by the same group of professional criminals at the beginning and end of the film, her life switched out as if it were a Ricoeur-ian metaphor expressive of "the tension between epiphor [expressing the existence of something] and diaphor [implying the possibility of something]." It is furthermore a picturization of *metalepsis*, which J. Hillis Miller defines as "that preposterous figure of speech that puts the early late and the late early," or, as Nietzsche states, "chronological inversion [*Umdrehung*], so that the cause [*die Ursache*] enters consciousness later than the effect." There is no accounting for the inner and the outer worlds (subject and object) outside of the phenomenal fiction (the fictional continuity) of the narrative form. Miller notes: "We cannot be conscious of our consciousness as such, as the latter only works in terms of comprehensible imaginary causal chains. We project backward a fictitious cause and only then can the thought or the feeling enter consciousness." *Is this what flashback is trying to tell the character who entertains it and through him, us?* "Inner experience," wrote Nietzsche, "enters our consciousness only after it has found a language [*eine Sprache*] the individual understands."[61]

Whatever language the Girl is hearing through her headphones is screening out the flight attendant's voice even as another flight attendant is removing *the temporary screen that had been set up so that the passengers could watch an in-flight movie.* "Thank you very much, hope to see you again soon," the Gilvray-face-wearing flight attendant impersonally radio-voices the departing passenger. "But why did she call me Susan," the confused Girl asks, I imagine, not because it is not her name but because she *has* no name. She (or I) must have me confused with some other film. "No, not confused," the former stewardess apparitionally turns and tells the camera. "At least no more confused than "sooner or later" is in denying time its present/presence." (To paraphrase Deleuze, the baroque night knows well that "hallucination does not feign presence, but that presence is hallucinatory.")[62] Husserl, leaning into frame ("I couldn't help overhearing. . . ."), offers that "this manner of givenness *of* the temporal experience is itself in turn an experience."[63] "You must have fallen asleep during the coming attractions," the stewardess in my scenario tells the Girl, who wonders what "coming attractions" even mean in relation to real life—as if the Girl even knows what "real life" means. It's all a language-game, isn't it? "There is," as the adage says, "no time like the present," because there is no other time and so no evaluative, but only representational (illusory) likeness. "The reality brought to language by metaphor . . . revealing itself only partially, ambiguously, and through symbolic indirection."[64] There is, in fact "no time like the present" because both the past and the future do not allow one to be in their midst, and yet there is in some sense no midst in which to be in the form of a discrete present. We do not time travel, so much as mind travel, the mind being the present's thickening agent, the moment's momentous-making mechanism that substitutes language for causality. The mind *is* the medium, the spectral archivist-clairvoyant enabling the Husserlian ego function of "living through" without necessarily having experiences, actively confusing the immediate *experience* of a real present with the *consciousness* that constitutes a "real present." And Ricoeur reminds us that Augustine posited "the threefold presents, the present of the past, the present of the future, and the present of the present." Husserl transformed this into the extended present, which includes the "quasi-presents" generated by the imagination "and which each unfold their own system of retentions and protentions."[65]

"One's justified belief that one existed a moment ago," suggests Albert Casullo discussing the a priori, "does not entail that one did exist a moment ago. It is logically possible that one just came into existence along with memories of the past." It is not a thesis to which Casullo fully subscribes, given the supporting evidence that life, including other people's lives, provides as memory. However, the Girl is flying in the interspace, which Kant arrives at via time. "It is not that time passes," he argues, "but the existence of what is changeable passes in time."[66] And so, I would add, the existence of what is unchangeable causes time to appear to recur. But appearance being manifold, having magnitude in Kant's construction, allows for time to act in different ways that determine how we perceive the figure in space, in the scene without necessarily taking into account how she sees herself (thus "the Girl's" generic appellation). Although Strawson argues via Kant that we appear in time and not *as* time, "in a temporal guise," we here broach the antinomy of the meaning of appearance and "the bounds of intelligibility." Kant *has* argued that space and time are in us, prior to experience; they are products of our a priori intuition.[67]

The Girl's mind appears to have been traumatized, but in a way that does not so much fix upon a memory as it enacts fixation *as* memory, with her as fixation's self-pursuing revenant. The Girl may be compared to Robinson Crusoe trapped on his small, circular island, whom Derrida suggests is pursued from the past or from the future anterior by the death he runs toward in the nominal future. "It is as if he were already dead and as if everything that happens to him were happening not for the first time, but as repetition, as *revenance*. Tomorrow is really yesterday, in a perpetual déjà vu. The future is already past." Like Derrida's Crusoe, the Girl's self-persecuting revenance may be her way of coming to death, accepting fear of her own death as opposed to death in the abstract, an event of which she may be unaware and is only made aware by writing, plotting, fantasizing her story. "I live my death in writing," Derrida observed. "I posthume as I breathe."[68] Here my own breathing grows heavy with the weight of what my writing knows. I think of Hamlet's performance of his own self-haunting and of a panic attack I suffered inside the mousetrap of an English king's labyrinth whose ominous telepathy negotiated my coming and going in place.

The Girl's mental space is blocked in the theatro-psychological sense like a Robbe-Grillet object in a *story-space* of logically affective detail. The characters who appear on screen abusing her are behaviors she introjects from some unnamed source, probably her rich but absent father "Dupont" (an evocative, symbolically monied name), whom she mentally holds for ransom with her head trauma. Despite being briefly called "Dupont's daughter," the Girl is nobody's relation, has no relation to time. She is really only her own aporia. If one accepts Vilém Flusser's subject-object-predicate ontological analysis of reality, then "the Girl" is an objectless subject who "lacks something against which it may be projected in a predicate," in her case, the retracted screen which leaves her adrift in a movie she is unable to identify as being such and "now."[69] I lose the object, do not see the truth of the object, I think in my interspatial mind, because my condition has no object and no justification. It is strongly indefeasible, a priori; it defeats "real" evidence with the obsessive-compulsive imagination's overdetermined belief. The mind always returns to the *scene* of its own consciousness-making, its crime, its head-case trauma, its "justified false belief."[70]

Somewhere between the first and last screenings of the Girl and her dead body's reflection in a mirror in what only appears to be the film's penultimate scene, the image, representation exposes its life-lie-ness, the Husserlian "inauthentic thesis [of] as though it were the case," and an "impotent mirroring."[71] But representation is constitutionally incapable of suffering alone, without the body that feels compelled to give false evidence against itself at representation's behest. Spinoza and Nietzsche argued, albeit differently, for the a priori body that puts us in mind of what a body is, of how the body endures, among other things being a body. The mind, Spinoza said, "can neither imagine anything . . . nor recollect past things . . . except while the body endures." The affective Cartesianism of "I think I have a body, therefore I am" makes it incumbent that we "*strive to imagine those things that increase or aid the body's power of acting.*"[72] The "foolish fact," as Nietzsche called it, of the body's durative (but not self-sustaining) power to act, to play itself, is what the Girl is *and* represents, which accounts for her denotatively functional name.[73] And what is time in this scenario? *Time is money*, ransom money given in exchange for keeping the Girl alive, if only "*for the time being,*" money changing time into nonsequential used small denominational currency (presents/presence), exchanging what is in hand for unstable "futures," of provisionality, precarity, of dread. The body is, becomes a nonorientable object in a premonition dream.

Even as we try to find our place in time, philosophy makes concerted efforts to keep time in its place. Via succession, determination, relation, and representation, we seek *to make time possible* in an empirical sense, knowing that time, as always, has its own flight manifest and means of escape. Our need to identify how and where we "fit" in relation to time takes something bigger than life (the outside of our outside) and reconfigures it as something small—as (a) life's container. At the same time, though, Aristotle argues in the *Physics* that time is independent from and superior to the things that it contains by virtue of the fact that it contains them.[74] A complex of thought-object relations of which transport puts us in mind provokes a hypnotic reverie on what Ricoeur calls "[the] problem of relatedness to the real." In this "relatedness" we glimpse the unreality of the past, present, and future as entities that can really only be understood aporetically, that is, as *obstacles to* understanding (the way in which Robbe-Grillet's objects are seen and his subjects unseen). Voice-overs, interior monologues, and other such narrative reconfigurations of human experience as a retrievable series of events produce the counter-effect of allowing us to hear our logical faculties laboring like a faulty engine.[75] The voice of time leaches out of the container that the physical mode of transport renders mentally real and physically unreal in time, so that the idea of the thing contained—a body, an object, a name, an identity—is put in flux, in play.

A mind in motion stays in motion; a mind at rest is an oxymoron. In both cases the body labors to represent what this or that means and in so doing to make time appear in terms of what it does to a body. The body of the Girl on the plane in *The Night of the Following Day* ventures forth into a world that causes it pain, bloated as the body is by a memory that is present in the recirculating "now" that the film formally (re-)creates as being commensurate with the body's fate.[76] For Husserl, memory is not only an act of retention but also "a retention of retentions," with all retentions dependent upon an uncategorizable present as their origin point and so necessarily the origin point of temporal series and succession. And even with this, not all memory is retention or else it would all be contained (memory being that which is remembered but also that which is altered or forgotten). The present, in turn, is infused not only with what is remembered but with the "remembered expectation" that is implicit in the form of its realization. (We cannot expect the present without a past and we cannot realize the past except as present.) Similarly, says Husserl, "the present is the actualization of the future of what is remembered."[77]

Now is "the night of the following day," but only if we say so (such self-referencing, Augustine argued, being essential to determining the present), based upon this sort of evidence without proof and that perhaps obviates the need for proof. In a sense, *The Night of the Following Day* corrupts any truth claim that can be made for the present, which, in its possible unsustainability, is, well, tense. Instead, the film, like Husserlian time in Ricoeur's paraphrase ("the interplay of protentions and retentions"), makes it so "every temporal thing seems to stand out against the background of the temporal form in which it is inserted by the interplay of intentionalities" it describes.[78] This separation of form and thing (*not* content) exposes the unreal not so much by definition but as problematic. In this sense (after Husserl), two impressions can have "identically the same temporal [or spatial, in the Hitchcockian example] position."[79] *The Night of the Following Day* may be said after Chudnoff to represent "one mereological sum" (a function of part-to-whole or part-to-part within a whole relations) that "can constitute two different structured wholes, at least at different times." Likewise, "one structured whole can be constituted by two different mereological sums, at least at different times." Here, "constitution at a time entails coincidence in location at that time."[80] Between the strangers on and strangeness of trains and planes, we create something like a vestibule in which to contemplate with aporetic expectancy the a priori's and the "as if's" of nominal arrival and departure. It is no wonder that our conversations concerning space and time are composed of non sequiturs even as the subject-object under discussion vanishes, no longer to be seen as it once was either by determination or intuition. Perhaps this is why Froy wrote her name on the train window. She saw no way out of the condition of not knowing other than figurative defenestration. As psychologically fatal as that might be, it does not approach the collective implications of the Girl on the plane who we imagine punching out her window and being sucked out by the sky, taking all content and context with her.

There is a scene in *Night* in which the stewardess/kidnapper Vi drives down a rainy street past the Esso Station we imagine appeared earlier in the French musical romance *The Umbrellas of Cherbourg* (dir. Jacques Demy, 1964). The rain expresses an incontinent body that cannot be contained within its borders. What are its borders? If this body is a monad after Leibniz and secondarily Deleuze, then the exteriority we see is just a circumstance of its interiority. It is environmentally sensitive, but as the retention and expression of environmental factors attest, the monad acknowledges no environmental influence that it does not contain and no discretely external environment that can contain it. Things are folded and unfolded so that a body is not just something that is but that someone has, possesses as his own, his body, her body, *my* body. The Deleuzian un/folding of the Leibnizian monad allows you to have your "have" and to be it too. The Girl's body is the one that dies and yet the Girl still retains possession of it on another plane (that we "again" see at "the end").

Redoubled time, like redoubled space, is coincidental. Vi runs into the same policeman for a second time after stopping by a café to get out of the rain and contends that this cannot be coincidental, that he is following her, and knows that she is up to something. Just because it's a small world, which clearly this French beach town is, does not mean that things transpire coincidentally, and just because things transpire coincidentally does not, of course, literally make the world any smaller. Only paranoia takes the nominal impossibility of coincidence literally, but, as they say, just because you're paranoid it doesn't mean you're not being followed, as day follows night and the night is of the following day. The heroine of *Cherbourg* is, like *Night*'s Girl, seventeen years old when her dreamlike journey begins. *Cherbourg* takes place in the beach town of that name in Normandy in the north of France. *Night* was shot in Le Touquet in Brittany, which is likewise located in the north of France, up the coast from Cherbourg. The director says that *Night* "was really an homage to the painter Magritte who came from that same region on the Channel in Belgium." The umbrella planted in the sand by the dying bowler-hatted sadist Leer (palindrome of the Reel), who "kills" the Girl, is meant to make this clear. (As a Boy I once absentmindedly ate Leer impersonator Richard Boone's autograph down to its final *ne* while watching my baroque night television.) In fact, the Chauffeur (the smiling criminal who greets the girl when she deplanes at the beginning and end of the film) drags Leer's body to the sea framed by the umbrella and the hat, as if Magritte's painting were being seen anamorphically, the sea washing up death, like Magritte's half-Girl/half fish upon the shore.[81]

The Magritte painting recounts the monadic dreams of the Craigian house of *Dead of Night* and the generic house by the sea in which the Girl is being delayed in time if not contained in *The Night of the Following Day.* As is proper to monads, the house is isolated and a figurative "dark background: everything is drawn into it, and nothing goes out or comes in from the outside."[82] Its surfeit of interiority is what Deleuze after Leibniz has in mind by saying that the monad has no doors or windows, which says to me that it is an interior *scene*, the scene of *it is*. All that is real in the Leibnizian system is the monad's recursive consciousness, which is synonymous with its scenic structure. "Chiaroscuro fills the monad," Deleuze says. Might we then call Leibniz a noir philosopher? "Contrary to Descartes," Deleuze argues, "Leibniz begins in darkness. Clarity emerges from obscurity by way of a genetic process, and so too clarity plunges into darkness, and continues to plunge deeper and deeper: it is natural chiaroscuro, a development out of obscurity, and it is *more or less* clear to the degree that sensibility reveals it as such." Leibniz's folds produce shadows and labyrinths, his monads are miniature worlds in human and urban forms. Leibniz speaks a singular as in baroque street language, likening a point of view to an undetermined street, a "street with no name" in noir parlance.[83]

Leibnizian compossibility attends in that it compels us to consider "the variety of all possible connections between the course of a given street and that of another." One could argue that film noir shows us what movement inside a monad looks like, "the obscure dust of the world, the dark depth every monad contains."[84] And it is Leibniz who gives the world the monad and the monad its dark world. The world for Leibniz is not, as it later would be for Wittgenstein, "everything that is the case," because the world is always as potential as it is real. An event that transpires in the world "participates in the becoming of another event and the subject of its own becoming," as in *The Night of the Following Day.* "Everything prehends its antecedents and its concomitants and, by degrees, prehends a world."[85] The kidnappers' plot falls victim to the world's and to its events' "chaotic multiplicity," within earshot of the sea, which functions as an objective correlative to the wave-like character of the event, "luminous and audible, and also prehensible as a complex of foldings and unfoldings," of noirish crosses and double-crosses.[86] "The caper," as Bud the Chauffeur calls it, is "a nexus of prehensions" that is missing a center.[87] The caper comes to an end when Bud kills Leer, who has already killed everybody else, and lays down his dying body where the waves break upon the beach, there to hear the "confused murmur coming from the innumerable set of breaking waves," as Deleuze after Leibniz called it. "I'm gonna give you time to think about it," Bud says, the sound of the crashing waves reminding us of Leibniz's notion that multiplicity when apprehended by or through the senses can be the event of its own undoing. It is as if the Chauffeur's gunshot shattered this particular seascape scene into the 750 puzzle pieces from which Perec's Bartlebooth had Winckler (re)compose each of his 500 different seascape paintings. How many *Nights of the Following Day* are there? How many pieces of time are we allotted to solve these puzzles?[88] Bud, who surprised Leer with his death by following him from the high ground to the low and then by hiding from him belly-down in the sea, right at the water's edge, lying down between two folds, rendered the dying man's perception of his own death hallucinatory. It as if the dying man were saying through the Girl on the plane's headphones, "I have been killed by a sound coming from waves, the sea, the folds of sleep," spoken like a Magritte figure becoming aware that he is dying recursively inside the picture, the painting, the frame.[89] The Girl has overheard the sound of Death *thinking*.

5

✦

Ipseity

He wondered, worried, feared he was mere appearance.
—William Gass, *The Tunnel*

Philip Marlowe is the first person we see in Robert Montgomery's *Lady in the Lake* (1947), writing a book of the same name in the first person. This being a movie, it is, of course, a picture book, but of a peculiar kind. Marlowe is, save for the film's opening, behind the camera, as is the actor Robert Montgomery who plays him. He is in the visible picture only when reflected in mirrors that otherwise function diegetically in a scene, and is otherwise seen and also heard when the characters address him as the camera "I." "YOU find a corpse and get framed!" the movie ads screamed at the time of the film's release. "Everything that happens to Robert Montgomery happens to you!" A film that claims to make more of "YOU" by a nominal trick of the camera eye/I makes this film actually *less real* than most movies purport to be. We know that this more of less-ness is at best a figure of speech, and at worst a benighted sense of illusion, like "reality," a term that works to hide *behind* and not beyond comparison.

Marlowe is discovered seated at a desk, holding a handgun (first seen atop the final credit card in the film's opening sequence), which he exchanges for a typewriter as soon as he catches the camera's eye that at this point coincides not with him but with his alter ego, director "Robert Montgomery." Marlowe promptly tells us (YOU) that he (a fictional character) has given up actual detective work in favor of *writing about it*. He challenges us to solve the crime he already has but warns, "you've got to watch them [the characters] all the time." Of course, we cannot hope to do this since the camera does not show "them" to us "all the time," that is, in real time. So, we are already embarked on a cynically produced fiction of Marlowe's writerly oversight. The first-person subjective camera approach that visualizes noir's traditional omniscient narrative apparitionally abstracts Levinas's face-to-face basis for establishing the identity of self and other, underscored by the film's stolen identity and misidentified corpse plot premise. The exposure of the rhetoricity of noir convention is well-served by the anamorphosis of the ostentatiously obstructed view of everything but its own limits and what these limits reveal. Although, as Barthes observed, "depth only occurs at the moment the spectacle itself turns its shadow toward man and begins to look at him"—as a missing person, "I" would add.[1]

Marlowe's presence in the film, much like the Ghost's in *Hamlet*, advertises self-necessitating spectral discourse, which in turn captures the film's anomalous Christmas-in-July setting.[2] His retelling of the story for the purpose of rewriting it turns Marlowe into his own ghostwriter of Christmas Past, Present, and Future, with each time (being) missing, not fully (a) present. Being missing is, after all, what the story is about. Marlowe has been summoned to and enters the offices of Kingsby Publications, Inc., a publisher of gory stories in the crime and detective, monster and horror genres, whistling the tune to Robert Burns's poem "Comin' Thro the Rye," which equates "person" with "a body." Marlowe's whistling then shifts into an unrecognizable eerie air that makes him sound in his unseen-ness like a ghostwriter whistling past the grave he dug for himself (his self). He proceeds into the office of Kingsby executive E. A. Fromsett, on whose desk is a cigarette lighter ensconced in a mock human skull. "The Artist" (Fromsett's illustrator) in the room puzzles over Marlowe's non-/presence in relation to a framed cover of the publication *True Horror Tales* (hanging on Fromsett's wall) that features a drawing of a skull. The Artist looks like he has seen the ghost of the self's evacuation, which he had believed was only a fiction. The Artist has glimpsed his own *psycho-philosophical dysmorphia*, drawn into the scene by Marlowe and the two skulls as an anamorphic design. Like Deleuze's Philosopher, the Artist is "the sensitive man, in that he encounters the violence of an impression. He is the reader, the auditor, in that the work of art emits signs that will perhaps force him to create." And, I would add, force him to be whom he has created. He is the horrific epiphany of self-realization of the not-I, "who scrutinizes the signs in which the truth *betrays itself*"—as death (as Marlowe), both an open question and a limit.[3] Can vision, the face and figure of the Artist silently asks, be reconciled with reality? And if I can (only) see myself as a character, in what sense am I real? How do I play the scene in which my artifice is so fully exposed? Will my acting "sincere" be perceived as overacting and make me a likely suspect in the story Marlowe is peddling, "based on an authentic case" from his own personal experience of himself as (being) suspect? Is his frank acknowledgment of himself in the/as a third-person meant to elicit a similar confession from me?—"YOU find a corpse and get framed!"

Fromsett tells Marlowe that "authenticity has very little to do with it," the "it" being writing, since writers don't trouble themselves with facts. "What do you think your story is full of?" "Short sentences," Marlowe responds. Marlowe's story, "If I Should Die Before I Live," sounds like E. M. Cioran could have ghost-written it. E. A. Fromsett uses the story as a pretext for hiring Marlowe to investigate a missing person's case that will become *The Case of the Lady in the Lake*. Fromsett's boss Derace Kingsby's unfaithful wife Chrystal is believed to have run off with a man named Chris Lavery to Mexico, *claro que sí* (of course). So, Fromsett intuitively decides to send one missing person (Marlowe) to find another. Kingsby enters the room, looking unsettled by Marlowe, whom he closely watches as if he has caught sight of himself in/as an impossible condition. He imparts some rough details of the case and then at the point of exiting, pointedly, point-blankly tells the detective, "Mr. Marlowe, I am glad to have *met* you." Kingsby meeting YOU affirms the film's rhetorical claim of putting the audience member *in* the picture as well as underscoring oppositeness/appositeness as being the picture's un/real subject. The strabismac eye/"I" dis-coordination that results from the spectator being unable to see himself in the picture or even to directly see the film's lead character except as he is only indirectly, abstractly seeing himself recalls the protagonistic condition that composes Robbe-Grillet's novel *The Voyeur* (1958), as well as the ocular condition from which actor Robert Montgomery himself appears to have suffered—write what you know, film who you are not.[4]

At Lavery's house, Marlowe is knocked unconscious by the missing person himself, when he (Marlowe) asks for the time. After regaining consciousness, we see Marlowe and Fromsett standing side-by-side examining the detective's mirrored black eye, conversing with one another as if in an auto-suggestive state that occupies only virtual space and time (which is all a "missing person" can give of himself, after all). When Marlowe returns to Lavery's house to get answers to the questions that indirectly rendered him unconscious the first time, he finds two things to be suspicious (one of which is not "the fact" that Lavery appears this time to be really missing): (1) A woman wearing a broad-brimmed, eye-covering hat and a pair of gloves, and carrying a pistol is scurrying down the house's interior staircase and chattering away to Marlowe about Lavery owing her rent and owning the gun that is currently in her possession (as if to say, "this is not a gun, in the sense that it is not mine, possession being nine-tenths of the law of identity"); and (2) *Everything* is out of place. Drawers are open and clothing strewn. Newspapers are unfolded everywhere, newspapers in which, Marlowe directly told us in the film's opening, YOU cannot read the truth. Marlowe dismisses the chatterbox despite the circumstantial appearance of her guilt, but as there is not yet anything visibly to be guilty of, Marlowe chooses not to get ahead of himself, even though we already know that Montgomery as "Marlowe's" director does just that. Ascending the stairs upon which "the landlady" (as she identifies herself) claims to have found the gun, Marlowe stumbles upon the bathroom murder scene. Marlowe notes that there are bullet holes in mirrors in which, we note, the detective's face *does not appear*. These holes of/in the un/seen analogize to the bullet-ridden shower door behind which is discovered the missing Lavery's dead body, the re-representation of the missing person.

Marlowe brings Fromsett the murder weapon wrapped up as a Christmas present in order to register her reaction to the news of Lavery's death. "You're afraid of life," Marlowe tells Fromsett in a voice that is less Kris Kringle than Emile Cioran. Only a Ghost knows how quickly life wastes itself on fear. The self-reflecting joke here is that Marlowe is the very (albeit nominal and mirrored) picture of mortality, beaten up and left unconscious on more than one occasion. *Lady in the Lake* ends in a cheap hotel room with a dead triple-murderess's body (the histrionic former "landlady" Mildred Havelend) lying on the floor (shot three times in the abdomen, twice after already being doubled over, folded), the dark shades drawn and Marlowe staring down the gun barrel of a bad cop named DeGarmot. DeGarmot literally picked up the trail of salt that Marlowe had improbably left for the good cops to follow, resulting in them following a trail that is no longer there. The dark room which was to be Marlowe's last becomes his next room instead when the good cops come through the one-way window, the one backing DeGarmot that he cannot see when facing the camera without the aid of a mirror, the one that cannot be seen *because* he is seeing Marlowe whose "presence" is unreality's abstract visual field which disenables ordinary sight. The bad cop sees without recognizing "Marlowe" as a sign of scenic unreality that defines the terms of his (the bad cop's) own life and death, or more specifically, his insubstantiality, his unreal presence/presentness. With no life remaining, the bad cop collapses and dissolves like a pillar of salt constituted by the impossible materiality that appeared to lead and now abandon him "here" as if he were a "real" person.

The cuts that periodically appear on Marlowe's face throughout the film may signal rifts in his facial self-recognition, what psychiatrists call "mirrored self-misidentification," a disbelief in the reflected image being one's own. This would roughly correspond with "mirror agnosia," a loss of understanding of what (a) "mirror" actually is.[5] Why would that be? Because when Marlowe is in the scene, he cannot see the visual field his *absence* embodies, the facial "cut" as edit. It is entirely possible that Marlowe (thinks he) sees someone other than himself, sees Robert Montgomery's stand-in, when he looks in a mirror. "There is," in any case, says Borges, "something monstrous about mirrors."[6] They render multiple not only the number of people there are but the number of people that replicate one another. Mirrors manufacture fictions, veridical hallucinations that forecast what will happen to a person even as it is happening (e.g., "you are aging," "you are dying"). Mirrors further afflict us with unreality, fill us with baroque astonishment of the everyday, encourage us with their reflections to buy into reality as metaphor without really telling us to what this metaphor specifically refers. They subvert the logical authority of numbers, language, names. We come to believe that "the act of counting modifies the amount counted," as we move our lips before the mirror in anxious anticipation of what the image reflected in it sum(mon)s up. The mirror demands a form of direct address that is not fully known to the speaker. It asks us to trust it as we trust ourselves, while showing us how untrustworthy we are in knowing who we really are. Grimacing at the mirror which performs a double-capture on film of the face's image and Montgomery's own double function as actor-director, Marlowe sees the cut-man whose function in boxing of the real and shadow variety is to suture discontinuity.

"Oh brother, that's a beautiful eye you got," the bad cop DeGarmot says of Marlowe's shadow-boxing (how else can you fight a missing person?) injury, his special name for Marlowe as a *private* eye being "Peepers." There are fewer shadows in this film than in other films noir for Marlowe to box, but a ghost knows how to pick his fights so that they will be not so much seen in real time as reflected in the results, not only of scenic effects but of ghost(writ)ing. The wound-producing fight then allows us to question in this context whether we are seeing monocularly, through a good or a bad eye, but also whether there is even such a thing as an eye/"I" being "good" or bad." This makes not just everyone but everything suspect. The self-denying actor Marlowe who may not allow himself to see Montgomery in the mirror face-slaps DeGarmot (who lives under the illusion that he is safe in his role) twice—a sign of repetition, of disdainful show. The slap administered to little Lee Earle "James" Ellroy by his mother prior to her murder knocked him off the living-room couch where he watched and straight into neighborhood homes, whose windows he peered through at actors who were real people on the (other) side, from which they called him "Peeper."[7]

Carcinogenesis

> Every disease is an identification.
>
> —E. M. Cioran, *Drawn and Quartered*

QUIET
ILLNESS
WITHIN

The sign composed of these three words is attached to the white picket fence of a picture-perfect suburban house on a tree-lined street in the film with the three-word title *Cause for Alarm!* (dir. Tay Garnett, 1951) that constitutes a call. The sign disturbs the opening voice-over of homemaker Ellen Jones, which says, "That Tuesday in July started out like any other day the past few months. There was no warning it was to be the most terrifying day of my life." Of course, we think, Ellen (despite the doubleness that her name and her voice-over suggest) cannot see what we can—the unsettling juxtaposition of the sign and the picture of the habitual that it inhabits, the sense of ILLNESS as a disturbance and not just a condition that can be normalized ("like any other day the past few months"), inhabited like a house in which you feel at home (which is less a simile than "a metaphor for metaphor").[8] In fact,

Ellen refers to how tired she was feeling on this particular day, how much her normal housework felt like drudgery. The sign-posted word "WITHIN" expands into the dysmorphic "ILLNESS" presenting as a body fatigued by its own routine, but also by the voice-over that breaks her routine "QUIET" to confess later rather than sooner what she thinks she should not even be telling us *now*. How else, though, can she put YOU in the picture, and by putting us in the picture, we suddenly realize that *she knows*.

The framing of interiority continues to sign to us from inside the picture once Ellen recedes inside the representational present in the form of the many wall-mounted framed pictures inside the home that are *kept just out of focus*. The Joneses' house is given the speaking number 116, recalling the number of the Shakespeare sonnet that famously begins, "Let me not to the marriage of true minds / Admit impediments." The sonnet's structural formality likewise admits no impediments in limits that render apposite what might otherwise (in another form) appear to be opposite (i.e., freedom and constancy: "It is an ever-fixed mark / That looks on tempests and is never shaken"). But this is for Ellen and her demented husband George nothing more than "a consummation devoutly to be wished," this surfeit from "the heart-ache and the thousand natural shocks / That flesh is heir to," the ILLNESS, a madness a mind like Hamlet's may counterfeit in self-regard or erroneously self-regard as being counterfeit.[9]

When Ellen calls upstairs to ask George if he had called her and whether he needs anything, he says *not now*, because he had "just begun work on an insurance report for the office." George is in fact penning an insurance policy for himself in the form of a letter to the L.A. District Attorney stating that his wife and his physician, who is also his close friend, are in love and are planning to kill him. Based on what we see in the film, this is as unlikely as insurance agent Walter Neff being cheated on by Phyllis Dietrichson *with her husband* in *Double Indemnity*. "The friend has been in love with her before I met her," the letter further says, throwing the particularity of Ellen's peculiar "today" into dialogue with George's *not now*, the un/real *no time like the present* and the counter-present of *no time* that George fears will soon be his. In the meantime, in the un/real present of overheard WITHIN(NESS) and VOICE-OVER, Ellen is made to feel "odd" by an im/material "something" in George's voice." This gets her thinking "about the first time we met," the glossy/gloss-over name for the time from which dates in George's mind the plan to rob him of his time going forward. Generally, it is the narrator who dies after the flashback, but how is George to know this? He has never acted in a movie, after all. Ellen recalls cute-meeting George, who for this purpose was lying under a hospital bedsheet feigning (a prognostic) illness. When George's friend Grahame enters the room, jokingly warning him, "Now remember, I saw her first," we are alerted not to the fallacy of memory's claim of being predictive so much as to the selective way in which it predicts in this case ILLNESS as a subset of marriage to the wrong man.

In the present, George fakes pain and then demands that Ellen call some doctor other than his no longer old friend Grahame. Grahame's arrival a full forty-five minutes later in his real-life doctor's role enables George's mind to see more clearly the apparitional scene of foul play, although this lateness is explained by Grahame's having been contacted while out on another call. What constitutes a "call" in this context? Is it an interpellation that misidentifies so that the wrong doctor (the one that is in love with George's wife), the wrong thought, the wrong reference, meaning, or conclusion comes to mind? Is this call, then, synonymous with an internal condition, an aberrant mental state? Grahame refers to George's heart condition, but it is his psychological condition that concerns him. George's thinking has moved from being a "self-reproductive" processing through thought (one thought "demands another in order to assure itself of itself") to an obsessive recycling of a single thought, "presenting reality to the Self distorted through the rules of thought," doubt becoming its own logic.[10] George's "illness within" has become *the film's* narrative condition. The letter George writes to the D.A. contains George's speculative theory of his imminent death—immanent death if you consider narrative to be an internal condition. George's desire to prove a murderous conspiracy is the narrative compulsion of a catastrophist mind without insight mirroring Ellen's need to confess her own disQUIETude.

George locks Ellen inside his bedroom and is getting ready to shoot her in "self-defense" (a telephone calls without being answered) when he suffers a fatal heart attack, dying on his twin bed. "That man lying there was George, my husband. He was dead. He died trying to kill me," Ellen's emotionally self-constrained, un-constrained by doubting, retrospective voice-over intones. She then proceeds to answer a series of calls from: the pharmacist following up on the evidence George left suggesting his wife planned to overdose him by doubling up on his prescription refills (making her into a victim of his excess); the non-death-inducing "Bang, bang!" of the neighbor boy's toy gun mimicking George's firing into the bedroom floor in the moment he died that gives the appearance of foul play; the loquacious postman charged with delivering the dead man's letter; George's unannounced Aunt Clara; and the sudden arrival of a notary after George's letter has been posted. Since Ellen's name does not appear on the envelope containing George's letter, it cannot be recalled, except in a flashback that is symptomatic of the excess Ellen can neither confess nor contain.[11] This instance of the missing person's voice(over) struggling to overtake some unconfessed guilt before the latter can be read as proof of some real crime again bespeaks ipseity or apartness rather than identity. Ellen's indictment demands no burden of proof beyond what the person missing from herself offers in the abstraction she presents. Who refers to themselves in a third-person voice-over in any case?

"Not enough postage, and we have to deliver them twice," says the postman, returning George's letter (his spectral remains) to Ellen because the D.A.'s office would not pay the cash difference (would not accept the spectral call).[12] The letter's proper addressee is no longer the dead man but the narrator, whose recollection of the plot has exhausted all other possibilities, closed down all other routes but this one, in which Ellen has emotionally recalled her husband's paranoia on the other side of (his) death. The letter, thickened by surplus, now outweighs the price of its stamp, its intention filigreed by baroque intervention, although perhaps weighing just enough for an envelope containing the events of "that one terrifying day." Ellen's likening this day to a dream is figuratively true (i.e., true enough in its likeness) given the ir/rational circuitry of the plot loop that coincides with the path the letter must take to produce the Nora-like (*Doll House*) suspenseful expectancy of its inevitable arrival. Grahame's tearing up and burning of the falsely incriminating letter recalls how Corneille's *The Cid* ended inside its allotted time frame, like the two-hour parking sign in whose gaze Ellen first begged the rule-bound postman for George's letter back. That letter, the narrator always comes to realize, is "I." As we enter into thought's deepest interiority, the self-contained monadic state, we catch sight of ourselves running in circles, trying to catch our own tale, our "self-sameness" minus a core self in its various reflections and narrative forms. The postman is my obsessive-compulsive disorder that is always checking on what my mind knows is always checking up on me. It is my way of personalizing and representing my fate, my unreality.

In the overhead establishing shot of Edward Dmytryk's *Murder, My Sweet* (1945), men sit around a table lit only by lamplight, the stage's blind spot reflecting (upon) private eye Philip Marlowe's temporary blindness. Three broad-shouldered police detectives interrogate Marlowe inside a room whose smoked glass door bears the palindromic number 404. Like this number, the detectives to Marlowe's left and right who face each other across the table look like one another's mirror image. The eyes of the third interrogator, sitting across from Marlowe, dart left and right, as might Marlowe's eyes behind his blindfold and my good and bad eyes that were blindfolded so that through sympathetic movement the temporary blindness I suffered in one eye did not fold into the other. The blood clot in my bad eye became my visible blind spot projected on the inside of my bandage like a flaw in the film that had burned on to the screen, like Marlowe's own burned retinas which necessitated his eyes being blindfolded in the first place, in the first scene that becomes when it recurs at the tail/tale end a film-long flashback.

Marlowe's private eyes are searching for the bar singer Velma Valento who has gone missing. The sign on the bar he enters to find her is meant to read "FLORIANS," but the neon is shot, exhausted in several places so that the sign now reads "F OR ANS," shorthand for "FOR ANSWERS," so Marlowe figures he'll start here. Marlowe visits the bar's former owner who makes up in thirst what she now lacks in memory. She doesn't usually sing to cops or private eyes, she says, "but when I like a guy and he buys me a drink, the ceiling's the limit," notably not the sky. She has already succumbed to the room's demands, given it her life, what's left of it, succumbed to the drink brought to the room with which the room plies her for compliance. "Now where did he go?" she says aloud to no one in particular, or maybe she does not say this aloud at all. "He was here just a second ago, sitting in the chair opposite me. We were talking face-to-face. Maybe it's the drink talking. Maybe he was never really here."[13] Reality always conspires against a mind in crisis. Funny thing, though—the moment after Marlowe leaves the room, she goes to the phone. "Suddenly, she wasn't drunk anymore," says Marlowe's overdubbed voice as he stares back into the room through the window. So, if she wasn't really drunk (her tolerance for liquor being very high), what caused her to hallucinate his disappearance before the fact? Does the hallucination belong to the blindfolded Marlowe and so, by extension, to the film itself? Unable to trust what he sees, his hearing has become acute. His memory therefore focuses less on what the eye actually sees than on what hearing might look like, if hearing could be seen, like a drunk old lady who *looks like* she is speaking on the phone. Synesthesia calling. It is worth noting at this juncture that the film's opening line, spoken to a blindfolded Marlowe by an unseen detective, is, "I remember you as a noisy little fella. Now you don't make a sound." And Marlowe's flashback narrative begins with him intoning, "Something about the dead silence of an office building at night. Not quite real." The office building at night is a surrogate image for what the blind man cannot see (glimpsed earlier in Walter Neff's late-night call to vision betrayed by danger's beautiful artifice), much like the dead silence reaches toward an absolute acuity that the sighted mind does not so much experience as metaphorically describe in the form of writing. "No matter what question one asks them, writings remain silent, keeping a most majestic silence or else replying in the same terms, which means not replying."[14] The cancer of writing is a silent killer, lodging first in the eye or perhaps in the voice but nearly always, it seems, hollowing out the core self. Struck across the face with a gun barrel, Marlowe drops into its depth, into the drunk old lady's syncope that suspends logical sequencing so that he always seems to be not here or there but somewhere else, diving into the "black pool" that visibly opens up at his feet where his "brains" are as if scrambled. "How do you get out of this funhouse, colonel?" Marlowe asks a butler, subverting conversational formality by upgrading the uniformed pawn in rank once he crosses the chessboard of the parquet floor. A cab driver in turn calls Marlowe "captain," which configures with the previous "colonel" in a vocabulary of colloquial quasi-referentiality. Marlowe then tells Moose Malloy, Velma's boyfriend, "You're crazy as a rabbit." A white rabbit, one supposes, since it is Moose who hires Marlowe and so first puts him on the clock. This "Moose" is more like his physical opposite, though, Carroll's dormouse (from the Latin *dormire*, to sleep). Much like the Hare and the Hatter slept on the dormouse, Moose sleeps on Velma, on who she really is, wearing the only apparent disguise of what she has become.

Spotlit by an overhead light fixture (secreted inside the film's previously cited overhead light source frame), Marlowe awakens from his involuntary drug trip in a strange bed and an even stranger place than "before" in which "the window was open but the smoke didn't move." He has, it appears, fallen through one of Alice's dark squares and down the rabbit hole. As in the upside-down room in which Sherlock Holmes found himself, the world has become still, "suspended" in Husserl's terminology (and as the form of Marlowe's own "out-of-play" voice-over narrative predictively acknowledges in its abstractedly past-presentness). Marlowe might easily be in one of Gregory Crewdson's movie-still photos with their eerily lifelike three-dimensional quality in two-dimensionally composed photo-spaces of a stillness made more absolute so as to be not merely recognizable but beyond the recognition they are about. "The doors are too small," says the drugged but mobile Marlowe, sounding again like Alice. "I can't remember things as I used—and I don't keep the same size for ten minutes together!" says Alice sounding a lot like Marlowe, leaving him to wonder whether it's not the doors that have gotten small but him. This thought reverses Norma Desmond's "I am big. It's the pictures that got small," but is no less delusional. "The stairs are made of dough," says Marlowe. It seems as though the faces and bodies in Marlowe's strange space are suspended in the smoke from Alice's Hookah-Smoking Caterpillar, who offers no answers, but instead asks difficult questions of the drug-induced private eye/I. The most difficult question the Caterpillar repeatedly asks Alice is, "Who are *you*?" "I can't explain myself," Alice answers, "because I'm not myself today, you see." "I don't see," says the Caterpillar, and Marlowe, his eyes only now figuratively bandaged in his interrogative anxiety dream inside a blindfolded film frame, nods sagely to himself as if he had found an answer.[15]

Marlowe is confused about time, but he remains clear about what he demands from language. "What were you saying?" he agitatedly asks the Doctor who drugged him. "I made no remark," the Doctor calmly responds. To this, ordinary-language philosopher Marlowe snaps back, "Remarks *want* you to make them. They've got their tongues hanging out waiting to be said." The patient who is, as the doctor would say, "presenting" the effects of "narcotic poisoning," a gumshoe whose word is his bond, here demands no less of words, that they follow through on what they promise, which is to be said, to show themselves, to present as figures in space, as components of figurative space, in fact. Words and the spaces they convey demand recognition. You cannot, in a Wittgensteinian construction, say that you did *not* say them, as you might say you did not *mean* them. Interestingly, the dialogue between Marlowe and the Doctor concerns his *not* talking while under the influence of drugs about a jade necklace he *did not* have. The object has gone missing from the speech of which it is the subject. The result is that meaning too has gone missing, or else has been suspended under the influence of a potent cocktail of injection and interrogation.

Although we are made to distrust the doctor's diagnosis of narcotic poisoning from a medical perspective, it actually captures the film's mindset and aesthetic, which is carcinogenic. The periodic encroachment on the film and story frame of what Marlowe sees and describes as being a "black ooze" captures the carcinogenesis that occurs when the smoking of cigarettes in the frame produces a field of smoke (or alternatively fog) that will not dissipate but instead hangs suspended in the air, in the story, an occlusion that is again vested in the compensatory interior vision of the blind man who is telling the story between smokes. This carcinogenic occlusion does not just frame the story, it *is* the story, Marlowe's story, and by extension the story of film noir. The nominal transparency of the flashback's narrative first-person voice and of its character tropes (gumshoe, fall guy, femme fatale) is an actual occlusion that the genre title, "film noir," confesses. This in turn extends and instantiates Lacan's belief that there is a "deceptive transparency in the very heart of the cogito."[16] The dark squares, the blind spots are difficult to avoid, because Marlowe cannot differentiate between his eye bandage's interior whiteness and his mind's even more interior blackness. Is he seeing white or only his mind's projection of what white might look like on a black background? Is his mind only screening whiteness as the thing his eyes are in fact screened from? Is this whiteness, like the papers and money he is given while sitting at his office desk, just one more thing, one *big* thing he hides under his desk blotter? Is this blotter just another sign of his visual occlusion that literalizes the memory loss that the noir flashback generally puts in motion in order to nominally reclaim?

Marlowe cautions someone that he should make his intended move "only if you want to wear your face backwards," a threat to face value ("because I no longer see it seeing me still, I therefore risk forgetting"), which coming from a blind narrator offers the compensation of having eyes in the back of one's head. ("Who comes before and who is after whom? *I no longer know which end my head is.*")[17] Marlowe's loss of sight has made his colloquial expression more exact and exacting, manifesting the cruel irony that the carcinogenesis of time and space brings. Throughout the film's flashback narrative, Marlowe passes unlit cigarettes under his nose, like someone who is trying to quit smoking but continues to manifest his desire as being acute to the point of refinement. Marlowe even lights a match on the butt-end of a statue of Cupid, further tightening the bond between his desire to smoke and smoking as pure desire, another form of alternative, blindside (backside) sensory acuity in the face of blindness. And I, blind to a carcinogenesis that recurred in me while writing, light a match in the dark and continue.

I am, like the writer in Dennis Potter's *The Singing Detective* (dir. Jon Amiel, 1986), a sick man, although as the real author remarks, "that *the disease* is mine does not make it autobiographical." Nagel, who published his philosophical text *The View from Nowhere* the same year, argued that "since we can't literally escape ourselves, any improvement in our beliefs has to result in some form of self-transformation. And the thing that we can do that gets closest to getting outside of ourselves is to form a detached idea of the world that includes us, and includes our possession of that conception as part of what it enables us to understand about ourselves."[18] On the surface, *Detective*'s hospitalized, psoriatic, parchment-skin-bound protagonist, weighed down by the moniker "Philip Marlow," is living a kind of a.k.a. existence that, however much it interrogates the idea of an authentic self, continuously suffers (from) its own subjectivity. Marlow's tormented alter ego movie-star turns in other self-imagined worlds cannot summon the impartiality of an objective worldview. "A rat always knows where it's tail [tale] is," Marlow proclaims as he is wheeled down to what he calls "the rat hole" of the hospital's basement ward. Marlow is a decidedly contra-Alice, his skin a wonderland of outward suffering and physical malice. Marlow's body is a child's model of the suffering world with an excess of dried glue calamitously visible on the outside. In the "rat hole," the hospital staff treats curtained and contained Marlow with a large dose of the institutional "we" that affects an empathy for the patient's embarrassed-to-be still living corpse. Marlow, who is bereft of his detective namesake's final "e," has this lack magnified by a body that fails the *I*-test from top to bottom. When Marlow asks whether he will ever be able to hold a pen again, the staff psychiatrist ("cryptically," Marlow notes) responds: "You ask those questions as if someone else was responsible for your condition, but no one is. Or at least in the unlikely event that someone, anyone is, then that someone cannot be anyone other than yourself, can it?"

Marlow is burning for a cigarette as a homunculus of his burning flesh. Apply one burning pencil point to parchment skin and write something different, for God's sake. "What kind of books did you want to write, in place of these detective not-quite novels?" the staff psychiatrist asks Marlow in so many words. "What were you in *a fever* to write?" he might have asked, might have put it to Marlow not so much in the form of a question posed by the Hookah-Smoking Caterpillar as of a proposition, a skeptical certainty about what is missing from Marlow's stories, other than the "e," of course, that gave him a name to overwrite under. While his physical condition draws attention, it is Marlow's voice that tells the tale. And the tale it tells is of the private eye being convention-bound, trapped inside a voice-over and its coterminal flashback. It is not simply that Marlow cannot escape his condition of psoriatic arthropathy, he conspires with his past so that it continues to fester like an idea in the story of the mind. It is, I say, an occupational hazard. Marlow's inner detective, who is little more than a genre trope, embodies the struggle between autonomy and "mere subjective appearance," as Marlow's condition expresses a not-doing that (willfully and maybe wistfully) disenables him from becoming (just another) part of the world.[19] Our being our own doing allows that we can be helped and also does not allow ourselves to be helped because we think it means giving up this "ownness." Patient Marlow's impatience with not being able to do things for himself at the most basic level is exacerbated by the inner life in which he appears to be autonomous. This internalization of an external perspective on himself gives Marlow the false impression that he "ought to be able to encompass [himself] completely, and thus become the absolute source of what [he does]." "At any rate," Nagel adds, "we become dissatisfied with anything less." Marlow's dream of getting outside himself is a bid for autonomy that is underwritten *and* undermined by his external view, his voice-over flashback.

Nagel writes: "The objectivity that seems to offer greater control also reveals the ultimate givenness of the self. . . . The process that starts as a means to the enlargement of freedom seems to lead to its destruction . . . skepticism and helplessness."[20] Still, Marlow is not so much a divided self as he is a self that is fully manifested as ipseity in relation to the "we." Marlow rejects the power of the "we" to absorb his singularity into its reality construction, which would make him into a "we-subject," a Marlo*we*.[21] This is what he cannot get his doctors to understand. Likewise, the medical community misdiagnoses the necessity of Marlow's thought as being mere neurotic fantasy, the continuity of childhood obsessions that must be rooted out in order to restore their patient to good health. They misread Marlow's "scenes," for which they lack diagnostic text, as being the mere manifestation of illusions. Marlow is, in his way, a speculative philosopher. Writing about Hegel, Karen Ng argues that "rather than beginning from the separation of Concept and reality, speculative logic begins from the absolute necessity of reality as always already determined by thought and of the activity of thinking that is always already the thought of the real, of the actual thing itself."[22] Scientific (and so, medical) analysis minimizes speculative philosophy's attempts to synthesize the possibility of knowing in how it presents. There is no cure for the present. Dark footsteps on rain-streaked pavements mark the sound of the narrator vainly attempting to step outside of himself, impossibility always being an act of vanity for the agent and agency of the voice-over. Marlow's memories may only be variant representations of an obsessive neurosis (a writer's tic), which causes him to associate thoughts with possible actions that are real or symbolic, like Freud's "Rat Man," whose obsessive infantile sexual fantasizing that his father would die (even though he was already dead at the time of Freud's analysis) led him to a figurative "rat hole."[23]

The further into his detective story Marlow gets the better he looks on the outside, the more his skin clears. Can the plot clear *and* thicken too? The characters in Marlow's reality begin to speak the words he is writing for them in the present tense. Are they legitimate or illegitimate fictions? Can reality be questioned in the same way, in the form of such a choice of alternatives? Can characters actually enter into our lives without a recognizable source? Is this, as Marlow calls it, madness? Or is this "*my unreality*"? Marlow's hands are still bandaged, as if giving him the appearance of being least suspect as the source of all this writing even as my hands are beginning to itch.

Prosopagnosia

> The human subject is a face.
>
> —Jacques Derrida, *The Animal That Therefore I Am*

Numerous films noir rehearse the theme of physical change of appearance without acknowledging that appearance is inherently the subject of change, an unreality that masks itself as the stable relationship of the self and the world. The bandaged face of Vincent Parry walks the streets of the real San Francisco in *Dark Passage* (dir. Delmer Daves, 1947) like a haunted a priori that passersby regard as being "the antithesis of the character of the apparent world."[24] The shooting of the first part of *Dark Passage* from the subjective viewpoint of the escaped convict Parry presents the audience with a face not meant to coincide with the voice we hear on the soundtrack, which is Humphrey Bogart's.[25] No great loss, say Bogart's anguished, self-regarding characterizations of men who are nothing much to look at. Parry asks Irene Jansen (Lauren Bacall), who is hiding him in her San Francisco apartment, whether she ever gets lonely living by herself. "I was born lonely, I guess," is her casual existential answer in a film in which loneliness echoes as if in a vacuum, but recalls Derrida's parsing Levinas: "the human voice is and says 'I am,' in the end, only in front of the other and after the other."[26] That Parry is a wrongly convicted criminal whose face is wrapped in bandages to conceal his identity in the process renders him less human, more animal-like and so ironically less subject to guilt because being without a face is, in Levinas's construct, "foreign to ethics" and so, it follows, less subject to the judgment of the Law. Even though, one should add, the mask's accentuation of Parry's eyes cannot claim indifference to good and evil, or as the court would say, an inability to distinguish right from wrong.[27] Nevertheless it is tempting to contrast Bogart's Vincent Parry in full facial mask with eyeholes, escaping judgment and Dick Powell's Marlowe (the role Bogart would make more famous in *The Big Sleep*, dir. Howard Hawks, 1946), with only his eyes wrapped as if to parody blind justice in *Murder, My Sweet*.

Irene tells Parry on returning to find him alone in her apartment that she thought she heard someone's voice. "It was me talking to myself," Parry tells her. "A habit I picked up in prison." The self-doubling of me/myself suggests a same-but-different presentational mode that is inscribed in the film's storytelling apparatus and that troubles the traditional indices of who, what, when, and where we are. Beyond this, talking to oneself destroys the face-to-faceness that Levinas believed is "the evidence that makes evidence possible." To not see the face, to deny the face-to-face is not merely to inscribe loneliness but the irrational and the unreal. Bereft of the other, we proceed to self-othering, to forgetting who we are, and we risk floating in a space that knows neither infinity nor infinitude, a space of not-thereness (e.g., the drunk old lady in *Murder, My Sweet*). "The attestation of oneself," says Levinas, "is possible only as a face, that is, as speech." Parry's run-on speech acknowledges that he is on the brink of switching out his real face for another's, for the other, eliding speech and change as possible forms of (self-) deception.[28] He instinctively knows that the face is epiphanic and so cannot remain silent even when the body is literally or even figuratively left alone.[29] The face cannot refrain from othering, from seeking out the other to define its being, since the other *is* who we are.

In one sense, the face can never be lonely, while in another it can never be anything but—wanting more and receiving less of infinity. Levinas claims that the ipseity of the self "consists in remaining outside the distinction between the individual and the general," refusing the concept of the individual and the general. The "I" does not just prefer to remain inside, "*it is interiority*" (my italics). The monad and ipseity take a more-*and*-less approach to the problem of identity, encapsulating it, interiorizing it to the exclusion not just of an exteriority but of a totality in which it refuses to participate. Both concepts dream the self in its own form-fitting house ("it is at home within itself"),[30] speculate upon what the self could be and not what it is in the reality of the world. Both the monad and ipseity go beyond self-sufficiency, since the latter allows for sufficiency as a qualifier to the self and so entertains the idea of the self being allied to a relative rather than to absolute value. The monad and ipseity are not carved out of being; they entertain being as a possibility with which they either choose or do not choose to engage: "The monads, echoes of the divine substance, form a totality within its thought."[31]

Parry fell into the habit of talking to himself in prison, where totality is a visible sign. He didn't belong in there, first because he was innocent and second but more importantly, because he does not recognize totality as a genus.[32] While I will not go so far as to say after Levinas that Parry enjoys the solitude that his rejection of totality constructs, as well as the solitude that obviates totality in the first place, there is a reason beyond wanting to change his material identity that produces the image of his face swathed in bandages. It is a sign of who he thinks he is and what he thinks he wants to be, which is alone. However, the remade face of Parry/Bogart in fact literalizes the Levinasian problem of who (else) it takes to be "me."[33]

Bogart-as-Parry's shadow celebrity profile does not so much have a face but rather "a face," as Norma Desmond physically and verbally maintained. The absent face that celebrity composes and maintains makes us all bear false witness to it, as did two-faced Madge Rapf (the sound a gun barrel makes through a silencer in an about-to-be-dead man's ear) to Parry's original face at his trial for his wife's murder. We later learn that Madge herself murdered Parry's wife, because she could not have Parry for herself. We begin to see here a facial overlay of Madge and Parry, along with the interruptive face of Parry's wife. This elides with the face-clock-face overlay-dissolve Hitchcock employed in the courtroom scenes of *The Parradine Case* (1947, the year of *Dark Passage*'s release), which also concerns a spousal murder trial. As fate (as literally as this figure can be expressed) would have it, Madge's death indirectly results from prosopagnosia, or face-blindness, specifically from her inability to recognize "Bogart" as the new jigsaw-puzzle face of Parry when it appears in the metonymic rectangular slot (rectangular screen shot) that is cut into her exterior apartment door. Madge has retreated to her apartment to hide from the man she helped put in prison and who recognizes her for what she has done. There, like another loudmouth, the aptly named Clarion who believes he can hide from death on a stage in Calderón's baroque play *Life Is a Dream*, death recognizes her all the more clearly in her uncharacteristic performance of the monad role. In fact, it was Madge's failed, belated attempt to claim the support of a previously unacknowledged community (unlike Parry, *no one* agrees to hide her, this "no one" being death's not-so-secret identity) that precipitated her retreat into a baroquely constructed aloneness that only the truly lonely know.

In truth, Bogart's face had never really gone away; it was just withheld until it is allowed to assert itself in the guise of reappearance—as in "What will Humphrey Bogart look like in this role when we inevitably see his face?" We already think we know what "Lauren Bacall" looks like, because her face is in plain sight. And yet, when a framed head-shot of her appears in her character's living room, a part of our brain says, "Oh, *there* you are." This is the kind of response that is elicited by any medium's conventions. The deeper question is whether Bogart's and, to a lesser extent, Bacall's action is a coming into presence or a coming into Being, coming to the realization that recognition (i.e., celebrity) has become their essence, the most elemental thing that stops them from accepting any role, closing the door on any real intimacy with the audience that helped make them who and what they are in the first (or second) place. Bogart and Bacall—two masks, celebrity skins that defy true facial recognition, because the faces that they had (contra Norma Desmond's assertion) stopped being truly seen the moment they became who they are—"Bogie and Bacall." Doctor Coley tells pre-operative Parry that he likes "to call a spade a spade," recalling with a straight face the surname of arguably Bogart's most famous role to date—Sam Spade in *The Maltese Falcon* (dir. John Huston, 1941). Is the doctor a Bogart fan who would transform as many faces as possible into Bogart's, or does he prize that face too much to re-create anything but the original?

"Don't try to talk," Coley cautions post-operative Parry, at which point the latter becomes a writer. The hands that are tied down at night to suppress normal reflexive behaviors now become extensions of Parry's head voice, the legibility of the voice-over, the previously suppressed identity of the star, Humphrey Bogart, whose voice we hear in our heads when we think of film noir. The writer's voice, as Blanchot tells it, beats itself up either for not confessing the truth of what is real or else for offering the false confession of its narrative as the only true reality with which he and we can know and together engage. Bogart's paranoid screenwriter character Dixon

Steele in *In a Lonely Place* (dir. Nicholas Ray, 1950) transforms "Don't try to talk" into the writer's comeback, pre-scripted by the self for the other, "Say it back to me. Let's hear how it [his writing] sounds." The line is always the same, both as written and in speech—"I was born when she kissed me. I died when she left me. I lived a few weeks while she loved me"—a self-parodying reduction of a life cycle to a narrative line and a theatrical manifest of what un-tempered (hot-tempered) Steele substitutes for real tempering. The line is his "lonely place," signifying "an internment within self-consciousness," his performance of capture, transforming Steele into a self-and-other strangling house-monad who is deaf to the line written by Levinas regarding the "voice" of higher being: "I have thought that it is in the face of the other that he speaks to me for the first time."[34] The writer, his weary eyes blind to the epiphany of the other's face, slaps it hard and recoils further into his own shadow, the thoughtlessness of light.

As Parry stares in horror at the empty space where the window glass has broken and Madge's lonely body has accidentally fallen through, he sees what on a stage the (window) curtain normally hides—the body rendered immaterial by its medium, the alterity of nothing which is death and disappearance. The fallen body's path is retraced in a series of steps, aided by two lap dissolves, covering a mere, nonrepresentational twenty-three seconds in the film. Parry's stutter-step escape retrospectively breaks down Madge's fall into a series of virtual stop-motion frames—virtual because while he continues to move he appears to be repeatedly stopping, almost as if he is retracing someone else's tracks, perhaps those of the original self that he can no longer face. There is a spatiotemporal interface in Parry's escape down the time-lapsed series of fire escapes, a sense of interval and interruption, as if his movement could or would be arrested in the process of desperately trying to avoid arrest. This only illusory (because edited) step-compression captures both the shortness of time Parry has been given to escape and the duratively experienced elongation of time it takes him to get down to street level, that is, his base.

But what is *our* base? We do not, after all, believe that Parry was *not* Bogart before his face was "changed." What *do* we know? Parry nominally escapes to P-E-R-U, whose total numerical value is 75 (P: 21; E: 05; R: 23; U: 26). Are there 75 steps in the sum total of fire escapes? We cannot put an exact number to it due to the cine-phobic lapses that rob us of memory-creation en route *as expected* by the anxiety of *not* seeing. Similarly, the facial "alteration"—which we cannot (bear) to see—of Parry's mug into Bogart's face only gets us to the image that we already know to be screen- and scene-worthy. This closed circuit of knowledge forms an episteme that vexes the identity of and so the relationship between the original and its representation. The original appears to subsume its representation into itself as if said representation were the original, as if Bogart was and is Parry, which is "in fact" the case. Humphrey Bogart died in 1957 at the age of 57, 57 being, of course, the inversion of the number 75, the sign here of where identity as a function of memory lapsed.

The aporetic nature of personal identity experiences memory as a limit, whereas memory is a time signature for change. Perhaps Alzheimer's de-suturing of memory from the self is a way of the brain acknowledging their essential non-correspondence. The neo-noir *The Memory of a Killer* (dir. Erik Van Looy, 2003) features an Alzheimer's-inflicted hit man, whose distance-making, memory-less profession predictively enacts his condition. When a hotel clerk asks him, "Is this your first time staying with us?" the hit man answers, "I speak Dutch," as if to say I cannot answer as myself, only as the spoken language that is the film's medium. Similarly, *Sunset Boulevard*'s Norma Desmond striving madly toward Max's filmless camera at Wilder's film's end wants no less than ipseity's monadic self-enclosure inside the medium. She wants *to be* the medium. In the noir-entitled *Fedora* (1978), Wilder's figurative sequel to *Sunset Boulevard*, Joe Gillis's William Holden here playing a(nother) screenwriter nicknamed "Dutch" pays to develop film for the movie's nominal title character who is pretending to be her mother, the *real* Fedora at the age at which she left films and who does not own a camera. Parfit has boldly stated that "personal identity is not what matters," by which he means that what we call "identity" is no more than a shorthand way of saying the connectedness of physical and mental events that comprise the givenness of the brain-body concordance. Objectively speaking, this "reductionist thesis" attests, we act without necessarily being self-possessed, with identity being an add-on, a performance and not a given in the story of our lives.

" 'Twas a story replete with twists and turns. It took place near Nice, by the sea. Maybe Menton. Alain Delon was involved, or a friend of Alain Delon," wrote Perec in what sounds like an overdub.[35] He is referring to René Clément's 1960's neo-noir *Purple Noon* (dir. René Clément, 1960), in which the sociopath Tom Ripley kills his rich friend Philippe Greenleaf over a game of cards and takes his life as his own. The death card for which Philippe's hand reaches is the ten of clubs, lying face up on the boat's deck when Tom stabs him in the chest. (I later came upon a playing card lying face down in the grass on the side of the road and without turning the card over identified it as being the two of clubs. Does this make me a fellow cardholder?) Ripley fails to realize that "the hand that recognizes [and reaches for] the being of the existent . . . at the same time . . . suspends being, since being is its possession." In other words, Tom Ripley cannot only *not* be himself in the person of Philippe Greenleaf (as the double negative suggests), he can no longer be himself either, once he has taken nominal possession of the other. After having disposed of the second body that was Freddy Miles, Ripley has a moment of not quite self-realization: "Wait a second," he says aloud, "Philippe is the killer! I had nothing to do with it." A so-called exemplar of America's adolescent, derivative culture, Tom Ripley practices signing

European old-money Philippe Greenleaf's name on the latter's bank statements. Ripley, like America a quick study in the power of destructive force and capitalist gain, nevertheless masters this rather ornate signature in record time. Certainly, Ripley is smart, but one suspects that the actor playing him (by virtue of the fact that *he is playing him*) is smarter. Delon must have used his own signature to double Greenleaf's and not Ripley's redoubling the Perecian affect of "Alain Delon was involved, or a friend of Alain Delon," as if it is Alain Delon who is caught in the act of being Tom Ripley pretending to be Phillippe Greenleaf.

This double-fake that transforms imitation into metastasis, specifically through the hand, recurs when the police ascertain that the fingerprints in Greenleaf's apartment match those that were found at the site of Freddy's murder. However, Greenleaf is already dead at the time of the murder, himself the victim of Freddy's murderer whose fingerprints are those discovered in Greenleaf's apartment and at the site of Freddy's murder. Since the police do not know that Greenleaf is dead or that Ripley has moved into his apartment (let alone under his name), they effectively conduct a double-blind(ed) investigation of the evidence, which unlike a double-blind study makes them susceptible to investigative bias and placebo effects. "I keep coming back to you," says the police inspector who is most doggedly on Ripley's case. "It must be intuition." But the "you" whom the inspector keeps coming back to is neither Ripley nor Greenleaf, at least as he tells it:

> *Inspector*: I'll fill you in on the details [of Freddy's murder] later, Mr. Risley.
>
> (Ripley ignores the Inspector calling him by the wrong surname the first, although not a second, time.)
>
> *Ripley*: I can't believe it.

Ripley can't believe what exactly? Certainly, that Freddy is dead in that he cannot be seen by the Inspector to believe it, since belief inculcates some measure of truth. But also, Ripley can't believe that the inspector has taken to calling him by the wrong surname. Is this the Inspector's way of telling Ripley that it is not really him, the real "him" in this case being Greenleaf? To Ripley's "I can't believe it," the inspector might well answer, "Neither can I," as in "I can't believe that you are actually and only Ripley and not a fake 'Greenleaf,' the fraudulence of this and of your 'I can't believe it' reaction to the 'news' of Freddy's death acting as a dissolvent of your own reality as Ripley" (thus, "Risley"). Of course, the Inspector might also be thinking of responding to Ripley's statement of disbelief, "Believe it or not," as in "Ripley's Believe It or Not," the sociopath's provocative unspoken challenge to prove a negative—that he is *not* pretending to be Greenleaf and so not *not "him"* (Greenleaf), which would also make him *not himself*. It is difficult to parse this as a proposition, but more difficult still (Kant would say impossible) to turn this proposition into a *nervus probandi* (nerve of proof) as to the suspect's true identity, since true identity is itself suspect.[36]

In *De Profundis* (1905) Oscar Wilde opined, "Most people are other people. Their thoughts are someone else's opinions, their lives a summary, their passions a quotation."[37] Like Borges and most especially his original copyist Pierre Menard, Wilde was fond of splitting the baroque subject's/object's singularity into what is and what it (also) appears to be. Borges applies Leibniz's argument that "there is no such thing as two individuals indiscernible from each other" to his side-by-side comparison of two seemingly identical passages from Cervantes's and Menard's *Don Quixote*.[38] Leibniz rejects the possibility of there being two indiscernible entities because it violates his guiding principle of sufficient reason, specifically "because, if there were, God and nature would act without reason in treating the one otherwise than the other." Wilde's paradoxical turn of mind actually affirms where he appears to reject this position by constructing in *The Importance of Being Earnest* (1895) John Worthing and his thought-by-him to be fictional younger brother "Ernest," along with Algernon Moncrieff and his fictional sick friend "Bunbury," as, in each case, a pair that is at once indiscernible from one another (since no one discerns that the latter is the former's invention who is actually identical to him) and is not indiscernible from one another (since one of them does not exist).[39] Wilde is here playing a language game in which he is personally invested—appropriating his socially and legally imposed "deviant" profile to language's deviation as a "detected alteration" that triangulates meaning in the [third] person of metaphor through the agency of the aptly named proleptically Froy-ish secret agent/writer Prism.[40] Through her forgetful authorial action of substituting baby John for her original manuscript and Wilde's resolution of error in everyone's favor, the play demonstrates that sufficient reason can be not only a criterion by which a thought or action is judged, but a mode for processing the possible compliance of necessity and contingency. This is, in effect, what makes the thinking of Wilde's play "deviant," "perverse." Leibniz's "grand principle of reason" says, "A is A and cannot be not A," but "Ernest" and "Bunbury" (two signs of *transference*) coexist in a state of being "A" and being "not A" at the same time, only in nominally different places. Their relationship is not real but metaphoric, as are all *Earnest* relationships that "hold two thoughts of different things together in simultaneous performance upon the stage of a word or a simple expression, whose meaning is the result of their interaction."[41] Particularly "Bunbury," like *Hamlet*'s "Ghost" (and *Don Juan*'s "Guest"), instantiates Levinas's proposition that "the power for illusion is not a simple aberration of thought, but a movement in being itself."[42] All three characters are exemplary intrafictional interlocutors of being/not being as a manifest (mental) condition.

Wilde's John and Algy are rewarded within the indexicality of fake identity whereas Ripley is not, because the latter targets mimesis rather than metaphor. The contested object is "likeness" as a form of the real, which *Earnest*-ness cannot sustain and Ripley cannot perceive as difference. In trying to realize himself as another versus John and Algy's re-creation of the unknowing self as the other, Ripley demonstrates how a sociopath thinks. If he were real within the fictional context of the play and self-determined, "Bunbury" might be a sociopath whose pretense overlaps with the identities that are called "John" and "Algy" and *Earnest* might be subtitled "*A Noir Play for Serious People*." Wilde already set the stage for the noir *Killer Bait* (a.k.a. *Too Late for Tears*, dir. Byron Haskin, 1949) in which a satchel of money is thrown into the convertible of a married couple, Alan and Jane Palmer, late one night on a winding road, who then deposit the satchel in a checkroom inside Union Station for safekeeping. The checkroom guards the original identity of all that it contains, making the object's nominal value (rumored by its safeguarding) worth another's earnest interest. From the imaginatively generative source of "Union," there commences a figurative vestibule scene of dually marked currency or compossibility, in which Jane conceals the expensive clothes she has purchased with the found money under her apartment's kitchen sink. There the realism of "the psychological phenomenon-individual" practices its own alleged concealment of motives. For this, Jane gets her face slapped several times by Danny Fuller, the man for whom she will later murder her husband and whom she will dress in the dead man's clothes to cover her crime.[43] The dead man's trench coat, which his replacement is wearing, contains not as expected the claim ticket for the remainder of the money that is still being held in the checkroom at Union Station, but a blank. Alan's sister Kathy discovers the claim ticket in the dresser drawer where the gun was kept wrapped up and left an impression on the cloth in which it was wrapped. Later, Jane returns the gun to its place, which shocks Kathy when she sees that it is no longer missing. Police Lieutenant Breach (a surname perfect for our purposes) tells Jane that her and Alan's car (which Jane abandoned at the beach) was seen being driven by a woman arguing with a man who looked like Alan. Jane claims to know that Alan was seeing another woman and describes her in a way that makes her sound like herself. Jane later tells Kathy that the police returned her car and there was a note in it from Alan that said he was going *to Mexico*. When Jane gets the claim ticket, she pays a man to get the bag for her, another body switch. The clerk who gives it to the man affixes a note to the bag to arrest the woman who comes to pick it up. After killing Fuller with the poison she had him buy to kill Kathy who was beginning to suspect her, Jane sets out for Mexico with the stolen money in the trunk of her car. She makes it across the border into Mexico and registers at the Hotel Reforma under an alias, but using her real first name, she is now "Jane Petrie," the surname being her maiden name, she says. Cornered in her expensive hotel room by "Don Blake," the brother of

Jane's first husband who killed himself, Jane draws a gun, and backing up in a police standoff falls to her death off her hotel room balcony with the money blowing around her body, tantalizingly out of reach of her "cold, dead hand," as they say in noir and its literary parodies.

The invisible filial relationship of John Worthing and Algernon Moncrieff, along with the visible but for a time illegible figurative relationship between John and his real and proper name "Ernest," announced but hidden in the play's title, contributes to the overall sense of a play of false indiscernibles that are designed to undermine God and nature, or "England," as the Irishman Wilde would have it. As Strawson has argued and Ricoeur confirms, "every individual entity . . . that can be identified can also be reidentified."[44] Neither Wilde nor his creations would stand up to close scrutiny as being who they are if paraded before eyewitnesses in a police lineup. Wilde, after all, was only prosecuted for Bunburying as the character "Oscar Wilde," who was by then a trope, a "figure of deviation" on the evidence of his play(s). As a figure, he, like his *Earnest* wordplay, deviated from even the "lexically codified usage" of the comedy of manners by affecting meaning with meaningful affect. Wilde's characters voice a perversely self-deconstructing insistence on the rectitude of presupposition for its own sake.[45]

In the end, it is the unpublished, uncited writer Prism whose redolently baroque agency collapses space, time, and identity in *Earnest* and in Ernest too, remaking Worthing from a two into a one whose worth has *meaning*. Here one recalls Kant's judgment that "fulfillment of duty consists in the form of the earnest will, not in the intermediate causes [responsible] for success." A man who because he no longer believes in the existence of God (the speculative proofs are weak) violates the laws of duty, which appear now to be non-obligatory, even imaginary, "would in his own eyes," states Kant, "be a worthless human being."[46] Jack's transformation, as superficial as Kant says it is, his worthiness not being tied to a supersensible but only dutiful in the sense of formulaic, genre-conventional idea, is already implicit in the play's title that offers a double life as a figurative theatrical madness. Jack's transformation, or rather the revelation of a doubleness that is in fact a oneness, is made possible in the realm of performance because, as Leibniz argues, space and time are not absolutes but rather "orders of existence."[47] That said, however much this revelation results in union and reconciliation, the spirit of the work as a whole and of the ending in particular is far more cynical, more probabilistic, Pascal would call it, more out of order in that Wilde not only makes a mockery of social class and class-based education as an organizational and even moral system, but throws doubt and certainty into a contest that neither side can win. When Leibniz asks the question, "why God did not create everything a year sooner," he sounds like Gwendolen telling Jack, "If you are not too long, I will wait here for you all my life" (III, 374).[48] Both utterances are illogical *and* self-aware, but the awareness frames the utterance rather than being contained within it. This framing makes both utterances appear to be irrelevant, even though they are not. More precisely, both utterances express a sense of time that does not properly take time's measure. Time's contentiousness is defined in terms of materiality, the things that exist *in* time, making the phrases "a year sooner" and "all my life" appear outside of time as its own abstraction, as in *The Night of the Following Day*.

Wilde forces us to consider that "the earnestness of life in its concrete richness," which Hegel said "leads the way to an experience of the real issue," is merely one of life's fluid practices and is not its own form of authenticity depending upon whether one views these performances as being "serious" or "trivial." Wilde (to use Hegel's words against him) has "open[ed] up the fast-locked nature of substance, and rais[ed] this to self-consciousness." Hegel's naming of "substance" as a kind of locked room mystery that must be traversed only from the inside to determine meaning puts us on notice, although it does not cause us to reject the noir room or the baroque house as signifiers, of substance's soul and the unitary conflation of character-room-action. Farce and comedies of manners are both fast-locked rooms, within which identities frequently shift and language plays. But in the end, the room, like "the house" against which we gamble, always wins. To borrow once again against Hegel's spiritual capital in order to derive a positive from his negative, the room, the house, the stage, "is conscious of . . . the finitude that is its own content."[49] Performance being obsessive-compulsive speaks of its yearning for freedom but is always checking the locks. For all their Bunburying, even Jack and Algy want to be married, and not just merely to satisfy social or even theatrical convention so much as to experience "the earnestness of life in its concrete richness." Under the sign of earnestness there is, in fact, a triangular relationship that exists between the sickness of Bunbury, the feverish experience and escapism of Bunburying, and the certainty of death. As Kierkegaard indirectly suggests, death, like earnestness, suits John and Algy to a "T" as fashion always does: "The idea of death may induce weakness in the more profound person so that he sinks relaxed in mood, but the thought of death gives the earnest person the right momentum in life and the right goal toward which he directs his momentum . . . Then earnestness grasps the present this very day, disclaims no task as too insignificant" (Wilde would say "no insignificance as too great a task"). The earnest person "rejects no time as too short" and "in the earnest thought of death [here read 'Bunbury,' a sort of imaginary 'testing by death'] he has the most faithful ally."[50]

The characters in *Earnest* speak (although not earnestly) of truth but do not speak the truth, except inadvertently, as when Jack who claims never to have had a brother or planned on having a brother in the future ends by saying in the face of the material evidence of Algy's filial relationship to him, "I always said I had a brother!" (III, 420–21). Consider too the following exchange, which contends with the truth that it expresses:

> *Lady Bracknell*: Good afternoon, dear Algernon, I hope you are behaving very well.
> *Algernon*: I'm feeling very well, Aunt Augusta.
> *Lady Bracknell*: That is not quite the same thing. In fact the two things rarely go together (I, 289–93).

Algernon is feeling well but Bunbury is not, health in Cioran's construction, "preserv[ing] life as such, is a sterile identity; while disease is an activity, the most intense a man can indulge in."[51] Algernon: "I have just had a telegram to say that my poor friend Bunbury is very ill again . . . They seem to think I should be with him" (I, 334–37). Algernon is, of course, with Bunbury in sickness and in health (to cite the play's central marital motif), although the healthy Algernon cannot allow himself to be mistaken for Bunbury, his creation who must always be ill. But using Cioran's reasoning, Bunbury is indeed Algernon's better half, not so much because he is imaginary as because he is unwell, this un-wellness being a sign of activity to counter the ennui of stationary, uneventful being, "the drying up of that delirium which sustains—or invents—life."

Wilde's performance identifications align, however unlikely, with Cioran's statement that "reality is a creation of our excesses, of our disproportions and derangements," which unreality, the sick and perverse unmask in an act of what appears to be an act of self-doubling fiction-making. "Frivolity," says the dour Cioran, "is the most effective antidote to the disease of being what one is; by frivolity we abuse the world and dissimulate the impropriety of our depths. Without its artifices, how could we help blushing to have a soul?"[52] I think it not to be too far-fetched to regard *Earnest* as noir's lighter double, the struggle between verifiable and unverifiable realities in which the self invests, the dupes and duping that life provides, the desire not to desire so much as to escape ennui and what Cioran calls the imprisonment of "a stupid perception" of what is and is not. "So it is that each night," Cioran writes, "facing a new day, the impossible necessity of dealing with it fills us with dread; exiled in light as if the world had just started, inventing the sun, we flee from tears—just one of which would be enough to wash us out of time."[53] The dread of self-disclosure concealed behind the trivial pursuit of lightness, of being "exiled in light" (doubling for and as performance), is a different form of shadow-play, one in which no one really dies because death is not realized and yet is no less real in the way that it consistently upsets the self's attempts to articulate what it is and where it stands.

Algernon does not respond to Lady Bracknell's question about whether he is *behaving* well (which he isn't and which is, in any case not so much the point as that he is [*being*] well), because that would necessitate bringing Bunbury to light as an imaginary manifestation of a symptomatic behavior that both is and is not his own. Similarly, when Bracknell hears Chasuble speak Prism's name, she inquires, "Is this Miss Prism a female of repellent aspect, remotely connected with education?" "She is," says Chasuble in response (we here mentally pause following "She is" as if she were as Bracknell has described her), "the most cultivated of ladies, and the very picture of respectability." Bracknell's response, "It is obviously the same person," reconciles the two indiscernibles into one, based upon the appearance of a logically impossible object much as Jack and Ernest, Algy and Bunbury contend for the same physical reality that they cannot du(al)ly inhabit (III, 321–25). Jack's opposition to Algy marrying Cecily and Bracknell's opposition to Jack's marrying Gwendolen stand in for Wilde's declaring the marriage of logic and meaning to be impossible. Wilde does so by making such marriages into mere formalities, things that are said (to be) not in earnest and "not [as] Ernest" as well. Thus, Cecily tells Algernon, who has named her "in every way the visible personification of absolute perfection," not to stop, as she is taking his words down verbatim in her diary and has "reached absolute perfection" (II, 422–25, 426–27). She has literally reached the point of writing down the phrase "absolute perfection" without any real hope of ever reaching that state, except in words only. Her earnestness attaches to doing, not to being, of which Bracknell might say (but only if she were being played by Wilde in drag), "That is not quite the same thing. In fact the two things rarely go together."

Kierkegaard believed that stage performance's transience and superficiality, its shape-forming and shape-shifting, its shadow-play of multiple identities serve the individual's desire *not* to access his actual self. Theater fulfills the fantasy of non-self-compliance, "the sophistical inclination of imagination, to have the whole world in a nutshell, this way, a nutshell larger than the whole world and yet not too large for an individual to fill it." The sense of not/being in the world is theater's gift to man, made anxious by his own freedom *and* his own mortality. This view is premised on the idea that man is by nature a melancholic self-doubter (which Kierkegaard viewed as a redundancy but not a repetition). This mental pathology mistakes earnest self-relation of the sort theater enables for an (artificial) actuality beyond which the imagination cannot reach.[54] "If the self is in despair," Kierkegaard writes, "is an *acting self*, it constantly relates itself to itself only by way of imaginary constructions, no matter what it undertakes, however vast, however amazing, however perseveringly pursued. It recognizes no power over itself; therefore, it basically lacks earnestness and can conjure forth only an appearance of earnestness, even when it gives its utmost attention to its imaginary constructions. This is a simulated earnestness." This earnestness/Ernest-ness is thus a "self-doubling" on the order of self-enjoyment rather than actual self-fulfillment. "The self in despair," says, Kierkegaard, "is satisfied with paying attention to itself, which is supposed to bestow infinite interest and significance upon his enterprises, but it is precisely this that makes them imaginary constructions."[55] Wilde's subtitling his play "A Trivial Comedy for Serious People" may then be speaking in appearance's code to despair's trivializing of a self that is never fully at home with, to, or for itself, as a private or a social function, of a self that is always in a state of visitation and self-dissolution.

Performance's repetition compulsion, "forgetting how to forget" not in the telling but in the doing, allows us to construct and deconstruct not so much our actual identity as our impulse to self-identify, to play safely with the idea of freedom of and from choice that Kierkegaard cites as a source of our anxiety. Theater is the play that has the imaginary of self-performance as its plaything. Marcus Pound writes: "The Kierkegaardian concept of repetition arises in the context of self-development. Repetition concerns the 'earnestness of existence.' In particular, it tries to resolve the dilemma of selfhood: how does one reconcile the fact that the self changes over time, yet maintains its apparent unity?" The apparent unity that dramatic character performs and contests runs up against the change and difference, the contingent multiple-selfing made necessary by lives lived according to social strictures.[56] Wilde's genius was to create a fantasia in which this process infected character through an illogical paradox of character and speech that elided social and dramatic convention under the guise of a common (heteronormative) assumption of earnestness. "A proper theatre public," writes Kierkegaard, "generally has a certain earnestness it wished to be—or at least fancies that it is—ennobled and educated in the theatre."[57] In other words, it knows what it (thinks) it knows, a knowing that Wilde uses to make liars of us all by getting us to sit still for and applaud the illogic of logical oversight on which such knowledge is based. Sherlock Holmes quickly sorted out the apparently illogical paradox of the upside-down room in which the room's furnishings were nailed to its ceiling. When Kierkegaard's narrator was presented with a room full of overturned furniture, he saw only "a repetition of the wrong kind" predicated on recollection of what something was or should be (e.g., a collection) and not what something (or someone) can or could be. One can imagine a production of Wilde's *Earnest* play in which the characters, like Richard Foreman or Guy Maddin characters devoid of Holmes's capacity for self-analysis, don miniature chair hats in order to acknowledge the world in/as a nutshell they can fill, but only with their heads that compete against one another to turn a phrase before the music stops and another chair is removed.[58] Maybe the objects should only be the words themselves, "chair" for chair—signs, but merely signage. "Prism" for prism, this last refracting our experience of Wilde's baroque play as an impossible object that is drawn in two dimensions but seen in three.

In *He Walked by Night* (dir. Alfred L. Werker and Anthony Mann, 1948), we learn that the L.A. police have a "modus operandi file." If this is true, might there be one for dramatic characters as well? Can a fictional character be said to have an MO? Isn't it "Ernest's" MO to be earnest, and the invalid Bunbury's MO to be in*val*id? Does a real object have an MO that makes it appear to be fictional? In *Somewhere in the Night* (dir. Joseph L. Mankiewicz, 1946) an amnesia patient who thinks his name is "George Taylor" sees a tree outside his hospital window and remarks, "For all I know, that's the first tree I ever saw. Still, that's what it is. That's what I call it." "Taylor" (not his real name) is on to something here. As Nagel suggests, when someone says, "Perhaps, I have never seen a physical object," he may be questioning not the object's existence but its fulfillment of "the spatiotemporal and mind-independent characteristics necessary to be a physical object—nothing of the kind that I take physical objects to be." That the particular object in question is the commonly used philosophical measuring stick "tree" is one thing; that the object is particular as in selected is another, since this relates to the absence in the amnesiac Taylor of some, but not all memory.

Taylor's knowing what to call a "tree" does not automatically permit him to understand what a tree is or to know where this "tree" falls within the time frame of his experiential life. (This excludes the very human aspiration to "go beyond experience," or, to paraphrase a horror tale, to walk beyond the range of one's light.)[59] As such, he cannot really know, as in determine, whether or not this "tree" has been planted in his mind by someone else (whether it is even his mental image to which he is comparing the physical object he sees), any more than he can be sure of what his real name is. This doubt concerning ownership of the image analogizes to the rift between mental image and representation of tree as an idea/concept and as a name/designation. Couldn't Taylor's doctors, in the interest of restoring his memory, have added things to and even subtracted things from what Taylor's present memory contained, in so far as they or he knew what was there in the first place? "Suppose I am a brain in a vat being stimulated by a mischievous scientist to think that I have seen trees, though I never have," asks Nagel in Taylor's stead (Taylor not being able [who of us is?] to say definitively of himself, "Perhaps I am a brain in a vat," or "That's the first tree I ever saw").[60] What if Taylor's doctors decided to call his lunch a tree, and a tree his lunch? How would he know that they were wrong? Seen against a speculative horizon, "who's to say that Hamlet is not really [just] a fir tree?" Ricoeur reminds us that "it is . . . the task of speculative discourse to seek after the place where appearance signifies 'generating what grows.' "[61] The tree (the "*perceived-tree as such*") behind the window might be a generative illusion (an intentional rather than an actual object), as Hamlet suspects, without necessarily knowing which side of the window he is on or whether the window has become a mirror. Perhaps this something we call "tree" is not a real tree at all, where the criterion for one's reality, the premise of self-perception, separates itself from the simple capacity to name what is seen (as Wittgenstein cautioned). We all live with doubt, and the amnesiac is a metaphor for who we are in relation to the things of this world, to the life that passes before us, takes us up and drops us off in "space" and "time" without a name. Ipseity is a branch of the tree "that displays itself by way of perception, by way of memory, by way of a picture." Similarly, as Nagel attests, "thought and language have to latch onto the world, but they don't have to latch onto it directly at every point."[62] There are trees that fall when we are not around and yet they not only fall but *are* trees even without us hearing, seeing, thinking, or naming them. So too, "each word [each name] inheres in a labyrinth of branching interverbal relationships going back not to a referential source but to something already, at the beginning, a figurative transfer."[63] Our words, our lives are figurative and labyrinthine, a self-contained metaphor in which the self is itself metaphorical.

The tree that Taylor sees through his hospital window might also represent as per Husserl not solely an object but a noema, meaning an object or mode of thought. This allows for there to be clarity where there is also abstraction, an intelligible representation of unreality, the idea of the object encapsulated in a real object in a post-Platonic world. In this formula, Levinas writes, "clarity is the disappearance of what could shock."[64] Whenever possible, the concept of reality resists the possibility of shock like the immune system fights off a virus. But what does such inoculation cost us? And if the shock prevails and is too great for our brain to process, does it opt for amnesia rather than unreality without realizing, that is, without consciously knowing that intelligible unreality represents gain, not loss, not something in the absence of its opposite (i.e., reality)? If we are to include amnesia and unreality in the same sentence, we might say that amnesia results in the forgetting of what we once knew, whereas unreality affirms the forgetting of what we already know. (We forget so that we can dream of there being a continuity from moment to moment in our lives that, said Nietzsche, does not exist. One moment is incommensurable with the next. Is this what the interplay of contingency and necessity in John Worthing's life suggests?)[65] Beyond this, though, "Taylor's" amnesiac forgetting is unreal, because it is un/consciously disingenuous and conflicted. His "amnesia" phenomenologically suspends the idea of "memory" in the glassy aspic of "window" and "tree," that is, as an *idea* of what this series of things are so as not to get caught up in mere representation, replication, and (by Husserl's lights) infinite regress. (Like brackets, quotation marks mark "reality's" suspension as phenomenological reduction.) Later Taylor visits a checkroom to retrieve the briefcase he left there for three years and seven months, "the longest," the clerk says, "I ever heard of anybody checking a briefcase, even a trunk, unless it's got a body in it." (How about checking a tree to see that it has a trunk in order to justify calling it a "tree"?) Obviously, Taylor has never heard of Prism or *The Importance of Being Earnest*, or if he has, he fails to draw the connection to a play that holds ipseity and real doubt in check for some time. "Taylor" is amnesiac because he is afraid of his own nature, which he gleans from an anonymous letter he finds in his wallet that he assumes he wrote angrily to someone who made him suffer and whom he hoped would be made to suffer in turn. "George W. Taylor" did, "in fact," take his name from the "W. George, TAILOR" tag on the inside of his suit (an act worthy of *Earnest*) on the night three years ago when he allegedly killed a man for a suitcase he later left at a checkroom containing $2,000,000 and the seed of his amnesia (which allowed him to forget *Too Late for Tears* three years later). And with this Prism's gathering headache speaks to the partially encrypted unburdening of a human memory mass of roughly equal weight to her own novel that she has been trying unsuccessfully to forget.

When, following a catastrophic train wreck in the Barbara Stanwyck vehicle *No Man of Her Own* (dir. Mitchell Leison, 1950), pregnant unwed Helen Ferguson hysterically realizes that she has been mistaken in hospital for the dead Patrice Harkness (a pregnant stranger she met on the train whose wedding ring she gave her for momentary safekeeping), her nurse asks her, "What's the matter? Are you afraid of your own name?" The real Patrice's in-laws have never seen her and this unseen-ness, this anonymity enables an identity-switch that commences a dark Bunburying that entails Helen's conscious choice to live with the wealthy Harkness family as Patrice whose child was lost and for Helen's own child to be substituted for hers. Then, out of nowhere, or out of a somewhere for which she had no contingency plan, Helen receives a telegram that says only:

> WHO ARE YOU?
> WHERE DID YOU COME FROM?
> WHAT ARE YOU DOING HERE?

These three questions that we all fear being asked and to which we must all respond (and which motivate actors to act) provoke Helen to exit the Harkness home. But before she can do so, she is again saved by the chance intervention of someone else's past. The Harkness family matriarch's private reading of the telegram Helen received elicits a sympathetic response in the form of a long-standing and secret heart condition that kills her. This involuntary surrogation of pain provokes Helen to continue surrogating herself to the role of Patrice, which she, at the same time, continues to resist. In a sense, Helen's inability to commit fully to living a dead woman's life saves her from self-delusion, as does the recurrence of her own past. These two forces collide when small-time crook Steve Morley, the man who abandoned her when she became pregnant, blackmails her into marrying him as "Patrice Harkness" so as to share in the wealth she (and he as her husband) will inherit when the elderly Harknesses die. Helen arrives late on the scene to discover Morley, whom she intended to kill, already dead. The before-ness of his passing could not help but intersect with the pastness of "Patrice," the woman whose name outlived her physical being. Here, as in other noirs, identity's ontological status is revealed. The late Patrice's brother-in-law Bill Harkness (who disposes of Morley's body from atop a railway bridge to cover his beloved Helen-as-Patrice's apparitional crime of being neither Morley's murderer nor the real Patrice) tells her in words that would strike Gwendolen Fairfax as perverse: "I don't care who you were or what you've done. . . . I love you, not a name." Personal identity, in any case, struggles to decide what it means to be "in character" and whether there is a plot on which our "character" depends to prove or make itself real.

There Is No Mirror

When he started going mad, Nietzsche needed to check mirrors to see whether he was still there and recognizable to himself.[66] A mirror is a dysmorphia-producing, anamorphic thing of madness that tells us, "It's not you, it's me that you see in reflection. *You* are apparitional. *You* are no one without *me*. It's why you keep coming back to look." Terry Collins (in *The Dark Mirror*, dir. Robert Siodmak, 1946) was born left-handed but she has learned to do things with her right hand, as effectively as Ruth, her twin. Each twin wears a choker with her name in metallic block letters, a fitting appointment given Simone Weil's assertion that "appearance chains being down" and that as anything other than itself it (appearance) is "error."[67] Although each sister addresses the other by the name that hangs from her neck, the name falls victim to appearance's untruth. Rorschach and polygraph tests administered to the twins by a Dr. Elliott (his own nominal doubling puts his own and his test's veracity in question) indicate that Terry is "insane," paranoiac, and manipulative. Terry convinces Ruth that she is sobbing *in her dreams*, which given that both Terry and Ruth are played by Olivia de Havilland, perhaps channeling her intense sibling rivalry with sister Joan Fontaine (who appeared in both the paranoid-delusion-inducing *Rebecca* and *Suspicion*), might here have been referring metaphorically to acting in films. "We had *names* then," the mirror silently spoke.

The Dark Mirror speaks not solely to the potential psychotic condition of the biological off-mirroring of twins but to what philosophers call "the unity of difference" that "suspends ipseity," whose "luminous locus . . . as the forgotten and irrevocable mother of identity" is otherwise too brilliant (in a literal sense) and too absent, too overlooked in the reduced overlay of self and identity.[68] That is, what is brought into view, however tenuously, by the film's underlying psychological dogma is a suspension of otherness as a mere mirror image of the self (or of the self as a personality/disorder). The conventional self-other binary is endlessly self-referential because, as is also shown to be the case in *Earnest*, it derives from the illusory belief in a "unitary selfhood," an "ideological construct" that holds not the real person but society and its characterological figures of speech together.[69] A facial recognition approach may be used to solve a crime but not a mystery. Ipseity cannot easily be sliced up as a captive hand to offer digital proof of life. Ipseity does not go looking for signs. "Self reference," on the other hand, is a quest for "how *not to* lose the means of referring to something other than one's identity." Ipseity persists, but only as "an illusion of identity in order to 'make do' in terms of calling oneself and being called."[70]

Hamlet's identity crisis—ironically echoed in *Earnest*'s John Worthing—is a self-fabrication insofar as "the notion of the self is a final result of multiple fabrications leading to the fiction of thinking and then to that of a thinker."[71] The Ghost, who speaks to Hamlet *as if he were his son and he his father,* haunts identity as much as representation, with the latter being the only verifiable (but inherently compromised) form of the two. Thus, the question the Ghost provokes, "To be or not to be," is a figure of speech concerning not self-ending but the possibility that the self is the non-corroborative issue of language as it is thought (up). The Ghost, who need not actually be seen, as in physically represented, is itself a figure of speech and the *passepartout* of this line of thinking. The Ghost in Grigory Kozinstsev's film *Hamlet* (1964) appears wearing a long "cloak of otherness" that billows from no identifiable directional source.[72] There is a wind blowing that night, since we see the capes of Francisco, Bernardo, and others billowing even before we see the Ghost. But their capes blow out from and back to their bodies and are not suspended from the body as is the Ghost's. This suspension suggests what we inherently know, that these characters cannot all be said to occupy the same reality. This might instantiate Philippopoulos-Mihalopoulos's filial terms "the suspension of suspension," "the inoperable unity of [a] difference," the sense that appearance being transparent is rendered unseeable in the spectacle of the Ghost's in/visibility. This spectral aporia gestures toward Hamlet's own "hybridity [which] points to a departure from the self, which is, however deeply rooted in the impossibility of ever having a full understanding of oneself." This is Hamlet's dilemma. He is not split in intention so much as he is psychologically and philosophically in transit within the apparent split of in/comprehension. His mind is being tested in ways that transcend his learning and its epistemological basis. The Ghost affects the figure of the father as instructor of what cannot be learned because it is not known.

Hamlet effectively tells the world, "There is something other I must become in order to be 'what the system is not.' "[73] Hamlet has entered into "an autopoietic system [that] is neither in the system nor in its environment, neither closed nor open, neither form nor distinction, neither neither nor nor, but a perpetual oscillation that cannot be traced except as a trace of a just present absence."[74] Hamlet is, then, not so much his father's son as his father's *Ghost's* son. Hamlet's "north by northwest" madness is the only directional account of the source of the wind that billows and suspends his "cloak of otherness" which imagistically captures without a mirror "the reality of ipseity" that his father's Ghost somehow performs as a means of passing on a new ontological and epistemological legacy to the son whose mind is processing toward the spectral, the televisual in the baroque night.[75]

Walter Neff and Phyllis Dietrichson enter the screen watched by Brian De Palma's eponymous *Femme Fatale* (2002). A door suddenly opening sounds like a gunshot that sets off a photo-flash, which in turn illuminates the room as if it were a set. We can now see that the television is backed by a Magritte-like green curtain that runs the length of the wall. The heavy curtain with its baroque folds suggests a Deleuzean theatrical intervention and some special effects trickery as per green-screen setups in which fake backgrounds that are seamlessly real in appearance are projected on studio sound stages. We are being baroquely reminded that we are viewing a scenic room inside a film frame from within both of which a film is being watched on a screen inside a smaller frame with a curtain that is dropped behind the small screen and scenic room. Added to this, the female figure is posed mostly nude in Venus-in-a-half-sheet fashion, her head propped up on her hand at *the foot* of the bed, marking a visual disturbance of sleep patterning. (Insomniacs do it—sleep—upside down.) The woman is watching *Double Indemnity* subtitled in French, but when the well-dressed man with the French accent enters, he speaks to her in English. He asks her, "Do you know what time it is?" and even though the woman is wearing a black watch on her left wrist, she remains silent, as if s/he isn't really there, in the time to which he refers.

Barbara Stanwyck is screaming through the wires that someone is going to murder her, but not so much in real time as in movie time, in 1 hour and 45 minutes, to be precise. But the femme fatale who is watching her in the wrong movie (i.e., in *Double Indemnity*, *not* in *Sorry, Wrong Number*) inside a movie of her own that misreads "45" as "54" (the running time of *Femme Fatale* is 1 hour and 54 minutes) cannot or will not take her call. Besides, the femme fatale knows that time is a hypochondriac, a complaint about passing and a passive complaint. The lit lamp on the dresser may only be there in order to dress the set so that we can accept it as being something other than what it is—a film, perhaps, or a dream whose light comes from one constant but miniaturized source, glowing at the margin. Maybe it's a Strindbergian sign of madness waiting to be thrown across the room in an act of self-exposure as in *The Father* (1887), or of a Heideggerian thrownness the woman is feeling but not allowing herself to show, although she will later or sooner be thrown over a railing not once but twice from a great height, the second time into a deep body of water only to re-break the surface on the way up in a limit-sized bathtub under another name, from which she like other corpses are reborn. Asthma sufferers like myself sometimes liken the physical experience of an asthma attack to trying to breathe underwater. Laure, the woman in question, at one point lies about being asthmatic, but maybe she really is asthmatic in her dreams.

Wearing night-vision goggles (standard issue for femme fatales) after her fellow thieves (one of whom is baroquely named "Racine") whom she has betrayed have cut all the lights, Laure *Ash* (the femme fatale being only a noir image of what there is no real hope of recapturing, as a "No Smoking" sign suggests) escapes the scene of a bait-and-switch jewel heist that she pulled off with another woman while everyone else at the Cannes Film Festival was watching the movie that actually premiered at the festival three years earlier. The pairing of nighttime and retroactive vision literally splits the scene/screen to show Laure's being telephotographed by Bardo from an impossible distance and a great height. This bifurcation will eventually transcend disguise and result in Laure's character apparently dividing into a second persona named "Lily." In the long view, Bardo (modeling the Buddhist in-betweenness of birth-death-dream for which he is named) is assembling a picture-montage of overlapping panels that appear to have been painted from his photographs (an evocative reversal of Winckler's puzzles made from Bartlebooth's paintings) that display images of Laure's body pulling away from herself, expressing her ipseity.[76] A TV talking head, recalling the smiling end of the Cheshire cat, asks Laure, who has been lying under a checkerboard-patterned comforter, "And if you could see the future in a crystal ball, or in the palm of your hand, or in a dream, would you change it?" When a reanimated from "death" Bardo (killed in a Laure-engineered double-cross) crosses paths again with Laure, he asks whether she and he (Bardo) have met before. Her response and the film's last line is "only in my dreams." Dreams, of course, offer us what Eyal Peretz calls a "futurity without content," much as the sudden, occasional appearances of bright light flashes that dispel the possibility of shadow in this neo-noir suggest the presence of an "absolute outside" that cannot be figured outside the frame of the self in the scene of the world.[77] Anymore, I would add, than can an absolute inside. Near the film's end, a truck driver hangs a miniature crystal ball the now bifurcated Laure/Lily purchased "as seen on television" on his rearview mirror, which prismatically refracts (Laure/Lily as Prism) the sun's blinding light and with "the maleficent power of [its] convexity . . . seemed to want to concentrate all available space into a single point."[78]

Film creates a bifurcated state of self-(un)knowingness that theatre double-exposes so as to make it seem necessary to see and to know that you are being set up (the right/wrong man theme), framed. If, as Hitchcock taught us (and taught De Palma), this is necessary and true, then we can become guilty in our thoughts, even though our eye does not appear to transgress beyond set limits. In Mark Robson's *The Prize* (1963), Paul Newman as the Nobel Prize-winning American writer Michael *Craig* arrives in the Stockholm that Paul Newman as American physicist Michael *Armstrong* in Hitchcock's *Torn Curtain* (1966, i.e., *three years later*) *only said* he was going to visit to cover his real espionage mission as a fake defector looking to steal a secret formula held in the mind of a noted German physicist who holds Werner (the uncertainty principle in quantum physics) Heisenberg's university chair in physics. In Stockholm, Craig discovers that the real brother of his fellow award-winning physicist *Walter* Stratman (Walter + Craig = Walter Craig in *Dead of Night*) is being impersonated by a stage professional whose name is withheld even in the film's closing credits. "Who are you tonight? Who are you *this* time?" are the questions anxiously posed by time, the anthropomorphized impersonator in a film that looks to "the future" and in voice-over by the Nobel Prize Committee chair Count Bertil Jacobsson, who worries over all the things that could (and do) go wrong "this time." The Count is essentially in-voicing an account of the film's plot mechanics, its iterative homage(-like) quality and of the "now-presence" that presents as a succession of past-, present- and future-nows of Hitchcockian representation. "The deepest truth of consciousness," assert Moran and Cohen in Husserl's name, "is that its origins lie in an upsurge of temporality itself, and this raises the question as to whether the source of this temporality has to be something non-temporal."[79] Time orders and structures narrative, as does the aptly named Count. But we can not only count numbers but count *on* numbers as degrees and degrees as modalities of experience and expression that are essentially nontemporal, that have the structure of representation (that offer an homage to representation and homage's own accompanying anxiety of influence) but aim at achieving meaning. Although it is not smart enough to know it, *The Prize* contrasts the administrative Count who acts on merely signitive intentions (numbering, ordering, recounting, representing) and the blocked writer Craig who acts on intuitive intentions, unblocking the real story and returning meaning to words (e.g., the return of "Max Stratman" to its original source). The Count's reiterated concern, expressed in an empty internal monologue that does not influence the outcome ("nothing of the object comes to life"), is "to make clear a thought to [himself] . . . [which] . . . can . . . be achieved . . . by a signifying presentation."[80] In the meantime, Michael Craig/Armstrong performs imagined guilt's (the traitor's and the undercover writer's) secret agency voiced over by a Count who is afraid to count on time given the interruptive, improvisatory agency of the free actor.

But we are not free, owing to our mind's confused state of being in a world we experience as an outside that is really inside our consciousness, a possibility that troubles both reason and belief. Oddly, it is Nietzsche who offers us reasonable counsel: "One should not understand the compulsion to construct concepts, species, forms, purposes, laws . . . as if they enabled us to fix the real world; but as a compulsion to arrange a world for ourselves in which our existence is made possible."[81] But can possibility or necessity turn off the interior darkness of this baroque night? If I could sleep, I think I would; but then again, I think.

6

✦

Habeas Corpus

At length, I consented to relinquish the corpse.
—E. M. Cioran, *The Trouble with Being Born*

Two Bodies

Like a name without a body or rather with *two* bodies, "Eddie" Spanier is punched in the face and sent flying through a paper wall inside the *House of Bamboo* (dir. Samuel Fuller, 1955).[1] The small-time gangster "Spanier" is the cover identity for the American military intelligence officer Eddie Kenner. After discovering the ruse (the paper wall entrance having earlier passed as real wall currency), mob boss Sandy Dawson sets up Kenner to take the fall for the jewel heist he was planning when Eddie's body dropped in. Posing an unconscious Eddie standing corpse-like inside the paper-bordered room of the theft weighed down by the jewels that are meant to offer proof of his guilt, "Eddie's" body literally falls to the floor before the police can shoot him, hitting instead Charlie who stood him up. "*You!*" the bullet hails the shadow on paper not knowing its name, mistaking the image it sees for the real thing, it whistles.

"How bodylike the book, how mindlike the text," Gass says and any author knows to be true.[2] Riding the London tube in *Swimming Pool* (dir. François Ozon, 2003), the mystery writer Sarah Morton is recognized by a fan from one of her book's author publicity photos. "You must have mistaken me with someone else," Sarah tells the poor woman. "I'm not the person you think I am." Nevertheless, Sarah's use of the preposition "with" instead of "for" suggests a certain coextension rather than substitution and even a Leibnizian compossibility. The figure who is hailed is Sarah in one life, in one reality, but not another, as Carlos Fuentes said we are "in your memory" and "in the time you cannot remember."[3] Sarah soon boards a train bound for her publisher John's vacant house in the French countryside so she can write, but it is the unacknowledged (by the author and her narrative) hailing of Sarah as "the author" on board the first train whose trajectory we see and hear.

Sarah notes that the vines on an exterior wall of the French summerhouse have grown or else been arranged in the suggestive shape of a flat tree that figuratively turns the wall into paper and we read in that she is writing. This "tree" is otherwise overlooked, an overlooking that shares its view with an eventful window overhanging a swimming pool. "The idea [for the new book] kept running through my mind while I was on the train," Sarah tells John when he phones. "You know, one of those stupid things that latch on and won't let go." The grammatical non-agreement between singular subject ("one") and plural verb ("latch") indicates some kind of writerly slip that John overlooks when he tells Sarah to "call when you're ready to read me something" and Gass says that in reading we become in our heads "the best book of all."[4]

That night, Sarah grabs a bulbless lamp in the insomniac time of *not* writing to see what character has entered the house. John's unspoken of daughter Julie is running a bath, her body smoking. At breakfast the next morning Sarah pushes away the ashtray she finds on the table with disgust. At lunch the next day, Sarah finishes her meal with a smoke that perhaps belongs to the new subject forming in the writer's mind emerging from the bath, like Laure in *Femme Fatale*, reborn. The writer is of two minds, using perfect French, for example, to say she speaks no French at all. Sarah's words and actions (her complaints, her insertion of earplugs) say, "I want to sleep," but her spying upon Julie and her lovers says "I don't," because "I would have to suspend my *conscious* writing." Writers make the best insomniacs. "I'm the walking dead," writes one. "It's like being punished for something, only I don't know what I did."[5] As read, "something, only *I don't know*" may easily become "something, *only I* don't know." The writer's complaint, much like the murderer's or the actor's, is "it's not me, it's my character." Who (else) do I need to convince? Windows are writing tablets for the likes of Sarah and Froy, whose tea-cosy patterning and detection the former hopes to artistically and personally overcome. (Sarah is tired of writing her highly successful Miss Marple-like English village mysteries.) Like Froy, Sarah is also a spy, mis/identified on a train. Her name is necessarily written to vanish reflection. Both can likely do their crosswords in ink, filled with inky blue pool water from Joe Gillis's pen.

Julie tells Sarah that her mother wrote a book that her father John hated, so she (the mother) burned it. It was a love story with a happy ending. "All he wanted was blood, sex, and money, which is what you give to him, isn't it?" Julie says. As Julie fills in her parents' history, Sarah becomes the compossibility of Julie and her mother reflecting (upon) a co-morbidity of living corpse and self-murderer as author of the work in progress, *Julie*.

Half-expecting in her writerly detachment to discover a corpse in the pool, Sarah finds it in the shed. There a rock came between Julie and Franck, who, as his name suggests (the "franc" inside the "Frank"), messed with a (sexual) currency of exchange (between Julie and Franck and Franck and Sarah).

Julie tells Sarah that she killed Franck "for you, for the book." Sarah burns Franck's clothing, but Julie tells Sarah that there's something she forgot to burn—"Your book. It could be used as evidence." When Sarah asks Julie whether she read the book, she says, "No, but I just can imagine." Sarah is now in her element, tidying up the details of a murder after the fact. "If you do exactly as I say," Sarah tells Julie, "I don't think there will be any problems." "Why," asks Julie, "because you write about murders in your books?" "Absolutely," Sarah says. Julie leaves in a nominal effort to outrun her fear of abandonment, leaving Sarah with these parting words: "I lied to you. My mother's book was not completely lost. It did burn but she kept a copy, which she gave to me. John doesn't know I have it. Perhaps if I give you these pages today, you will bring her back to life. So, the thing's *by you*. Take them, steal them. They're yours.—Julie." Not "Yours, Julie," but "*They're* yours.—Julie." Although the ear can be forgiven or else credited for reading these two sign-off phrases as being not so much the same as of a piece, the penultimate piece of a puzzle, in fact.

Back in London, John has finished reading Sarah's manuscript of which he disapproves. "Well, I don't understand what you're trying to say. And I don't recognize you in it . . . It's too abstract. Where is the action, where are the plot twists?" "So what's your advice?" asks the author of the mother('s) manuscript. Sarah has, in fact, already published the book with another house, making John's opinion of it (avenging his late wife, the late wife's revenge) irrelevant. The book is, of course, *Swimming Pool*. As Sarah passes through John's outer office, his daughter enters. Her name is in fact "Juli*a*" and not at all the amateur femme fatale Sarah wrote about in her book. Julie does not exist in the real world apart from the writing, much as the book appears to the author who is reading it to have been written by someone else.

Deleting scenes is one way of rehearsing the disappearance that writing affects. A scene deleted from the finished film shows a train-bound Sarah observing a "Julie" manqué (played by a different actress) being told that her ticket requires stamped authorization, requiring an additional charge.[6] The scene has been cut to conceal not so much its unauthorized content, which is metaphoric, but to cut the cut, the edit that sutured the scene of Sarah sitting in her window seat at home to her sitting in the window seat on the train. Because, quite likely, it is in that interval, in the interspace that she writes her story. All of the scenes that follow as the central plot of the film constitute Gwendolen's "something sensational to read in the train" in *Earnest*. Sarah is Bunburying like Wilde's bachelors, which befuddles Froy, the prototype for the protagonist whom Sarah is struggling to abandon, into not recognizing her surrogate author.

Surrogacy's authorship is likewise the point of Henri-Georges Clouzot's *Diabolique* (1955), in which the heartless schoolmaster Michel Delasssalle advises his sick wife Christina (she suffers from a heart condition, as did the director Clouzot's wife, who played her) not to worry about (her) appearance.

Michel's later "death" temporarily stands in for Christina's death, of which Michel and his mistress Nicole (Christina's co-conspirator in *Michel*'s death) are authors as of some strange metempsychosis. On board a train en route to the death scene the two women have planned for him, Michel catches the attention of a young woman who will reappear as a needlewoman in a later scene, giving the latter the déjà vu sense that carries over into dream. Christina and Nicole hear the whistle of the train crossing the Ackerman Bridge, as if as in *Sorry, Wrong Number* the murderer were coming for *them*—which, it turns out, he is. Awaiting Michel's arrival at Nicole's house, Christina nibbles on small pieces of the baguette that Nicole brought from the store and which Christina earlier appeared to be throwing into the swimming pool.

Nicole stops just before knocking on her upstairs tenants' door upon hearing what turns out to be the final lines of a radio broadcast of Alfred de Musset's play *Don't Trifle with Love* (1834): "I'll find her a husband. I'll redeem myself. She's young she'll be rich and she'll be happy." In Gass's essay "The Book as a Container of Consciousness," I misread the word "radio" as "ratio" in the passage "Add radio to print and the word became ubiquitous. It overhung the head like smoke and had to be ignored as one ignores most noise."[7] Such misreading doubles down on the distraction that radio presents as so much noise to the non-sleeping writer (the upstairs husband is writing Nicole a letter of complaint for interfering with his sleep) while offering itself up as distraction by allowing us to see where we went wrong, but also where we went right. "Ratio" enters into the word-game of relation—(in Aristotelian philosophy) "proportional metaphor," similitude, specifically to the ir/rationality of the scene taking place downstairs that is murdering (another man's) sleep. "She's interfering with my enjoyment!" the upstairs husband proclaims, euphemizing the complaint of his downstairs counterpart. The dead and the living talk out of two sides of their mouth, alibiing one another as an absent presence—the upstairs couple can testify to the murderous downstairs couple not being where the dead body is, which will be moved to the swimming pool under cover of banging pipes and draining water. The upstairs husband complains to his wife that he still can't go to sleep, because "when she [Nicole] opens the drain, the noise will start again." There is an alcoholic teacher at the school who is surnamed "Drain"—a cruel joke told two ways. This reinforces the even crueler doubling of the upstairs husband who wants to but cannot sleep and the other, now murdered husband downstairs who as he went under, protested, "I don't want to sleep. I don't want to sleep." Michel was lying in the bed that Nicole earlier told Christina is "ours," meaning, one supposes, theirs. Christina is a Pisces, a water sign.

Going through the soon-to-be dead man's inside jacket pocket (where as we know, noir objects hide), Nicole discovers Michel's return train ticket and burns it, so as to conceal death's interruption of return (strategic to the "corpse's" plot). The two women transport Michel in a large wicker trunk to the school's swimming pool, which Nicole warns Christina not to stare at, because "we're not supposed to discover the body." Christina in turn upbraids Nicole for turning the aftermath of Michel's death into a kids' game: "You took one of your word problems with leaking taps, and tanks that fill up and empty and you planned a murder from it. In real life this kind of thing does not exist," Christina asserts. Well, perhaps in "*real*" life it doesn't, a chorus of bookish voices led by Sarah Morton reply in so many words, in so *many* words.

Michel's prototypical "George Kaplan" brand of dead man's suit returns without him, leading his murderers to the dry cleaners that dispensed it, where they discover a key to room 9 of the Eden residential hotel and the aforementioned needlewoman metonymically weaving together the writerly plot. A corpulent man in an apron, a rough approximation of Hitchcock performing a cameo in someone else's film (he had wanted to make *Diabolique* but Clouzot beat him to it), meets Christina in Michel's hotel room, where he has been cleaning the bathroom, the tub. He admits to never having seen Michel, because clearly, he tells Christina, "his life is somewhere else." Christina confesses to Inspector Fichet to killing Michel, who is not dead, so her words do not hold water (in a house the policeman says, dreams too much of it). Murder is like a bad syllogism: its logic, like the corpse's is a posteriori. "It's not time to die," Fichet assures Christina, while failing to get Michel's lighter to light, an action replayed three times in Hitchcock's *Torn Curtain*, signaling getting not at something, but at nothing, at death. "Lighters," writes Jack Pendarvis, "are born of broken things," from the components of broken pistols, perhaps.[8] Fichet departs and a more focused light draws Christina down hallways and through doors that apparently open of their own accord. Behind one of these doors, Christina hears someone she thinks is Michel typing. The answer to the riddle, "How can a dead man be typing?" might be, "When someone else is doing the real writing." Michel's murder is past imperfect because it is not real, and Michel and Nicole's murder of Christina by shocking her into a fatal heart attack (the real murder plan), although real is imperfect because they get caught by Fichet who suspected them ever since *he* first appeared. But neither of these crimes is really what the story is after, only what it appears to be about.

As school closes and its faculty and students depart, the schoolboy Moinet, who earlier claimed to have seen the presumed-to-be-dead Michel, now tells Monsieur Drain that Christina is alive. Drain (his name evoking "the kids' game": "You took one of your word problems with leaking taps, and tanks that fill up and empty and you planned a murder from it") insists once again that this is impossible but again Moinet, whom Drain labels a "mythomaniac," sticks to his story, because we believe it is *his* story. "I saw her. I know I saw her," Moinet says as he again goes to stand in the corner, facing the wall, as his punishment for lying to cover having shot out the same window a second time with a rock launched from his slingshot. "Don't tell them what you saw," *Diabolique* tells its audience in just so many words at the end, as if speaking with one voice to counteract Moinet's actions. What did Moinet initially see? He saw, through the window of a closed door, two women, Nicole and Christina holding a small bottle which Christina's refusal to smell indicated *something bad about the contents*. A moment later, we saw Moinet disappear from behind the door's glass frame and Michel appear in his place. The misbehaving schoolboy used his time in the corner (a six-hour stretch at one point; the length of Sarah Morton's train-and-chunnel ride from England to France?) to extrapolate the film's story from this interior scene in which he himself appears like the figure in Escher's uroboric spectator within the frame activating the picture he is viewing in the 1956 etching *Print Gallery*. From the moment Michel enters "the scene," everything we see and hear is Moinet's invention, but because there is no indication that perspective has changed, we cannot separate un/reality and doing so becomes irrelevant. It is, as Wittgenstein asserted, all a language game. Wittgenstein's famous *Tractarian* statement, "The world is everything that is the case," is an a priori statement with a grammatical shadow. "Case" in German (Wittgenstein's native language) is "fall," as in the partial sentence, "In case I die."

In the approach to this house (the school) in which people dream too much of water, there is a pothole filled with standing water, and bobbing on the surface is a child's small paper boat. If it were to be unfolded, would we find the story of *Diabolique* written in Moinet's hand, as perhaps we do this book's text folded inside Arkadin's paper airplane? While Michel is looking out the window that breaks, Moinet's schoolmate Patard is defacing the wall in which the window is lodged. Patard's drawing depicts a man in a hat and three-buttoned coat. The man's two arms are held up from his sides, perhaps in alarm or surrender. The ambiguity of the gesture is worth noting. The man's right hand has a line drawn through it, perhaps to suggest he is holding a cigarette. His torso is rectangular, as if the stick figure had impossibly swallowed a swimming pool. Patard draws the stick figure directly after, and perhaps as a response to the story, Moinet tells him and another boy about having seen Nicole and Christina with the "dark little bottle." We note that Patard is visually framed on either side by Nicole and Michel, who are, "in reality," planning a murder. Michel is holding a cigarette in a holder in his *left* (i.e., sinister) hand, indicating a possible misapprehension of his role (the "victim" is, in fact, the murderer). His cigarette draws no light from his lighter, which works only *after* his "death," which does not transpire inside the frame fatale. Instead, his alleged corpse resurfaces, bobbing on the water like a schoolboy's paper boat. The camera irises in on the figure of Moinet returning to his corner, his story that it was the dead Christina who returned his slingshot to him having not gone down well with Drain. Maybe Drain is right, and Moinet *is* a mythomaniac, but considering that it is namely the devout, dead Christina who is his story's protagonist, Moinet's final alibi suggests that unreality may in fact be a form and a way of lying away the limit-giving concreteness that is otherwise all that a life without faith can offer. When Michel stands up in his watery bathtub grave, shocking his wife Christina to death, he peels off the fake eyeballs that she earlier thought she saw roll to the top of his head. Is this what dreaming is in paraphrase—our vision rolled up inside our head?

De/composition

Sigizmund Krzhizhanovsky writes in *Autobiography of a Corpse*: "Relations, acquaintances, and even friends have an extremely poor grasp of non-obviousness; until a person is served up to them in a coffin as a *cadaver vulgaris* under a trihedral lid, with two five-kopeck pieces over the eyes, they will go on pestering that person with their condolences, questions, and 'how do you dos.'"[9] As vampire lore foretold and Greek tragedy confirmed, in the shamefulness of its neglectful abandonment, the corpse recurs, comes back. The exposed corpse is like Derrida's postcard: "Anyone who intercepts it and reads it can take it as addressed to him or her." The corpse invites "disinterred iterability" on the part of its recipients, who mistake receipt for authorship and ownership. "Someone or other chances upon [it] and says, 'It is intended for me. It has chosen me and I choose to be chosen by it. I say, 'It's me [*c'est moi*].'" But the corpse, like a Derridean dead letter, "creates the recipient . . . by chance or even by error." The corpse, whose identity and biography are of secondary importance to the characters who trespass upon it with their secret anxieties about death as their near relation, instantiates Derridean subjectivity that "becomes an effect, "a place," or a function rather than an originary cause."[10] The corpse/corpus is never itself so much as a constellation of the other(s) who write (de/compose) it (as you have done, my readers. This is what has been at stake in the book. You have been its stakeholders).

The trouble with "Harry Worp" (*The Trouble with Harry*, dir. Alfred Hitchcock, 1955), identified only by the name written on an envelope inside his suit jacket pocket, is that he has migrated from the bathtub previously glimpsed in *Diabolique*. "*What's he doing in our bathtub?*" the guileless child Arnie asks local painter Sam Marlowe, who tells him "that's where frogs belong," and with this we imagine Moinet making frog-eyes at this other small boy. As a boy, I often attended double features at the movie theaters. Usually I came to see the western, but once I, inexplicably, stayed for the horror film, perhaps as a psychophysical prompt to the strange mind-body kinesis to run toward what I most feared. The film was *Scream of Fear* (dir. Seth Holt, 1961), starring method acting patriarch Lee Strasberg's daughter Susan as a wheelchair-bound young woman who keeps seeing her father's dead body popping up everywhere in and around his house and estate. There are watery deaths, a sympathetic chauffeur who turns out to be a criminal, complicity, role-playing and switched identities, and a wheelchair thrown off of a cliff (perhaps) to a beach below. I do not know what frightened me more, the father's ubiquitous corpse that moved according to some secret directive of the "there is" (*il y a*) or the fact that one body could as easily replace another (a drowned girl's body in southern France replaced by her friend's nearly drowned body in England). I am fearful of the corpse that is/not mine, of its having been neutralized as much by Being as by no longer being. I see in its frozen-open eyes the insomniac's alarm at night vision infusing the nominal day, provoking a scream of fear to oscillate between the two of us, neither one of whom can find asylum in which our fear can be successfully ministered.

"What's the trouble, Captain?" the spinster Miss Ivy Gravely (who thinks she killed Harry after the wild man attacked her on the road) asks Wiles (who thinks *he* killed Harry with an errant shot meant to bag a rabbit), when she comes across him dragging the corpse into a nearby copse. (Gravely refers to it as "my body," and being named after the grave, she should have first claim on it.)[11] The trouble is that Wiles has lied about his past life as a ship's captain who has "faced death many times," and so his buried past forges a pact with the corpse of *clandestination*.[12] There is an ethical violation at work here that exceeds the responsibility to bury the dead, as if remembrance alone were a ghost protocol of the deceased's unintelligibility. Wiles tells Gravely to run along, because "you don't want to be an accessory after the fact," with "fact" standing in linguistically for "evidence" of both the thing and the suspect thing that is being and has been un/done. This un/doing of evidence presents itself *before* the fact in the beer can and "NO SHOOTING" sign Wiles encounters on his way to discovering Harry's corpse. The two objects that are *not* Harry have been shot with the only two bullets Wiles fired, transforming Harry into an "after the fact" as far as Wiles is concerned (this, doubling the after-the-fact-ness that attaches to every corpse). And yet, perhaps because Wiles is played by the same actor (Edmund Gwenn) who lured the protagonist "John Jones" (a one-off for "John Doe") to a would-be accidental death in Hitchcock's *Foreign Correspondent* (1940) and "Gravely" is played by an actress (Mildred Natwick) who could have doubled for the fake (high-heeled) nun (played by Catherine Lacey) assigned to watch over the corpse-like Froy in *The Lady Vanishes*, "What's the trouble, Captain?" is, in effect, a "how do you do" and a "here I am again" addressed to the both of *them* by the *cadaver vulgaris*. Wiles pulls the corpse by the arms and Gravely nudges it in the side with the toe of her square, mid-heeled sensible shoe, embodied reminders of where his hands (grabbing air while missing Jones and falling from a high tower) and her feet (betraying her deadly ruse to Froy's allies) have been. Harry's corpse re-grounds them via disinterrance in time that evokes a longer, winding thread of relationship.[13] The corpse is that which re/appears after the fact of what Wiles calls the "unavoidable accident" of death. The corpse, which does not (as opposed to *can*not) forget it was once alive, is its own a priori, since to be alive is *not* to be a corpse, is noncontinuous with the name "corpse." Only in its archaic usage was "corpse" a sign of a body that was either *living or dead*.[14] There is, in effect, no pastness for what was not before, except for other people who attach chronology to time as if it were (a) "fact."

Deputy Sheriff Calvin Wiggs presents Marlowe with "evidence" that the latter's sketch matches the description of the now missing corpse. "I do know the face of a dead man when I see one, and this is it," Wiggs says, even as Marlowe is changing the features of the face in his drawing, destroying evidence in the process (the drawer consigning "evidence" to the drawer, a figurative self-consignment). The source of Wiggs's verbal evidence was a tramp, who stole dead Harry's shoes, which does not trouble Marlowe at all: "If the shoes fit, he should keep them," he says in a variation of "if the shoe fits, wear it," which could be read as an owning up to some unspoken guilt, punishment, responsibility. However, unlike a true noir protagonist, this Marlowe feels no need to walk around in the dead man's shoes, which were oddly filled in any case by the uncredited actor Philip Truex, signaling the "x-ing" out of "truth" and the suggestion of its ex-ness or pastness. This was Truex's final appearance on film, so the actor was in a sense already rehearsing his own ex-ness as a model mode of demise.[15] Harry was apparently making his way back to Jennifer Rogers, Arnie's mom and both Harry *and* his brother's "ex," when he was killed, as if realizing his own desire only belatedly.

> *Marlowe:* Perhaps I'll come back tomorrow.
> *Arnie:* When's that.
> *Marlowe:* The day after today.
> *Arnie:* That's yesterday. Today's tomorrow.
> *Marlowe:* It was.
> *Arnie:* What was tomorrow yesterday, Mr. Marlowe?
> *Marlowe:* Today.
> *Arnie:* Oh sure, yesterday.
> *Jennifer Rogers:* You'll never make sense out of Arnie. He's got his own timing.

If there's no getting to the bottom of time in the form of a grave in the small, model world where Harry is causing such trouble, the corpse must be outsourced in terms of causation to a new form of grammar. Names like "Wiles" and "Gravely" perform a Wittgensteinian secondary function as a sourced rather than a source truth.

> *Wiles:* If it's murder, whodunit?
> *Marlowe:* Did it?
> *Wiles:* That's what I said.

Grammatical misdirection from verb to noun, from matter to mystery is likewise premised on the absence of real time, a fact to which Hitchcock returns when the "trouble" with Harry is readdressed by restarting the film's narrative (underscored by the same musical theme) in which Arnie discovers the corpse. Only "this time" ("today," which is actually "tomorrow"), Marlowe, Jennifer (the future Mrs. Marlowe), Wiles, and Gravely have placed the body so as to exonerate themselves from the before-the-fact narrative ("yesterday") in which they were implicated as "accessories after the fact" ("tomorrow"). The source of the idea is fittingly Arnie's mother:

> *Jennifer*: Wouldn't it be nice if Arnie found him all over again. Then he'd run home and tell me and then I'd phone Calvin Wiggs.
> *Marlowe*: Yes, and Arnie could explain quite clearly to Calvin . . .
> *Jennifer*: That he found Harry tomorrow.
> *Marlowe*: You mean today.
> *Jennifer*: But to Arnie, tomorrow is yesterday.
> *Marlowe*: Let's go get Harry.

"Causality in nature is nothing more than a stable empirical regularity of co-existence and succession," Husserl wrote.[16] In Hitchcock nature stands witness to causality's undoing. Likewise, recurrence relies upon someone's forgetting, "corpsing" in the performance of the role.

The restaging of Arnie's discovery of Harry's corpse enables the film's final line—"The trouble with Harry is over"—to be read, but only by the audience who actually *saw The Trouble with Harry*. The "trouble" with Harry is his "wholly otherness" (after Derrida), which infuses the narrative with its wandering (like Arnie's) unpredictability.[17] The signature of the abstract non sequitur with which the story has been overwritten makes it a kind of silent voice-over narrative in which the "I" replacing the "He" diverts responsibility and its attendant guilt to a self that we might want to but cannot distance. Our experiencing of the narrative has been conditioned from the film's opening scenes in which while exploring the wilds of his small town's environs, Arnie, toy gun in hand, "hears" three gunshots (it would have taken Wiles a third bullet actually to have killed Harry) and a noir voice proclaiming from some illusory distance to no one in sight, "Okay, I know how to handle *your* type." *Who* might that "type" be? The imaginative type who creates a crime scene where there is none? *What* might that type be? A writer?

With this only partially, even subconsciously in mind, Arnie's adult protectors—his mother (whose idea it is to restage the narrative) and future stepfather—alleviate themselves and symbolically "Arnie" of a nascent "trouble" that childhood affects, that being an inability to differentiate the really dead and the only fictionally living, the real and the unreal. The adults at the scene, including Wiles and Gravely, are likewise demonstratively anxious for Arnie to reset the clock of their residual fear of death and dying. From their scene of concealment, they side-coach Arnie but so as *not* to be heard in a subliminal, psychoanalytical way:

Jennifer: Go on, Arnie. Run home and *tell* me about it!
Wiles: Don't *touch* him!
Gravely: Please, Arnie, run home and tell *your mother*.
Marlowe: Beat it, you little creep! (He instantly witnesses Jennifer's face become like a dark shadow.) I mean, "Hurry home, son."

There is something altogether fitting in Marlowe's exchange of "son" for "creep," marking the belatedness of responsibility the speaker feels in the moment after he has first spoken. At the same time, one hears in this the faint echo of an absent God calling Harry's spirit home from where his corpse continues to homelessly reside. Science, in the person of the distracted, poetry-reading town doctor Greenbow, has already apologized to the corpse for not having seen it in its path for what it was and is. Greenbow determines that Harry died from a heart attack, although not necessarily from "natural causes," since what is causal can no longer be determined in any case. In "the end," Harry's corpse is the objective correlative for the modes of seeing what life and death are in relation to the abstract-concrete spectrum of human consciousness and perspective that together bury-unearth-rebury what we take for knowledge.[18]

Such is also the case with Hitchcock's *Rebecca* (1940), which features the subconscious still dreaming itself as water. When Maxim de Winter first meets his future "Mrs."—only his first wife, Rebecca, is afforded a first name—he is contemplating throwing himself off a cliff and down to the roiling sea below. His not yet future "Mrs." tells de Winter that her father was a misunderstood painter who painted one tree over and over again. He sounds not just like an artist seeking perfection as his daughter suggests, but like a philosopher caught up in what Gass calls "the fever of first principles." It is a term he uses to characterize Wittgenstein, who notably sought to make philosophy poetic and who, Gass notes, identified "knowledge with virtue . . . and the right to exist with the claim of creative accomplishment."[19] The artist father "had a theory that if you should find one perfect thing, or place or person, you should stick to it." Such loyalty to a subject makes a virtue of art and of philosophy, as the singular "tree" attests. It is a sentiment with which de Winter, whose steadfast attachment to his late wife Rebecca strongly concurs and his behavior, it turns out irrationally, supports. The late artist's daughter likewise sketches, but by her own admission "can never get the perspective right." How could she when de Winter, seeing in her the image of his dead wife, makes her promise "never to be thirty-six years old."

After a whirlwind courtship, they marry and the new Mrs. de Winter first sees de Winter's Manderley estate in a heavy downpour, which appears to submerge her in a deluge of what is for her unrecalled memory. The grave housekeeper Mrs. Danvers tells the new Mrs. de Winter that only the drowned Rebecca's bedroom overlooks the sea. Poor Maxim's memory is so water-colored, it has lost all ballast. His new wife inadvertently plays into this theme. Upon answering the phone, the second Mrs. de Winter, in a meek state of self-denial, tells the caller that "Mrs. de Winter's been dead for over a year." She only hears herself say this a moment too late, as if she is later than "she," later than herself as she is later than Rebecca whose apparent reiteration she has become. Her nerves unsettled by her own words, she accidentally breaks a family heirloom and then hides the pieces of the broken cupid (no less) in a drawer inside a writing desk. Any attempt at new (self-)authorship is at this juncture uncertain and concealed from public scrutiny. When Danvers asks her to choose a sauce for lunch and adds that the first Mrs. de Winter "was most particular about sauces," the second Mrs. de Winter responds, "Let's have whatever you think Mrs. de Winter would have ordered." Being later than late, there is no place to hide the living corpse of the second Mrs. de Winter, except in the third person, a mythic self-construction.

Danvers walks the second Mrs. de Winter through the ostensible story of the exquisite-beyond-words Rebecca that is told by her room in all its beautiful possession(s). But Rebecca, it appears, was possessed of a beauty that was only superficial, which metaphorically accounts for her drowning in the watery depths bordering Manderley. Danvers speaks hypnotically to the young wife about resting in Rebecca's bedroom and listening to the sea. The still un-self-possessed young woman feels herself drowning before she can even appear, except as "she," the late, non-identical third person, Rebecca. "Could we have a costume ball, just as we used to?" she asks her husband, notably linking the "we" of the present to the "used to" of the past. "I feel we ought to do something to make people feel that Manderley is just the same as it always was." Maxim tells her that he is the only one who is not required to dress up for the ball and wonders whether his new wife might go as "Alice in Wonderland," indicating that he regards her as being both a child and an outsider for whom Manderley seems unreal.[20] But "Manderley" is not so much unreal as it is a code for the interspace (in) which unreality and reality cohabit. Danvers, of course, knowingly talks the innocent young woman into dressing for the ball as Rebecca's double. This sends Maxim's mind into a spin, in whose aftermath the new bride comes to realize that being Rebecca's "second" does not "become" her since only her death after Rebecca, acknowledging the impossibility of representing her, can.

As the painted subject, Rebecca (and by extension her successor) is "consigned . . . to appearance," which in philosophical terms equates with untruth. Unlike in "real life," though, in art appearance signs itself. The paradox of the portrait painting is that it co(n)signs its subject to an inherent constitutional inadequacy that contradicts its implied idealism, simultaneously presenting both this idealism and *even this inadequacy as being unachieved*. But Maxim's violently negative response and instantaneous rejection of his second wife wearing Rebecca's costume only *appears* to be a response to her representational inadequacy and her cruel decision to remind him of this. Maxim is suffering not from a crisis of memory (he remembers how he really feels about Rebecca) but *his own crisis of representation*. This speaks to Barry Stroud's statement: "We can directly compare one picture to another . . . but we cannot hold our current beliefs about the world up against the world and somehow measure the degree of correspondence between the two."[21] In the mythomaniacal world of "Rebecca," Maxim no longer cares about what the world or reality "is," and allows others to determine it for him. He is a man who has lost his context to a frame.

In contrast, Danvers's plan of enticing the second Mrs. de Winter back into the sea and her as yet undiscovered lateness is perversely, unexpectedly (although with a certain symmetry), and figuratively fulfilled. In the attempt to save a sinking boat at sea (a scene suggestive of genre-painting), a second boat containing Rebecca's real body/the real Rebecca's body is discovered below. It now appears that Maxim had identified some unknown woman's body as being Rebecca's and had it buried in the family crypt. There it lies under an assumed name like some testament to these water people's collective mythomania. Maxim twice flicks his lighter and finally relates to his still innocent wife the salient parts of "the (w)hole story," the central theme being his murderous hatred for the adulterous, unloving Rebecca and the doubleness of her death. The talk turns to cigarettes and to the ashtray he has filled with his cigarette butts that recycle Rebecca's own from the night he confronted her alone in the very place where he and the second Mrs. de Winter now stand, the cottage where Rebecca held her extramarital trysts. Maxim only thinks he killed Rebecca, striking her where she stood threatening to produce an heir with another man who would succeed Maxim at Manderley. Maxim then carried her unconscious body to a boat, which he prepared to sink. At the inquest that follows, it is learned that Rebecca had visited a doctor on the day of her death under the presciently grave name "Mrs. Danvers," unconsciously replicating the even more presciently misidentified "Rebecca" buried in the family crypt. The progressive cancer Rebecca's pregnancy posed for the de Winter legacy was, the doctor determined, in fact real and terminal. Maxim realizes that he did not so much kill Rebecca as assist in her suicide that same day. In effect, the second Mrs. de Winter's sense of being later than late was a clue to the story of the first Mrs. de Winter, who is "killed" after her death sentencing and represents her own (i.e., "Rebecca's") second death. Unable to live with the new couple's happiness, Danvers burns Manderley to the ground. A rose on what had been Rebecca's bed and an embroidered "R" on her former pillow case predict the burning of "Rosebud" in Orson Welles's *Citizen Kane* (1941), a scene which likewise marks the literal beginning and figurative end of a story of self-mystification and collective mythomania.

Danvers's attempt to assist in the second Mrs.'s suicide seems to affirm the thesis that the housekeeper will not allow her to replace the irreplaceable, although it may serve mainly as a prolepsis of Maxim's similar role in relation to Rebecca. But the narrative is "in fact" plotting against itself, nuancing replacement with continuity between the first and second Mrs. de Winters as what Nagel calls a "series-person." A series-person extends what Parfit interprets as Nagel's belief that a brain can continue to live in someone else's body following the original body's death and decay. This, I think, is more a matter for metaphor than for science, as Parfit makes clear by choosing the mythical phoenix that rises from the ashes to represent this continuity. *I* can be a series-person in the form of the "Old-I" and the "New me." Personal identity here becomes less important than the relationship of embodied brains.[22] With this in mind, the name-sharing of the old and new Mrs. de Winters reinforced by the latter's lacking a personal name and the resulting pronoun confusion makes sense. When the second Mrs. de Winter proclaims, "I am Mrs. de Winter, now," she is in effect saying I acknowledge that I am a series-person, "I" am "she,'" as one would answer a question of identity in the third person, the third person in this case being a continuation of the first. Rebecca's failed attempt at producing an heir to Manderley and the de Winter name is meant to tie up the ostensible plot while contributing to its unspoken nuance.

At the same time, Nagel argues, "only I can really speak in the first-person Cartesian style," even though from the world's perspective there is no room for me as an "irreducible first-person fact." Nagel calls this "a sharp intuitive puzzle." The autobiographical premise of *how* I got to be me is replaced by the fundamental question, *why* I get to be me. "I" and "me" constitute a problem of agreement between subject and predicate, in a sentence where even verb tenses give me trouble. Nagel writes that in "a fully objective description of the world" (the world absent my perspective or else with my perspective neutralized in the level relationship of the one to the many), "there is no room for the identification of a particular time's . . . presence, pastness or futurity." An uneasy Nagel acknowledges that whatever status time loses as a lived-in state or condition does not obviate the effect of its passage. Nagel and Parfit also both refer to what the latter calls "*Further Fact View*" of personal identity, which says that the latter "does not just consist in physical and/or psychological continuity." There is more to this than meets the "I"—a mystery that is more metaphorical than metaphysical, which is not to say that it is all *merely* semantic.[23]

The assertion "I am Mrs. de Winter," Nagel might suggest, is "a special kind of statement, it states no special kind of truth—for it is governed by truth-conditions that are entirely explicable without indexicals."[24] And with this argument, the statement "I am Mrs. de Winter" burns to ashes or else dissolves into the puzzling anonymity of the first speaker's voice, the female voice-over that began the story in the rain with the statement, "Last night I dreamt I went to Manderley again." What should we call the dreamer? Whose voice do we really hear if not the Writer's speaking in the first-person present, which Nagel presents as a paradoxical case that is an essential part of a centerless world that excludes it, "an ordinary person" and "a particular objective self, the subject of a perspectiveless conception of reality"?[25] The question as to whether the voice-over—which commingles objective and subjective form, motive, and perspective—is the province of or a model for the (still) living or the dead is not easily parsed, nor should it be. Who *are* "*you*"? (Thomas) Nagel writes, "The statement 'I am TN' is true if and only if uttered by TN. The statement 'Today is Tuesday' is true if and only if uttered on Tuesday."[26] My sister and I were engaged in a conversation that had nothing at all to do with the day of the week. When we posed a question relating to this conversation to our hearing-impaired mother who was present for but not aurally privy to it, she answered with a question of her own—"Tuesday?" I wish that I had responded, "Yes," because "I *am* Tuesday," hiding the fallible body's memory of itself in time.

My Compliments to the Boys in the Guilt Code Department

We make light of the body in a vain effort to offset its recalcitrant heaviness on the one hand and its immanent pessimism on the other, although "the one hand" and "the other" belong to the same grave corpus. We might describe Frank Capra's *Arsenic and Old Lace* (1944) as "A Screwball Comedy Noir," which employs the bony knees and sharp elbows of farce to lighten death, as if the latter could be sketched on paper and dry-erased at the edges. A newspaper photographer at the marriage bureau in *Arsenic* asks his reporter sidekick, "I wonder if any big shot is getting married today." Immediately, they sight Mortimer Brewster, a "dramatic critic" who wrote the book on marriage as "A Fraud and A Failure" and who looks suspiciously like Cary Grant in his dark glasses in his standing-in-line-at-a-Hitchcock-ticket-window scenic context. There is a sort of pre-*North by Northwest*-ern scenic madness about recurrence that does not yet know its name. Witness the loud sneeze emitted by Reverend Harper that is overheard and referred to as being possibly pre-pneumococcal by two people during their dialogue in the cemetery abutting the Brewster family home. The sneeze interrupts the Reverend's laying down the law to Mortimer's aunt Abby regarding the inappropriateness of Mortimer marrying his daughter Elaine. The sneeze replays the propulsive sternutation of an Englishman taken into the hands of the law while investigating an abduction (the body's physiological response to sneezing) in the original *The Man Who Knew Too Much* (dir. Alfred Hitchcock, 1934). Mortimer's delusional cousin "Teddy Roosevelt" Brewster, who is nearby, believes that it is he, not the Reverend, who sneezed, marking a displacement of the body but likewise the contagion of death that is in the house by a graveyard that advertises room for rent.

When Mortimer tries to get Happydale Sanitarium to accept his brother Teddy (so that his aunts' murders of lonely old men who Teddy then buries in the basement can be blamed on the demonstrably "true" madman), he is advised by the hospital's director, the cadaverous-looking Mr. Witherspoon: "Well, you see Mr. Brewster, we have several Theodore Roosevelts at the moment, and it would lead to trouble." The trouble with Teddy, though, is symptomatic both of something and someone else, an idea that has already been put in play when "his" sneeze came out of the Reverend's nose. This nose will later come back in the larger-than-life model of Lincoln's nose in which Roger Thornhill was originally meant to hide near the end of *North by Northwest*.[27] "Lincoln" himself, that is, the role of "Lincoln" (like that of "Roosevelt" and "Washington"), will appear in *Arsenic* in the person of Mortimer's deranged, long-lost brother Jonathan, who is played by the Lincoln film impersonator Raymond Massey. The joke here is that while Lincoln was naturally homely, Jonathan's terrifyingly ugliness is handmade, his face stitched together as if he were Boris Karloff in his most famous role of Frankenstein. By his own admission, Jonathan's cohort Dr. Einstein, played by the original *Man Who Knew Too Much*'s villain Peter Lorre, drunkenly modeled Jonathan's most recent face after a horror movie he had just seen. Lorre, who characteristically overplayed his roles, is told by the very Cary Grant-like Mortimer Brewster with third-person irony to "stop underplaying, I can't hear you."[28] (*"Stop underplaying," I tell the corpse. "I can't hear 'You!'" its silence returns.*)

I first saw *Arsenic and Old Lace* in a Soviet Palace of Culture in the 1970s. Rather than Russian actors dubbing the actors in the film, a single disembodied non-actress on a live microphone hidden somewhere in the theater overdubbed them all. Her monotonic, one-voice-fits-all Russian-language delivery blanketed the screen with what Blanchot calls the narrator's "disinterested interest" ("the rule of nonintervention"), the voice-over advertising a non-deferential relationship to the dead.[29] The eccentric character voices of Grant, Massey, and Lorre were turned down on the film's soundtrack so that the narrator's voice could tell us only what we needed to know and not what we needed to hear. In the 1953 comic noir *Beat the Devil*, director John Huston appears to absent time by *dubbing death*. Billy Dannreuther (Humphrey Bogart, looking as usual half-dead) is believed to have died in a car accident but has not, although on his return, he is mistaken for his own ghost. Peter Sellers added some uncredited vocal dubbing for the role of Billy after Bogart himself was involved in an actual car accident while on location, knocking out some of his teeth and impeding his speech. The syncope of halted speech brings forth vocal dubbing that previews disembodiment. (Bogart died four years later in his sleep.) "I suppose seeing you alive is different than thinking of you dead," Mrs. Gwendolen Chelm tells Billy. Gwendolen, who is enamored of the equally married Billy, sounds very much like Wilde's Gwendolen Fairfax, who marries her "Ernest," the former orphan John Worthing. Billy tells his Gwendolen that he was an orphan until the age of twenty. "In point of fact," as Mrs. Chelm is wont to say, her own husband is later also thought to have died but does not, with the result that he beats the crooks to the good fortune that was meant to be theirs. However, in that fortune's news is communicated via a telegram, how do we know that it wasn't sent by a ghost?

When *Arsenic*'s Jonathan tells Einstein, "This time I want the face of an absolute nonentity," we think maybe he means Humphrey Bogart rendered not as himself but as the facially unbandaged Vincent Parry in *Dark Passage* of whom we say, "That *looks like* Humphrey Bogart." Were these distinctive actors being misrepresented by some unsympathetic agency, or were they, as real fakes, like Perec's art forger Winckler, seeking only their own image, face, attitude, and above all, their "own ambiguity"?[30] Teddy's equally mad aunts are anxious about Jonathan's presence in their house not because he is a murderer, which because they cannot understand what murder is they cannot see, but because of what the neighbors might think of "people coming in here with one face and leaving with another." "Where'd you get that face?" Mortimer asks his initially unrecognizable brother Jonathan. "*Hollywood*?" (He actually got it from Broadway, where the real Boris Karloff—whose birth name was William Henry Pratt—originated the role of "Jonathan.")[31] In the movies, Nora Desmond told us, the stars whose names were associated with classic Hollywood had "faces." (Peter Conrad observes that "the cinema encouraged the separation of heads from bodies, or of faces from the minds behind them.")[32] The Lincoln-esque Massey died in movietown Los Angeles *of pneumonia*, perhaps from the cold he caught in the Brewster house from the Reverend, but being an actor known for impersonating a president, more likely from "Teddy." Or then again, it may have been more a result of having caught the "Lincoln" bug.

Einstein believes that "at least people in plays act like they've got sense," a statement which Mortimer undermines by enacting the self-imperiling stage directions to a play *Murder Will Out* that have him as the character being tied (by Jonathan and Einstein) to a chair with murderous intent while commenting, "This fellow doesn't even have the sense to be scared." This slyly acknowledges "Mortimer Brewster" as the character Cary Grant is playing while also playing "Cary Grant," the person who Archibald Leach became and the man who "Cary Grant" said publicly that even *he* wanted to be. No wonder Hitchcock dreamed of casting Grant as Hamlet and when asked his name, the tied-up actor says, "Usually I'm Mortimer Brewster, but I'm not quite myself today."[33]

Self-modeling and substitution are the noir disorder of the day. Teddy regards his toy-model ship "The Oregon" as being important, because "it goes to Australia," which was, of course, settled by criminals and so reinscribes the characters' production code (and Jonathan's specific "Melbourne torture method"). Later, in Billy Wilder's *Ace in the Hole* (1951), disgraced big-city newspaperman Chuck Tatum reacts to being stuck in "Land of Enchantment" New Mexico's "too much outside" by producing a miniature wooden ship inside a bottle. In *Arsenic*, "Panama" after the real Teddy Roosevelt's famous canal serves as a substitution code for the basement where "Teddy" digs his approximation in the form of graves where his aunts' victims are buried (the grave as the ultimate lock). These bodies in Teddy's delusional mind succumbed to yellow fever contracted in the real Panama, although the illness of illusion was "more likely" spread by a sneeze in Brooklyn that helps make the film's code intelligible. *Arsenic*'s object-action code is co-morbidly pathological, though not always psychotic. In Gogolian fashion, Mortimer absent-noirly dons a dead man's hat to leave the house on one occasion and earnestly tells the two men who plan to kill him: "When I get back, I expect you to be gone. Wait for me!"[34] On another occasion, Jonathan tells his aunts that another man's corpse will get along fine with Mortimer. "They're both dead." Turnabout is fair play in language as it is in representation. A harried Mortimer tells this same cabbie who has been waiting for him with the meter running for much of the film's running time to call him a cab. The comical double-take here is that the cabbie summons Mortimer *another* cab and does not, as he might, given the story structure's DNA, literally call Mortimer (himself) "a taxi."

Teddy cannot be admitted to the sanitarium because he signed the admission papers "Teddy Roosevelt." Mortimer convinces Teddy to sign with his real name by working out for him how "Roosevelt" is code for "Brewster":

> *Mortimer*: Don't you see. Take the name "Brewster." Take away the "B" and what have you got?
> *Teddy*: Rooster.
> *Mortimer*: Aha. And what does a rooster do?
> *Teddy*: Crows.
> *Mortimer*: It crows. And where do you hunt in Africa?
> *Teddy*: On the velt.
> *Mortimer*: There you are—Crow's Velt.
> *Teddy*: Ingenious. My compliments to the boys in the code department.

It turns out that sanitarium director Witherspoon is also a would-be playwright, although the play he tries to get Mortimer to read is not nearly as good as the one he may already be writing in his head from (t)his madhouse-perspective, *Arsenic and Old Lace*.[35] The play ends with Grant's Mortimer reenacting Hamlet's north-by-northwest madness so as to divert Detective Rooney's attention away from the thirteen corpses in the basement; the Brewster sisters voluntarily committing themselves to live alongside Teddy at Happydale so he will not be alone (consistent with ending men's loneliness as their rationale for murder); and Einstein faking his own "doctor's" signature on the admission papers to make them legitimate, even as a concurrent verbal report over the phone describes Jonathan's accomplice "down to a 'T.' " And even as Mortimer's own signature as "next of kin" is delegitimized by the aunt's telling him he is not a biological Brewster. Can we trust this to be true, or does the aunts' madness serve here as cover for the legitimate, new-life-giving wedding gift—freedom from the fear of hereditary insanity—they are bestowing upon Mortimer? Such is the unreality they inhabit, that the aunts might not know themselves. Mortimer tells the cabbie who calls him by what is no longer his real name, "I'm not a Brewster. I'm the son of a sea cook." To this the cabbie responds, "I'm not a cab driver, I'm a coffeepot." To illustrate this "fact," the cabbie puts "one hand" at the end of a crooked arm at his side and dangles "the other" in the air, as if to make light of the same grave corpus by turning himself into a model of something else.

The *rope* Jonathan uses to tie Mortimer to a chair in his unrealized murder scene formerly bound the curtains hanging behind the *chest-or-trunk* (object-torso)-like window-seat in *Arsenic* and arrives late on the scene in Hitchcock's *Rope* (1948) as the actual murder weapon. Brandon Shaw and Phillip Morgan, *Rope*'s thrill-seeking trunk murderers/stranglers are both bachelors, recalling the Brewster spinsters, their lonely, family-less victims, and their nephew Mortimer's previously well-publicized bachelorhood.[36] But isn't the corpse in the trunk (whose girlfriend comes looking for him) the ultimate bachelor? Brandon's sociopathy is ironically mirrored by Philip's current, guilt-induced "antisocial behavior," as Brandon calls it. But making death into an event and a physical centerpiece, complete with candelabra, is all Brandon's idea. The budding professional pianist Phillip is far more reticent, preferring to emulate the man in the first *Man Who Knew Too Much*, who removes his cherished decorative objects from atop the piano where they usually sit when trouble comes. "There's trouble coming soon," that film's protagonist speak-sings in mock hymnal fashion to his (sneezing) partner in the hope of preventing death from becoming an event, let alone a recital. The fragility of objects stands in for and conceals life's deeper fragility in the (literal) case of death. When Brandon refers to their murder victim David Kentley's penchant for whiskey as being "out of character," Phillip promptly responds, "Out of character for David to be murdered too." And out of character for Phillip to admit to being a murderer. He is, after all, as Brandon asserts in a farm story he tells and that Phillip claims is untrue, a "chicken strangler," which temperamentally he is.

Is this where I confess to being haunted in my sleep by a murder I committed in my own reckless youth? I cannot remember who I killed or why. I think that I did not do this horrible thing alone, but I cannot recall anything other than "the fact" that I did it. This is an obsessive-compulsive behavior, I know, but that does not make me any less a chicken strangler denying sociopathic thoughts, nor does my failed memory disprove the veracity of these thoughts on some level of unreality that is nevertheless real to me. Parfit (sort of) for the defense (of my apparent but fictional criminality):

> Locke's claim [that someone cannot have committed some crime unless he now remembers doing so] is clearly false. If it was true, it would not be possible for someone to forget any of the things he once did, or any of the experiences that he once had. But this *is* possible. I cannot now remember putting on my shirt this morning.[37]

At least one sociopath agrees: "You know the most interesting thing about doing something terrible? Often after a few days, you can't even remember it," says Tom Ripley.[38] I dreamed last night that I was in possession of two sets of skeletal remains, one belonging to a celebrity, the other to "a nobody." This only apparitional murder is, no doubt, an effort to displace my own death scene, which is now more rapidly approaching, but also to account for the small but enduring life-traumas I have suffered that require some condensed, fictional-physical form (or *idea of* a physical form) to lend ballast to my sinking feelings. These feelings cannot be laid upon someone else, so I have reenvisioned myself as having *been* someone else (a murderer) and *another* someone else (the murderer's victim). It is, in effect, my attempt to plan and execute the perfect crime, to justify my guilt while code-covering its sources with an inexplicable, heinous act for which I *should* feel guilty. My congratulations to the boys in the code department for figuring this out.

"*Death is the beginning of the life of the mind*," Perec wrote of his murderous art forger Gaspard Winckler. The mind's refusal to accept the logic and clarity of the murderous act is reflected in its composition of Winckler's tortured quasi-syllogistic defense by reason of inevitability: "I killed Madera. I killed Anatole. I killed Anatole Madera. The killer of Anatole Madera was me. I did murder. Murdered Anatole Madera. Everyone murdered Madera. Madera is a man. Man is mortal. Madera is mortal. Madera is dead. Madera had to die. Madera was going to die. All I did was speed things up. He was under sentence." This is in effect another unsuccessful obsessive-compulsive rope-trick that hangs its designer with his own words. The boys' (including the late David's) former teacher Rupert Cadell (who at one point mistakes a dead man's hat for his own) recalls how the figure of a chest (in turn, a figure of death, which is itself a figure) obsessively recurred in boyhood bedtime stories Brandon told others.[39] In one of these stories a spring-locked number traps a young maiden inside. It would take an actual murder, though, for Brandon to get his motiveless obsessing over an object and his mentor's chicken strangling academic Übermensch-ing (superior beings have the right to kill inferior beings) off his mind and his chest. Brandon tells Rupert, "You often pick words for sound rather than meaning," something that Brandon has secretly proved to himself that he does *not* do. "*Habeas Corpus!*" Brandon's murder says to his old teacher. "*I've done my bit, now you do yours. Show us who you killed. Produce your work!*" For murderer-as-artist Brandon, though, it is not just committing a murder that indicates your superiority, but the superiority of the particular murder itself. He gets this from De Quincey, who wrote: "One murder is compared with another; and the circumstances of superiority, as, for example, in the incidences and effects of surprise, of mystery . . . are collated and appraised."

Rupert will have his revenge upon Brandon (and upon any perverse embarrassment he feels about having been so academic in his surrogate desiring) not by committing a murder, but by solving one. In this play's third act (like *Arsenic*, *Rope* was originally a stage play), Rupert, who suspects that a murder has occurred, returns to the apartment on the pretext that he has left his cigarette case behind (the same genus as Walter Neff's imaginary cigars).[40] Rupert proceeds to read the room for clues like the (murder) scene it is (while prompting the boys with re/acting cues) and performs the prestige part of their magic act by making the object (the corpse) they made disappear, reappear. Once props that are inherently fakes (corpses, trunks, ropes, books—models) begin to speak, they become the devices of their would-be manipulator's undoing. De Quincey remarked that had Descartes actually been murdered and not "all *but* murdered—murdered within an inch," "we should have no Cartesian philosophy. And how we could have done without *that*, considering the worlds of books it has produced, I leave it to any respectable trunk-maker to declare."[41] The object can do without the Cartesian cogito. The rope, which Brandon co-opts to be the measure and meaning of his philosophical corpus, enacts its revenge, returning to cinch the case against him (and the ancillary Phillip) and the bookishness of his murderous design (in the shape of a trunk). Rupert effectively turns Brandon and Philip into *The Lady Vanishes*' two very English fools Caldicott and Charters, who nattered on about "something emerging very clearly" and about the Indian rope trick that "never comes out in photographs." Clarity is for the murderer-as-artist Brandon what Perec's artist-as-murderer Winckler ("I killed Madera . . . just to see what would happen") called "certainty without mediation."[42] The thing that has emerged very clearly in relation to Brandon, the only real certainty, is the rope, the story's central device that now hangs around his and Phillip's necks like the twin nooses of infinity, which cannot be seen, captured, or controlled. "A fine caricature of fate," as Winckler would call it.[43] The rope had left the room wound around a stack of books that Brandon gave to the already late David's father at the party to cap the secret celebration of the fatal act that Brandon vainly imagines can establish murder as a modality that is superior to death. It is what Quine would call "a doomed attempt to capture the *doing* of the action in a new kind of causation" that extricates agency from the life-death continuum of event-to-event. In this, Brandon is "tripped up by his own rope-trick," which brings him no relief from the events that are generated not really by him but by the revenge of the book that has him as its subject.[44] We know who owned the books that Brandon gives to Mr. Kentley, but not who wrote them. And here my criminal mind says, "*I wrote them. I confess. You are reading one of them now.*"

I Confess

Guilt is the homunculus that sits inside us, "the wrong man" who is too often mistaken for us as a life-size double but is proportionally more like the silent tongue inside a bell. In Hitchcock's *I Confess* (1953), the homunculus is Father Michael Logan's internalized guilt about having to keep secret murderer Otto Keller's confession to himself. "The wrong man" scenario's mistaken identity precipitated by the serendipity of appearance theme (Keller committed his murder dressed in a priest's cassock) covers up the complicity of rule-based behaviors of the real murderer (who continues to tend the dead man's garden) and the accused, along with that of the detective investigating the case, who cannot tell one "priest" from another. Murdering someone in a cassock is here akin to Groucho Marx's saying he shot an elephant in his pajamas, then, "What he was doing in my pajamas, I'll never know." The wrongness of this statement (and of a priest, in this case, the falsely accused Logan, committing murder while wearing what for him would be a priestly *non*-disguise) is what makes it so ludicrous and yet so self-satisfyingly arrogant in what the sentence intends and achieves. Groucho's joke, characteristic of structural language-based comedy in general, represents the triumph of the inessential over the essential, rendering the logic of the sentence suspicious by varying the thought it articulates. Since it is essential to Logan to preserve the bond of trust signified by confession and the confessional, he cannot be other than who this trust says he is. He cannot be "the wrong man," even though his freedom and possibly his life depend upon him *being* "the wrong man." The paradox this presents leaves the man of faith speechless and philosophically dumbfounded. How can I be the person I am not, and continue to be the person who I am?

A stage (site of "I am/not" performance) spells "curtains" for the cornered-into-confessing murderer Keller, who thought he could expand the sanctity of the curtained confessional to keep his secret hidden. Keller, who concealed his murder in the folds of a priest's cassock, is oddly unable to part the folds of the stage curtains that have been figuratively sewn together by needlewoman-spy Froy, who locates him in the field of *clandestination*. As Parfit suggests in relation to a science fiction scenario: "There are two kinds of sameness, or identity. I and my Replica are *qualitatively identical*, or exactly alike. But we may not be *numerically identical*, or one and the same person."[45] A cassock clothes a single priest but is also the clothing of any number of priests. At the same time, "the Cassock" could name a particular priest infused with universal meanings or implications in a film or play. But this number does not coincide with the numerically identical that suggests singularity, the very thing that the aforementioned universality in its symbolic value makes impossible. You cannot actually *be* the thing that you stand for, if the thing that you stand for is another (mode of) being. Similarly, Logan tells a detective he "can't say" to the question "Do you know?" "I'll never know," Groucho says, because the evidence (the elephant in my pajamas, the priest in my cassock) is unintelligible in that it does not follow rules. Evidence, Husserl argued, is not self-evident but rather "derivative," "mediated," and "synthetic." It must be constructed as a certain logic mediated by the imagination that makes intuitive connections that may be called either reason or faith.[46] Husserl opposed the French philosopher Octave Hamelin's belief that "the essential function of reason is the construction of reality according to rules," which reduces scientific logic to the arithmetical, and specifically the geometric, which was not incidentally thought by some to be God's baroque plan.[47] There is to this day an O. Hamelin listed in the directory of Quebec City, Quebec, where *I Confess* is set. Any attempt to suggest that this is evidence of some kind of support of my Husserlian intervention would of course be illogical in any rule-based way save my own.

Hitchcock's *Suspicion* (1941), which brooks no real confession, begins with the dark, disembodied voice of Johnnie (Cary Grant) apologizing to his future wife Lina, who are for now two strangers on a train: "Oh, I beg your pardon. Is that your leg? I had no idea we were going into a dark tunnel. I thought the compartment was empty. Oh, so sorry. I hope I didn't hurt you." Johnnie's before-the-fact apology covers all the times he *will* pull Lina's aforementioned limb, figuratively speaking, and also hurt her. From the start, sexually repressed and preternaturally suspicious Lina (initially viewing Johnnie *through her reading glasses*) recoils from Johnnie's touch as if it alone could kill her. The plot turns on whether or not it actually will. It is not so much Johnnie's irresponsibility (his constant borrowing money, gambling) that is childlike in Lina's already made-up mind (Francis Iles's 1932 novel *Before the Fact*, being the film's source), but Johnnie's darkly playful withholding of his intentions to make things "right" until after he makes or appears to have made them wrong. He demonstrates a perhaps self-destructive willingness to let appearances (of his wrongdoing) stand, as if they were speaking for themselves. Anything else would make him look "bad," in a psychological rather than a legal or moral sense. Whether or not he is capable of murder is only the ostensive question. The more important question that only Johnnie can pose to himself from inside his pose is: "*Who would I be if I were <u>not</u> guilty, if I did not feel this guilt? What might that make me do to justify it?*"

Psychology sees circumstantiality as an obsessive attention to minor details so as to talk around the point of a conversation's central theme.[48] Circumstantiality is flawed not just from an evidentiary perspective but from a logical perspective as well. And the relationship between evidence and logic is, as so many "wrong man" cases have demonstrated, highly suspect, an a posteriori deduction drawn from "given circumstances" passing as a priori knowledge. Froy, a.k.a. the actress Dame May Whitty, here playing Lina's mother, may know more about this than she can say and still remain in character. She now appears to be content playing a homebody doing her needlepoint. I am suspicious as to why she is there in the *second* place. Certainly, guilt and suspicion are both part of some larger design. Johnnie's guilt and Lina's suspicion complicitly sabotage themselves and one another, like alibis that coincide *and* contradict. "Johnnie, if I had only known," Lina tells him on realizing that he meant to kill himself, not her. "This is as much my fault as it is yours."

As is by now well known, the film originally ended with Johnnie killing Lina and his subsequent posting of a letter Lina wrote in which she named him as her murderer (replayed unironically in *Cause for Alarm!*). That ending fulfilled the demands of Johnnie's actual guilt and Lina's suspicion, as well as of his prior guilt-driven behaviors and her a priori suspicion. The suspicion that nearly sabotages their relationship recalls Badiou's pronouncement after Hegel that "the passion for the real is also, of necessity, suspicion. Nothing can attest that the real is the real, nothing but the system of fictions wherein it plays the role of the real." Lina finds her ideal mate in Johnnie, whose suspect behavior rewards her negative assessment of her guilty desire for him. "Dying well," says Badiou, "is the only thing that escapes suspicion."[49] Lina's self-sacrifice is not offered in order to discover truth so much as to serve "the necessity of semblance, which, has perhaps always constituted its own real."[50] Hitchcock's famous internally bulb-lit milk glass (with which Johnnie allegedly plans to poison Lina) is this "necessity's" delivery system, which recirculates the many instances of Johnnie's refusal to face reality, and Lina's misappropriation of "the real" as "true," faithful to a particular standard of what reality looks like, as in resembles, and how its agents should *act*.

In the film's original trailer, Lina directly addresses the audience as if we were real: "There was something strange about Johnnie Aysgarth. I knew it long before I married him. These are facts, the evidence before the crime. I wanted you to know in case I met a violent end." Lina is not so much prophetic as she is authorial in voicing her concerns (she is in fact quoting herself from her unsent letter), as if she had written the book on M-U-R-D-E-R, spelled out "like letters she sent to herself."[51] This is what guilt is, in so many of the pieces that constitute the puzzles that the apparitional F-R-O-Y stands in to solve on our behalf.

Himself

> It's a bright, guilty world.
>
> —Michael O'Hara

Nagel suggests that "the objective self functions independently enough to have a life of its own. It engages in various forms of detachment from and in opposition to the rest of us, and is capable of autonomous development." This, says Nagel, "places us both inside and outside the world and offers us possibilities of transcendence which in turn create problems of reintegration."[52] If we lived our lives attending to the sound advice of our own voice-overs, we might know more sooner, although the voice-over would argue for later. Michael O'Hara's (Orson Welles's) voice sounds displaced, external to himself (expressing the objective self), as if parodying the voice-over that starts his *The Lady from Shanghai* (1947) on its circuitous course.

(The voices in virtually all Orson Welles-directed films sound like this, perhaps given his start in theater and especially radio.) The voice sounds as if it were speaking not of (any) him but as "himself," as the stage Irishman says when speaking in the third person. Welles acted onstage in Ireland as a young man and perhaps intended this role as a sort of virtual return to "himself." O'Hara is a seafaring man, who will soon take the plunge and find himself in deep water. He can only hope not to become a corpse bobbing on the water's surface, like Gillis would in *Sunset Boulevard* three years later. But then, O'Hara's voice already advertises a self-acknowledged unconsciousness it no longer possesses, making it untimely before the fact of speech, unreal in relation to the narrative it is relating to and to which the flashback images will "now" (as in "then") relate. Pursuing the pursuer, the eponymous key-lit-eyed femme fatale "Rosalie," as he calls her after a romantic fashion ("Elsa" is what she calls herself, "Mrs. Bannister" what others call her, Rita Hayworth as the actress was called by her ex-husband Orson Welles), is like trying to catch but not be caught by your own reflection, when your eyes have migrated to the sides of your head to avoid seeing all there is to be seen, like the fish out of water O'Hara already has been and will be again when the film begins and ends.

In another variant of third-personhood, Elsa's wealthy lawyer-husband Arthur Bannister's law partner George Grisby hires Michael to kill him: "Mr. Grisby wants me to kill Mr. Grisby," as Michael himself tells it, in what sounds like but is not a rhetorical statement. The "victim," Grisby explains, will pay his murderer Michael from the large insurance settlement the *surviving* law partner can claim. "According to the law," says Grisby, "I'm dead if you say you murdered me, but you're not a murderer unless I'm dead," that is, unless a corpse is produced. So says "himself," the third-person voice of O'Hara's own logic-overriding desire for Bannister's wife as a death benefit.

"I've never seen an aquarium," Michael tells Elsa, now sounding like the fish out of water he is. The two lovers kiss in profile, like two wall-eyed fish, like two one-eyed Jacks whose being seen nevertheless conceals something. That the camera shoots stars in profile to capture their "good side" is doubly ironic, since it also puts us unconsciously in mind of the frame. Grisby is in fact planning to frame O'Hara by killing Bannister himself and pinning it on the Irishman by planting the latter's yachting cap at the scene of the crime. (But why *wouldn't* O'Hara's hat be there? Bannister employs him to sail his yacht. An object left at a crime scene is only incriminating insofar as it is *un*familiar, does *not* belong where it is found, like a fish out of water or a noir *without* a hat.) When Broome, the detective whom Bannister hired to keep an eye on his wife, confronts Grisby with his knowledge of this plan, Grisby shoots *him*, and off-camera Elsa shoots Grisby for killing Broome instead of her husband as *she* planned. "I'm dead already," Broome tells Elsa, who offers to call a doctor for him, the corpse-in-waiting being unable to know a murderer when he sees one, because it is not *his* murderer, not *his* bullet. "The wrong man was arrested," Michael says of himself in voice-over, "the wrong man was shot." Self-reflection shows itself here in its fracturing, like the funhouse mirrors that are waiting to be famously shattered at the film's end.

Outside the courtroom where Welles's Michael is being tried for Broome's *and* Grisby's murders, Mr. and Mrs. Bannister smoke in the shadow of a NO SMOKING sign. (There are no NO SHADOWS signs in conventional film noir.) The narrative began with Michael offering Elsa his last cigarette, which she took and carefully wrapped up in a handkerchief, because, she said, she did not smoke. (Perhaps she was saving it for her inevitable execution, wrapping it up as she did inside what could serve as a makeshift blindfold.) She later asks *him* for a cigarette, because she's "learning to smoke now." This "now" you see me, "now" you don't (see me smoking gambit) conceals the real Elsa while exposing just enough of *her* "edge" to garner interest minus suspicion. A cancerous-looking Elsa's facial skeleton that does not appear in the film's final cut features a cigarette still clenched between the death's head's teeth.[53] The skeleton, as always, makes death seem rhetorical, and the cigarette a rhetorical flourish more than a signature cause. It is of a piece with the fracturing of meaning by syntax. Grisby told Michael that he wanted to disappear because he is unhappily married, but Michael learns from Elsa (herself a duplicitous source) that Grisby has no wife. At Michael's trial, the defense attorney Bannister undercuts D.A. Galloway's rhetorically solicitous desire to cut a policeman's testimony short so that he can get home to his wife and children by getting the policeman to admit that he has none, a variation on Pirandello's dramatic cases of un/real conjoining in un-(w)ho(l)ly matrimony. The plot is now down two imaginary wives, which, of course, makes for two imaginary husbands as well. Elsa tells Michael that she learned about love from the Chinese, as if this meant something *because it sounds like it should.* And Bannister invokes his right as a defense attorney to cross-examine *himself*. This is in all senses a *show trial.*

"The way I understand it, he'll be alright if we keep him moving," a court officer says of Michael, who ingested some but strategically not all of Bannister's pain pills just before the verdict was read in court in order to forestall anybody hearing it. "If he goes to sleep, he's done for," a second officer says, invoking the story's original title, *If I Die Before I Wake*. The anxiety surrounding sleeping and (not) waking finds each man speaking for himself as another, as the victim of a murder without a body, a murder inside the head "himself." "Don't move," Elsa tells Michael upon awakening. "Don't *you* move," Michael says in return, as if whispering to a corpse. "I must be dreaming," *I, myself* say inside my head. Will this dream forestall some unnamed punishment's certain arrival with death being the final sentence? What am I accused of having done? Did I take another man's life? His wife? Should this other man have been born in my place? Should I take, have taken a bullet for him? What if I take some pills before the verdict is read in open court and don't wake up? When Michael awakens, he finds himself (in the concrete realization of Marlowe's narcotized suspended state of distended and replicated forms in *Murder, My Sweet*) inside the MAGIC MIRROR MAZE. There Elsa's and Bannister's narrative dissembling is decomposed through the simulation of distorting mirrors that conceal him and her from himself and herself. "Killing you is killing myself. It's the same thing," Bannister tells his corrupt eidolon, the clay-footed Elsa, at which point each of them fires at the other's fractured image as if at once and for once they were one, the two-in-one capacity of "myself" as another.

Herself

"*We might be right back where we started,*" Rita Hayworth said to Glenn Ford, who was the man in the picture. She could not remember *Gilda* (dir. Charles Vidor, 1946), but she does recall being slapped. Actually, she recalls someone showing her a picture of herself being slapped by Glenn Ford, which may well be what she remembers, but maybe the picture was from the *Gilda* retread *Affair in Trinidad* (dir. Richard Sherman, 1952), in which her costar was again Glenn Ford. There were some tessellating picture frames that captured the vibration of the single slap, perhaps because she had connected the two films with their two separate slaps to make a mental sequence. She doesn't know whether that was when her condition worsened, not from the actual slap but from the multiple replaying of those pictures inside her mind, like so many bullet-shattered mirrors.[54] Apparently she dropped a single glove and some odd duck picked it up and regarded it as a *unicum*, a one-of-a-kind figure of uncommon loneliness, although he allowed that "any object whatsoever can always be identified uniquely."[55] Her image, as former husband Orson Welles had shown, even when tessellated, still testified to the uniqueness of its mirrored subject, the desire for which (as for whom) was not abated by the image's multiplicity and or the doubtfulness of its veracity. As her mental faculties reduced and scattered to the far corners of her mind never to return, she rapidly shifted gears moving through interspace, from amnesia en route to Alzheimer's and oblivion. She is soothed by the comforting voice(over) of her former husband, Orson Welles, whom she betrayed with her failing memory.[56] "The only way to stay out of trouble," he said, "is to grow old, so I guess I'll concentrate on that. Maybe I'll live so long, I'll forget her. Maybe I'll die trying."[57] Funny that it was he who spoke of forgetting. Of course, it was not him but himself, Michael O'Hara, who said this in the voice-over that followed her "death," the voice-over signifying that he had not yet merged his subjective and objective selves. Some part of what remains of herself thinks about what remains of himself as voice-over, which will no more outlive him than the objective self it affects as a form of personal expression.[58]

Myself

"*You!*" I said as the corpse-whisperer, my access to her earned as one of the sleepless, as the ghost of who I am. How long had she been displayed in the *ekkyklema* of the open coffin, as the payoff of death's puzzling, citational non/appearance, this guilty spectacle that I had been called to witness in the dead philosopher Cioran's house in Romania? Cioran, a long-dead Transylvanian and noted insomniac, hailed me through this dead woman: "Yourself a specter, how would you see others as alive?"[59] There was in all of this a certain non-deference to death that would appear on the face of it to be non-normative. Normativity, though, depends here on whether the corpse can be said to represent my neighbor in the wider and deeper sense that Levinas suggested, the ethical, pre-ontological sense despite the physical evidence of my never having known her. Was the non-knowledge of my own death that my presence asserts overcome in my whispered moment by what Levinas called "an eventuality transferable onto oneself"? This transference, he wrote, "is not mechanical [*une mécanique*] but rather belongs to the intrigue or the intrication of My-self [*Moi-même*]." Was my non-deference not to death but to "the nonsense of death," in my inability to know, localize, or objectify it to my own satisfaction as if it were only self-citational, death-dealing like a noirly advertised psychosis? [60] In noir places, a mobster can say about a corpse signed and surnamed "Marlowe," "Give him some air, give him plenty of air" (*Slightly Scarlet*, dir. Allan Dwan, 1956). The corpse leaves no forwarding address and cannot be so addressed, but the belief that death can be reduced to a joke, says he can. "The end," as Levnias tells us, "is but a *moment* only of death, a moment whose other side would be not consciousness or comprehension but the *question*, and a question distinct from all those that are presented as problems." Theater is poised between the intentionality of its problem-solving reductionism and the question that may break through at any moment, as a moment that is not death's capture but its performed transcendence.

If my visit to Cioran's house had been a dream, I would have staged it as I found it, with life going on in the next room, most inappropriately, it would seem, with people feeding and watering themselves as if no proximate corpse existed. But then, "each death," Levinas reminds us, "is a scandal," so why wouldn't the corpse expose itself or be exposed to me?[61] Exposure is what makes a scandal what it is—public and un/ashamed. The question, "Whose body is it?" speaks not just to identity but to ownership and broaches issues that may be either metaphoric or rhetorical. Who *holds* the body, under what circumstances and by what right? The writ of habeas corpus urges these questions toward a speedy and decisive ruling at a court trial. It is aimed at those who would conspire to not let the body appear. But what if the body's appearance is an a priori fact and the body cannot be made *to disappear*? What if the body has a hold on those who would conspire against the continuity of its appearance, which under normal circumstances would define its personal identity? What if the body is *dead*, and what if, as Strawson argues, the dead body can be thought of as a disembodied person, "retaining the logical benefit of individuality from having been a person"?[62] What is this person owed, and how does even an unconscious awareness of this owing inculcate feelings of guilt and fear in the living?

Racine's baroque *Phaedra* (1677) is set inside and outside "a palace," through which a bed-*ekkyklema* moves ghostlike the queen's tortured body twisted in her sheets. "The bed [Perec wrote] is almost a sign of catastrophe." The wall is what Deleuze calls in reference to Leibniz "the viniculum . . . a membrane that works as a sort of grid filtering the monads that it receives as terms." The viniculum "determines an individual unity of the body that belongs to it; this body that I have is not only the body of a man, a horse, or of a dog; it is my own body."[63] Phaedra is subjected to her body. Hippolytus disregards the body as one would a subjectless object, a mythical abstraction. Together they make a corpse of the cursed thing. He prefers to remain an Amazonian affiliated monad, "convey[ing] the entire world independently of others and without influx," withholding his body even from himself as if it were not his, as if it were *not*. "The world," Deleuze writes after Leibniz, "is actualized in souls and is realized in bodies." But there is in this a split between the body's realization of what the soul perceives and "the realization of phenomena in the body" as being the body's (own) reality.[64] "The bed-monad," as Perec calls it, further elides subject-object so that "almost a sign" can be rewritten as "a sign," with the accompanying awareness that "almost a sign" does not consciously achieve reduction ("a palace" for "a place").[65]

What kind of stage object can *almost* escape its signage? What kind of tragic dramatic character can *almost* escape her fate? Phaedra's bed is forever in the breach, it *is* the breach that death is, the corpse displayed on the *ekkyklema* inside Cioran's house, as breach of façade, my own appearance constituting in some sense a breach of etiquette, in non-deference to death. "*Three walls I have memorized. / Fourth—I cannot give a guarantee*," wrote the tragic, suicided poet Marina Tsvetaeva, thinking of her life as Phaedra, nearly stripped of her belief in the stage imaginary.[66] In this suspension of *belief*, the indexicality of performance recedes back into unconsciousness where our guilt, the original breach, sharpens and deepens what we cannot say but already know. "Two kinds of mind: daylight and nocturnal," Cioran observed. "They have neither the same method nor the same morality. In broad daylight, you watch yourself; in the dark, you speak out."[67] Phaedra's nocturnal mind is housed inside a non-nycthemeral play, whose reality is not (neoclassical claims notwithstanding) sequential, "the night of the following day" here signaling not sequence but eclipse. She is Blanchot's "*insomniaque du jour*," who as Simon Critchley says, never sleeps, her "stupefied" eyes blinking back the light that offers neither respite nor revelation from the endless night from which the mind never escapes. This sounds a lot like *You,* like *Me*.[68] Her full-time wakefulness is a life lived in reverse, a death that cannot be sequentially arrived at and not overcome. The corpse's silence before my interpellation constitutes a "pure question mark, the opening onto that which provides no possibility of a response." My hailing returns to me as *You*, as an affirmation of the who that I am.[69]

Forward and backward sequencing are part of the same logical timeline, which the catastrophe of Phaedra's bed elides into a vertically indexical space of physical simultaneity, palace/a place. She figuratively shares her bed with Artemis and Aphrodite, the frame figures from Euripides's earlier version of the story, as well as with her own sister Ariadne, who, by freeing Theseus from the Minotaur's labyrinth with a skein of thread, tied Theseus to Phaedra in a drama that culminates its own monstrosity. Breaches of vows and of allegiances to deities and to bloodlines ("Every no rises out of the blood") produce an obsessive circularity of thought and feeling that, like the uroboros, consumes its own tail/tale.[70] "I cannot meet you in your future," Hippolytus as Cioran tells Phaedra, his insomniac reflection, "because the whole of the future is already here."[71] His speech redraws the labyrinth, which is Phaedra's family business, linking her and her sister Ariadne to Hippolytus's father Theseus, who indirectly killed them both.

Phaedra fears the "abhorred and tainted blood" (2.5.48) that her family legacy brings to life, but still reluctant to vacate the stage in my staging, she stabs herself with a retractable prop gravity knife in an only apparent bloodletting. "What's this, my Queen? [her nurse Oenone cries] / Someone is coming. You must not be seen" (2.5.48). But Phaedra *wants* to be seen, unembarrassed as she is for herself, unable to part with this "pain [a.k.a. performance] behavior" that ever is a retractable blade. "Everything turns on pain," Cioran wrote, "the rest is accessory, even nonexistent, for we remember only what hurts. Painful sensations being the only real ones, it is virtually useless to experience others."[72] A contemporary, self-confessed agoraphobe, a house-and-bed-monad, draws the skein of thread closer to his own (family) home: "The family was like a ball of yarn in the center of which all its secrets were tightly bound. It felt as if even the slightest tug on the outer strand could unravel the whole thing."[73] Ariadne might have said as much of her own family's yarn, its labyrinthine threading of self-sacrifice as recoverable loss, a theme of psychoanalysis that Barthes describes as "an approach ready to acknowledge the fear of the world."[74] Phaedra, who fears the world, is a proper psychoanalytic subject, as is Hippolytus, who fears the other, and yet they are not on the same page.[75] Each says s/he fears transparency, but each more accurately fears that ambivalence is not as true a thing as the thing it secretly desires. Seneca's Phaedra says it best: "*this thing I want—I do not want.*" But is Phaedra speaking as herself or as a corpse, which can want for itself without being able to do for itself? Must someone else speak for the corpse, express its desires? "To me," the corpse says. "To me: some bread . . . some quiet . . . And perhaps. . . ."[76] The corpse speaks in the dative case, of reception, of something being given and in keeping with this indirectness and in the dilation of an elision, of that something *being* a given.

"*This thing I want—I do not want*" expresses not just behavioral ambivalence but what Levinas sees as being the turn from comedy to tragedy: "When the awkwardness of the act turns against the goal pursued, we are at the height of tragedy." In arguing that we are "responsible beyond our intentions," Levinas makes the more profound point that "our consciousness [and therefore our mastery] of reality does not coincide with our habitation in the world." Are Phaedra's anymore than my own feelings reducible to comprehension, which is to say, can words make sense of reason, or are they (meant to be) beyond sense, beyond reason, beyond metaphor, the staff of life upon which the mind actually leans for its sense and reason?[77] Asleep on my feet, I recite or imagine myself reciting lines. Discovering that I will truly have to invent my lines instead of acting as if I were reciting them, I come up with a compromise. I continue to speak, but only in order *to speak about* speaking my lines. "I go through the motions of taking off my glasses (even though my eyes had no need of them at that period.) This gesture of removing something I am wearing in front of my eyes constitutes the moment of awakening, as if it corresponded to the real action I perform when opening my lids."[78] This is the dream speaking, but it is the dream of waking life too.

I dream, says Phaedra, that King Theseus is Schrödinger's cat, for a time indeterminately n/either living n/or dead. In the meantime of experimental personhood, I act ecstatically outside the constraint of my own death, and by so doing mentally disallow Theseus's return. I hallucinate Hippolytus as being both a Theseus surrogate and an anti-Theseus, a nonhistorical figure, a way out of my life by imagining it having been otherwise. Even so, "I do not forgive myself for being born. It is as if, creeping into this world, I had profaned a mystery, betrayed some momentous pledge, committed a fault of nameless gravity."[79] "*This thing I want—I do not want*" is a pretty good expression of self-arousal as self-denial, don't you think? It is, I think, also symptomatic of my actor's condition, but if I admit to the saying I must also admit to the doing of the thing. Even dropping out the Artemis-Aphrodite frame (as Racine did), "the jealousy of the gods survives their disappearance" inside my own frame fatale.[80]

Possibility and Necessity are the gods' new (as in modern) names only sometimes rising above language to make us aware of what we inherently know—Ricoeur's "manner of being that is one's own . . . constraint."[81] By the time Phaedra comes to speak Racine's language, "*This thing I want—I do not want*" speaks to the constraint upon freedom of thought, not of belief, which is why he writes a play and not a homily. Phaedra's corpse is also a corpus—not just the body but the work, not just the outcome-image but the function, not just the scene but the mise-en-scène, its own incompossibility, cold to the touch. Trapped in the body, it is nevertheless "impossible to say how long this finitude might extend." This is the interspace above whose entrance is printed in blood: "*I sought in doubt a remedy for anxiety. The remedy ended by making common cause with the disease.*"—Cioran (my italics).[82] Having reached the stage, Phaedra has achieved her fate, a predetermination to confess, to not be *un*confessed. She fits inside the frame of what Cioran calls French history's "bespokenness," in which "everything . . . is perfect from the theatrical point of view. It is a performance, a series of gestures and events which are watched rather than suffered, a spectacle that takes ten centuries to put on."[83]

In the end, Phaedra pursues not death, only stage-death, "a time where time does not exist." "The more injured you are by time," Cioran writes, "the more you seek to escape it," with which I self-identify as being a trauma scenario.[84] A stage-death is only rhetorical, a death citation, a death notice. Poisoning herself (with the potion Medea brought to Greece no less) to satisfy neoclassical tragedy's moral imperative, Phaedra slumps in her bed, only to arise from the *ekkyklema* in my staging and breach death itself. She now draws down upon a rhetorically contrite Theseus, who is mouthing the platitudinous promises of reconciliation with the living and the dead by, of all things, the prompter's box (the very sign of a secreted rhetoricity). Picking up the prop knife that has been stored inside the prompter's box with which she made a show of stabbing herself earlier, she kills Theseus with a single thrust, the blade not now retracting akin to the non-lighting cigarette lighter that suddenly lights.

Nietzsche characterized the modern artist of his day as possessing the physiology of and talent for dissimulation of a hysteric and a morbid vanity that was "like a continual fever that requires narcotics and does not shrink from any self-deception, any farce, that promises momentary relief" from his "continual need for revenge for a deeply ingrained self-contempt." The particular artist Nietzsche has in mind here is the actor, "the absurd irritability of [whose] system, which turns all experiences into crises and introduces the 'dramatic' into the smallest accidents of life," he says, "robs him of all calculability: he is no longer a person, at most a rendezvous of persons." In discussing the background of his *Birth of Tragedy*, Nietzsche states: "The antithesis of a real and an apparent world is lacking here: there is only *one* world, and this is false, cruel, contradictory, seductive, without meaning—A world thus constituted is the real world. *We have need of lies* in order to conquer this reality, this 'truth,' that is, in order to *live*—That lies are necessary in order to live is itself part of the terrifying and questionable character of existence."[85] Phaedra cannot tear herself from her stage-world without (dramatically) tearing herself apart. But to do so is simply to realize the metaphoric value of tragic *sparagmos* as a means of manifesting performance's recurrence as a behavioral tic. Phaedra's is a noir baroqueness, believing that "pleasure . . . is always suspect, both in itself and in its manifestations."[86] She craves not the sword's engagement, but the aporia, the impasse, the retractable blade of pain's performance.[87] She is horrified that others continually mistake this for some superficial love-sickness, something purely decorative like a sword (k)not. She is even more horrified that she does too. That's the problem with beds taken for signs and not for monads.

"If we could see ourselves as others see us," Cioran writes, "we would vanish on the spot." And yet, we should not dwell in self-remorse, which Cioran states, "is for those who do nothing, who cannot act. It replaces action for them, consoles them for their ineffectuality." Phaedra hands off Oenone to death because her nurse has become a figure of remorse, reason's weak handmaiden, her face a mask not of tragedy but of bathos. Despite her emotional affect, Oenone stands as an indictment of the *raisonneur* who allows the reasoning process to overwhelm itself with ineffectuality, thus rendering it servile. Kierkegaard's discussion of "the completely inclosed person," who only a confidant saves from suicide, may offer another explanation that is actually more in line with the tyranny of the protagonist's self-contradiction ("*this thing I want—I do not want*"): "It would be a task for a poet to depict [the] solution to a demoniac's tormenting self-contradiction: not to be able to do without a confidant and not to be able to have a confidant," Kierkegaard wrote, describing a condition of abstract "corpsing" (forgetting and denial) of (the) living in the first person.[88] I recall Borges describing a mountebank who is hired to impersonate the mourner in the ritual for an effigy standing in for the real (dead) thing. Does this doubleness allow for the possibility of the mourner lying in for the corpse? I imagine writing in the visitor's log, "Never have I seen a woman so uncomfortable in her own coffin."[89] I, who have my eyes closed, pretending to sleep, offer no sign that I have heard the person who whispers in my ear, *You!*

Barthes calls *Phaedra* "the panic drama of defenestration, of opening," which "employs an abundant thematics of concealment."[90] To a certain extent, we defenestrate thought with our writing, our voices. What I have been doing here (what *I am* doing here, in the sense of my mise-en-scène, my emplacement) is creating a syllogistic aura from the evidence I have made available to myself from the few citations with which I began. I have drawn a circle that draws me in, that is, nominally includes or absorbs me, but in unreality creates me at the outset. I am not a metonym of the circle, nor is the circle a synecdoche in relation to something else. I am the circle, or more properly the ellipse with its two mutually regarding center points. I am the strange loop of which Douglas Hofstadter speaks. I have drawn the voice up from the page to the surface that is unreal, given its lack of logical thought prerequisites. The thought is a shadow that is commensurate with myself but bigger, outside myself as well, so that it not only announces my presence but the anxiety of presence whose unreality is manifest where there are, owing to what is thought to be missing—no scenes. It is my subjectification (self-creation after Foucault) through death in the symbolic order (death *of* the symbolic order) that I have created from the play's and the world beyond the play's (i.e., my world's) signage chasing itself in and out of shadow. No, that is a disingenuous statement. I subject myself to "death" so as to destroy the world of the play, to unleash the chaos of unreality into the world. No, not even that. "My death" testifies to the unreality that I already experience in the guise of being in the world and the play-acting that I do in it so as not to feel so "thrown." "Pretend" (to be happy), my father used to tell me to counteract my then (and for a long time thereafter) undiagnosed conditions. He would apply his fingers to the edges of my mouth to force a smile that was not otherwise forthcoming. A paradox arose within me. How could I continue to live the unreality that was my sole possession, *my* unreality, and still hail the world via its signs? One answer is, of course, by writing this book. I saw someone walking toward me today balancing a book on his head. I wonder if it was this one.

The 100 Steps

I first saw *The Friends of Eddie Coyle* (dir. Peter Yates, 1973) with a dark hood covering my head, put there by a blackout that cut the electrical power to the theater. In this context, noir-unreality was suddenly made available to me as a manifest experiencing. Actually, the dark hood was put there during a home invasion that threatened my life and the lives of my family. I don't know what they really wanted. They kept insisting that I take them to the bank and open the vault for them, but in what must have been a dream or the film, I don't know which bank they have in mind or what they even mean by "the vault." Is it my memories they're after, I wonder? They suddenly change their directions, telling me to walk away from where they are seated in my car to a 100 count, at which point I can safely remove the black hood and turn around. My mind asks in the third person whether the man who is counting to 100 is simultaneously counting down the time he has left on this earth. Is he taking comfort in the finitude of subtraction, or is he cutting his steps so as to get there later rather than sooner? Is he embarrassed to be here, at the brink of allegedly certain death, or is he relieved that his anxious anticipation of his death is soon to be over? The man reaches the 100th step, removes his hood, and turns around to see that the car has vanished. What now? The anxiety starts all over again. "How am I to get home?" he worries. "I no longer know where I am. Is my family still alive, and if so, how can I possibly get back home to see them? Will there be door locks or windows to replace when I get there? How am I to find someone to do the repairs before night falls, so that we don't suffer a second break-in that I can anticipate? Anticipation is always the worst part, the embarrassment of one's own incapacity to do or fix the thing that you know needs to be addressed but for whatever reason is not done. Anxiety is the fill-in-the-blanks answer to why you can or could do or did not. It is a way of fitting yourself with finiteness, framing yourself and breaking your own alibi in the moment that you give it.

Eddie Coyle is thought to have sold out his criminal "friends" to the cops. He is taken on a ride from Boston to Quincy, Massachusetts, after being treated to a night on the town that has left him drunk and sleeping in the front seat of a car with one of his friends, the real snitch and his future assassin, seated directly behind him. The car drives through a dark tunnel and Eddie dreams of the man in the black hood who thought he was about to die. Eddie does not put his and the hooded man's stories together, though (it being *my* dream). Eddie does not see why one man dies and the other one is saved. Eddie is shot, his body slumps in his seat. "Is he dead?" the Kid driving the car asks the shooter. "If he's not now, he's never gonna be," the shooter says. Does Eddie know this, or is he still waiting for the black hood to come off? Eddie Coyle is watching the movie of his life in a blackout, or so he believes. A man's got to believe in something.

NOTES

Chapter 1

1. Emmanuel Levinas, *Totality and Infinity: An Essay on Exteriority*, trans. Alphonso Lingis (Pittsburgh, Pa.: Duquesne University Press, 2004), 192; Raúl Ruiz, *Night Across the Street* (2012).

2. *Crime Wave* (dir. André de Toth, 1953).

3. G. W. Leibniz, "A New System: Of the Nature and Communication of Substances, and Also of the Union That Exists between the Soul and the Body," trans. Jonathan Bennett, 2006, 4, http://www.earlymoderntexts.com/pdfs/leibniz1695c.pdf.

4. Lois Parkinson Zamora and Monika Kaup employ the term "*Artificialization*" in "Baroque, New World Baroque, Neobaroque: Categories and Concepts," in *Baroque New Worlds: Representation, Transculturation, Counterconquest,* ed. Zamora and Kaup (Durham, N.C.: Duke University Press, 2010), 11.

5. Edmund Husserl, *Ideas I*, trans. Daniel O. Dahlstrom (Indianapolis, Ind.: Hackett, 2014), §114, 223.

6. Paul Schrader, "Notes on Film Noir," *Film Comment* 8, no. 1 (spring 1972): 11.

7. Emmanuel Levinas, *The Theory of Intuition in Husserl's Phenomenology*, trans. Andre Orianne (Evanston, Ill.: Northwestern University Press, 1995), 48.

8. G. W. Leibniz, "Principles of Nature and Grace, Based on Reason," in *Philosophical Essays*, trans. Roger Ariew and Daniel Garber (Indianapolis, Ind.: Hackett, 1989), 210; Gilles Deleuze, *The Fold: Leibniz and the Baroque*, trans. Tom Conley (Minneapolis: University of Minnesota Press, 1992), 76.

9. Friedrich Nietzsche, "On Truth and Lies in an Extra-Moral Sense," in *The Portable Nietzsche,* ed. and trans. Walter Kaufmann (New York: Penguin Books, 1982), 46; Gilles Deleuze, *Proust and Signs: The Complete Text*, trans. Richard Howard (Minneapolis: University of Minnesota Press, 2000), 94, 95, 97, 101.

10. Ruiz adopted the idea of "inverted perspective" from Pavel Florensky. Raúl Ruiz, *The Poetics of Cinema 1: Miscellanies,* trans. Brian Holmes (Paris: Dis Voir, 2005), 34, 35, and 44.

11. Paul Ricoeur, *Time and Narrative*, vol. 1, trans. Kathleen McLaughlin and David Pellauer (Chicago: University of Chicago Press, 1990), 326.

12. I am cognizant here of George Lakoff and Mark Johnson's "container metaphors" that extend to the insides and outsides of all manner of objects and substances. George Lakoff and Mark Johnson, *Metaphors We Live By* (Chicago: University of Chicago Press, 1980), 25, 29, 30.

13. Rémi Brague, "L'Être en acte," in *Aristote et la question du monde* (Paris: Presses Universitaires de France, 1988), 492, quoted in Ricoeur, *Oneself as Another* (Chicago: University of Chicago Press, 1995), 314 n. 18.

14. William H. Gass, *Finding a Form* (Champaign, Ill.: Dalkey Archive, 2009), 339.

15. Husserl, *Ideas I*, §31, 53 and §113, 220; Georges Perec, *La Boutique Obscure*, trans. Daniel Levin Becker (Brooklyn, N.Y.: Melville House, 2012), 194; Edmund Husserl, *Cartesian Meditations*, trans. D. Cairns (The Hague: Nijhoff, 1967), 182; Dermot Moran and Joseph Cohen, *The Husserl Dictionary* (New York: Bloomsbury, 2013), 147, 167, and 251.

16. Žižek cites the gull that falls out of the sky and attacks the heroine of Hitchcock's *The Birds* (1963) at sea as an example of a thing that disturbs the frame it also engenders, that, in effect, it is (as we see things in the film from a bird's-eye view). Slavoj Žižek, *Absolute Recoil: Towards a New Foundation of Dialectical Materialism* (Brooklyn, N.Y.: Verso, 2014), 109 and 110. "Finding meaningful connections between unrelated events; Clear and frequent déjà vu experiences or experiences of unreality" are cited as symptoms of attenuated or mild psychotic disorder: http://www.cedarclinic.org/index.php/understanding-early-psychosis/early-signs-of-psychosis.

17. Immanuel Kant, *Critique of Judgment*, part 1, trans. Werner S. Pluhar (Indianapolis, Ind.: Hackett, 1987), "Introduction," IX, 37.

18. I will have occasion to discuss Thomas Nagel's theory of the objective self at various points in this book.

19. Kant, *Critique of Judgment*, part 1, §10, 65.

20. Seneca, "On the Shortness of Life," in vol. 2 of *Moral Essays*, trans. John W. Basore (Cambridge, Mass.: Harvard University Press, 1932), book 10: 3.1–4. Translation modified in Jacques Derrida, *Aporias*, trans. Thomas Dutoit (Stanford, Calif.: Stanford University Press, 1993); Paul Ricoeur, *The Rule of Metaphor*, trans. Robert Czerny (Toronto: University of Toronto Press, 2012), 226.

21. Moran and Cohen, *The Husserl Dictionary*, 114–15.

22. Ricoeur, *The Rule of Metaphor*, 240; Immanuel Kant, *Critique of Pure Reason*, trans. Marcus Weigelt (New York: Penguin, 2007), 586.

23. Husserl, *Cartesian Meditations*, §8, 20.

24. Husserl, *Cartesian Meditations*, xxxiv, §1, 59 and 60 and 342 and 344.

25. Husserl, *Cartesian Meditations*, 517, 522–23, 527, and 533–34.

26. Husserl, *Cartesian Meditations*, 235.

27. "Whatever we may know of matter is nothing but relations," Husserl, *Cartesian Meditations*, §8, 81, and 263, 280, 285, and 359–60; Levinas, *Totality and Infinity*, 92.

28. Kant, *Critique of Pure Reason*, 319 and 355.

29. Kant, *Critique of Pure Reason*, 504.

30. Kant, *Critique of Pure Reason*, "Preface to the Second Edition" (1787), 30 and 252. As Kant observes, "we do not seem to be content with hearing only what is true, but want to know a good deal more."

31. Friedrich Nietzsche, *The Will to Power*, trans. Walter Kaufmann (New York: Vintage, 1968), §479, 265, §482, 267, §484, 268, §659, 348.

32. Nietzsche, *The Will to Power*, §488, 269, §530, 288, §532, 289, §535 and §536, 290–91.

33. Nietzsche, *The Will to Power*, §490, 271, §516, 279, §518, 281.

34. Nietzsche, *The Will to Power*, §520, 281.

35. Nietzsche, *The Will to Power*, §528, 285, §586, 319 and 321, §588, 323, §602, 326, §617, 331.

36. Ricoeur, *Oneself as Another*, 117; Ricoeur, *The Rule of Metaphor*, 47.

37. "Images, I think, elicit a kind of attention that returns again and again to an originary non-linguistic ground, where articulatable meaning seems conclusively inaccessible. Hallucination may be the echochamber of that particular anxiety." James Elkins, *Why Are Our Pictures Puzzles?* (New York: Routledge, 1999), 16.

38. Albert Casullo, *A Priori Justification* (New York: Oxford University Press, 2003), 26–27.

39. Husserl, *Ideas I*, §136, 271, §137, 273, and §153, 309.

40. Husserl, *Ideas I*, 15.

41. Aristotle, *Poetics,* in *The Basic Works of Aristotle*, trans. Ingram Bywater, ed. Richard McKeon (New York: Random House, 1941), 1457b6–9; William David Ross, *Aristotle* (London: Methuen, 1949), 1457b7.

42. "Borrowing" here relates to Ricoeur's explication of Aristotle's use of the word *epiphora*, meaning "displacement" or "movement 'from . . . to . . .' " in defining "metaphor." Ricoeur, *The Rule of Metaphor*, 18.

43. Ricoeur, *The Rule of Metaphor*, 21.

44. See, for example, *The Woman in the Window* (dir. Fritz Lang, 1944), in which a woman's portrait that is much admired by the film's protagonist—a college professor—comes to life (i.e., he meets the artist's model for the painting), mis/leading to murder in that the encounter turns out to have happened only in the professor's dream. Maurice Blanchot, *Aminadab*, trans. Jeff Fort (Lincoln: University of Nebraska Press, 2002), 3, 6, 22.

45. Willard Van Orman Quine, *Word and Object* (Cambridge, Mass.: MIT Press, 1960), 12 n.4.

46. Ricoeur writes that in the *Nicomachean Ethics*, Aristotle asserted that "metaphorical transposition serves to fill the gaps in common language." Ricoeur, *The Rule of Metaphor*, 325 n. 19.

47. Martin Heidegger, *Schelling's Treatise on the Essence of Human Freedom*, trans. Joan Stambaugh (Athens: Ohio University Press, 1985), 170–71. Heidegger cited and discussed in Lee Braver, *Groundless Grounds: A Study of Wittgenstein and Heidegger* (Cambridge, Mass.: MIT Press, 2012), 194.

48. Alain Robbe-Grillet, "The Dressmaker's Dummy," in *Snapshots*, trans. Bruce Morrissette (Evanston, Ill.: Northwestern University Press, 1986), 3.

49. Thomas Nagel, *The View from Nowhere* (New York: Oxford University Press, 1986), 223.

50. Quine, *Word and Object*, 44.

51. Levinas, *The Theory of Intuition in Husserl's Phenomenology*, 84, 86, 88, 89 and 90.

52. Ricoeur, *The Rule of Metaphor*, 196 and 197.

53. Ricoeur, *The Rule of Metaphor*, 213; Casullo, *A Priori Justification*, 36; John L. Pollock, *Knowledge and Justification* (Princeton, N.J.: Princeton University Press, 1974), 320, paraphrased in Casullo, *A Priori Justification*, 63.

54. Werner S. Pluhar, "Translator's Introduction," in *The Critique of Judgment*, xxxviii.

55. Compare Welles's disappearing mass image in *Arkadin* with that of Welles's bloated police captain Hank Quinlan in *Touch of Evil* (1958), where mass (mere form) had displaced space ("a form of sensible intuition"), rendering the baroque

mannerist, not just particular but peculiar in its self-regard. *Mr. Arkadin* (dir. Orson Welles, 1955); Kant, *Critique of Judgment*, §318, 187 and §365, 243.

56. Pluhar, "Translator's Introduction," xli.

57. Pluhar, "Translator's Introduction," xciii and xcv.

58. Pluhar, "Translator's Introduction," lviii.

59. Kant, *Critique of Judgment*, 103, 104, 105.

60. Ricoeur, *Oneself as Another*, 5

61. Ricoeur, *Oneself as Another*, 103, 104, 105; Kant, *Critique of Pure Reason*, 411.

62. G. Von Wright, *Explanation and Understanding* (London: Routledge and Kegan Paul, 1971), cited in Ricoeur, *Oneself as Another*, 110, 111, 150, 325.

63. Ricoeur, *Oneself as Another*, 3.

64. Edmund Husserl, *Phantasy, Image, Consciousness, and Memory (1898–1925)*, trans. John B. Brough (Dordrecht, Neth.: Springer, 2005), 690.

65. Husserl, *Phantasy, Image, Consciousness, and Memory*, 692.

66. Emmanuel Levinas, *God, Death, and Time*, trans. Bettina Bergo (Stanford, Calif.: Stanford University Press, 2000), 146, 147–48, 150.

67. Levinas, *God, Death, and Time*, 157, 158. Kant writes that "an object is *monstrous* if by its magnitude it nullifies the purpose that constitutes its content." Kant, *Critique of Judgment*, 109.

68. Kant, *Critique of Judgment*, 149 and 198.

69. "The sublime . . . is an object (of nature) the presentation of which determines *the mind to think of nature's inability to attain to an exhibition of ideas.*" Kant, *Critique of Judgment*, §261, 120, §262, 121, §268, 127, 128 and §272, 132.

70. Kant, *Critique of Judgment*, §217, 405. The floating hat image comes from the short film *Bum Rap—A Noir Fantasy* (dir. Andre Hunt, 2013), available for viewing on YouTube, https://www.youtube.com/watch?v=PH7vdg8m9MY.

71. Kant, *Critique of Judgment*, §205, 394.

72. Kant, *Critique of Judgment*, §453, 343.

73. Jean-Luc Nancy, "Urbi and Orbi," in *The Creation of the World or Globalization*, trans. François Raffoul and David Pettigrew (Albany: State University of New York Press, 2007), 34.

74. Levinas, *God, Death, and Time*, 208.

75. Emmanuel Levinas, *Ethics and Infinity*, trans. Robert A. Cohen (Pittsburgh, Pa.: Duquesne University Press, 1985), 157; Maurice Blanchot, *Pure Immanence: Essays on a Life*, trans. Anne Boyman (New York: Zone Books, 2005), 51; Emmanuel Levinas, *Alterity & Transcendence*, trans. Michael B. Smith (New York: Columbia University Press, 1999), 157.

76. Nancy, *The Creation of the World or Globalization*, 35

77. Maurice Blanchot, "Two Versions of the Imaginary," in *The Station Hill Blanchot Reader*, trans. Lydia Davis, Paul Auster, and Robert Lamberton (Barrytown, N.Y.: Station Hill, 1999), 418, 419, and 424; Husserl, *Ideas I*, §114, 223.

78. Gilles Deleuze and Félix Guattari, *What Is Philosophy?* trans. Hugh Tomlinson and Graham Burchell (New York: Columbia University Press, 168).

79. Deleuze and Guattari, *What Is Philosophy?* 189.

80. Levinas, *Alterity & Transcendence*, 24.

81. Levinas, *Alterity & Transcendence*, 27; Levinas, *God, Death, and Time*, 139.

82. Likewise, the sea in Melville and the mirror in Woolf. Deleuze and Guattari, *What Is Philosophy?* 168–69.

83. Deleuze and Guattari, *What Is Philosophy?* 183.

84. Levinas, *Alterity & Transcendence*, 104–5, 126–27, 127–28.

85. Levinas, *Alterity & Transcendence*, 140.

86. Blanchot, *Pure Immanence: Essays on a Life*, 51.

87. This peculiar handshake occurs between a wealthy industrialist and a low-level civil servant in *The Mask of Dimitrios* (dir. Jean Negulesco, 1944).

88. A number of films noir feature characters who are hard of hearing, pretend not to hear, or have their hearing compromised by getting slapped, among them: *T-Men* (dir. Anthony Mann, 1947), *Out of the Past* (dir. Jacques, Tourneur, 1947), *The Big Combo* (dir. Joseph H. Lewis, 1955), and *The Brothers Rico* (dir. Phil Karlson, 1957).

89. Gilles Deleuze, *The Fold*, trans. Tom Conley (Minneapolis: University of Minneapolis Press, 1993), 81.

90. Jorge Luis Borges, "The Circular Ruins," in *Collected Fictions*, trans. Andrew Hurley (New York: Penguin Books, 1999), 96.

91. Borges, "The Circular Ruins," 98.

92. Levinas, *Alterity & Transcendence*, 67.

93. Deleuze after Leibniz, a "hypothetical necessity" in *The Fold*, 101, 156–57 n. 4.

94. Deleuze, *The Fold*, 130 and 131.

95. Robert B. Ray, *A Certain Tendency of the Hollywood Cinema, 1930–1980* (Princeton, N.J.: Princeton University Press, 1985), 160.

96. Mladen Doler, *A Voice and Nothing More* (Cambridge, Mass.: MIT Press, 2006), 61.

97. Deleuze, *Spinoza: Practical Philosophy* (New York: City Lights Publishers, 2001), 20.

98. Sigmund Freud, "The Uncanny" (1919), in *The Uncanny*, trans. David McClintock (New York: Penguin Books, 2003), 124. The Japanese roboticist Masahiro Mori coined the term "uncanny valley" in his essay "The Uncanny Valley," trans. Karl F. MacDorman and Takashi Minato, *Energy* 7, no. 4 (1970): 33–35. My thanks to Hans Vermy for introducing me to this concept.

99. Christopher Fynsk, "Foreword," in *The Station Hill Blanchot Reader* (Barrytown, N.Y.: Station Hill, 1995), x and xv.

100. Maurice Blanchot, "The Song of the Sirens," in *The Station Hill Blanchot Reader*, 447.

101. Blanchot, "The Song of the Sirens," 447.

102. Blanchot, "The Song of the Sirens," 447.

103. Blanchot, "The Song of the Sirens," 443.

Chapter 2

1. Kant, *Critique of Pure Reason*, 38.

2. Martin Heidegger, "Building, Dwelling, Thinking," in *Martin Heidegger: Basic Writings*, ed. David Farrell Krell (New York: HarperCollins, 2008), 356.

3. Heidegger, "Building, Dwelling, Thinking," 351.

4. G. W. F. Hegel, *The Encyclopaedia Logic, Part 1*, trans. T. F. Gereats, W. A. Suchting, and H. S. Harris (Indianapolis, Ind.: Hackett, 1991), §11, 35.

5. Kant, *Critique of Pure Reason*, §5, 68, §26, 162–63 and 249.

6. G. W. Leibniz, "On Freedom and Possibility" (1680–82?), in *Philosophical Essays*, trans. Roger Ariew (Indianapolis, Ind.: Hackett, 1989), 19, 20 and 21.

7. G. W. Leibniz, "On Freedom" (1689?), in *Philosophical Essays*, 94.

8. Architecture is about "identifying, and ultimately releasing potentialities hidden in a site." Bernard Tschumi, *Architecture in/of Motion* (Rotterdam: NAi, 1997), 21.

9. G. W. Leibniz, "Discourse on Metaphysics" (1686), in *Philosophical Essays*, 39.

10. Friedrich Nietzsche, *Also Sprach Zarathustra* (1883), trans. J. Hillis Miller, in *Ariadne's Thread: Story Lines,* by Miller (New Haven, Conn.: Yale University Press, 1992), 15 and 16.

11. Michel Leiris, *Nights as Days, Days as Nights*, trans. Richard Sieburth (Hygiene, Colo.: Eridanos, 1987), 36; Perec, *La Boutique Obscure*, 186–87.

12. Soren Kierkegaard, *The Sickness Unto Death: A Christian Psychological Expedition for Upbuilding and Awakening*, trans. Howard V. Hong and Edith H. Hong (Princeton, N.J.: Princeton University Press, 1983), 55.

13. See Ian Hacking's work on the growing importance of numbers (influenced by the mathematician-philosopher Gottlob Frege), specifically statistics in Western democracies, expanding and individuating (even creating) the number of people to be counted at a time when detective fiction also developed (ca. 1830–48). Ian Hacking, "Biopower and the Avalanche of Printed Numbers," *Humanities in Society* 5, nos. 3/4 (summer/fall 1982): 281.

14. Joan Copjec, "The Phenomenal Non-Phenomenal: Private Space in *Film Noir*," in *Shades of Noir*, ed. Joan Copjec (New York: Verso, 1993), 169.

15. Hans-Georg Gadamer, *Truth and Method*, trans. Joel Weinsheimer and Donald G. Marshall (New York: Bloomsbury, 2013), 382 and 383.

16. Joe Gillis is reading Irwin Shaw's novel *The Young Lions* outside Norma's bedroom while waiting for her to wake up and put on her face. The book was made into a film eight years later (dir. Edward Dmytryk, 1958) costarring Montgomery Clift, who would have his face rearranged in a car accident two years earlier, exacerbating the actor's natural reticence to face the camera and the camera's fascination with him.

17. Free Dictionary, http://www.thefreedictionary.com/prolepsis.

18. Jorge Luis Borges, "The Garden of Forking Paths," in *Collected Fictions,* 120 and 121.

19. Free Dictionary, http://www.thefreedictionary.com/life-sized.

20. Free Dictionary, http://www.thefreedictionary.com/lifelike.

21. Kant, *Critique of Judgment*, 111.

22. Severo Sarduy, *Written on a Body*, trans. Carol Maier (New York: Lumen, 1989), 111 and 113 n. 7, 130.

23. Sarduy, *Written on a Body*, 100.

24. Mallarmé ("an allegory of itself") (unidentified source) and Adams Sitney, "Afterword" to Blanchot, *The Gaze of Orpheus and Other Literary Essays*, quoted in Pierre Joris, "Translator's Preface," in Maurice Blanchot, *The Unavowable Community* (Barrytown, N.Y.: Station Hill, 1983), xxii.

25. Maurice Blanchot, "The Malady of Death," in *The Station Hill Reader*, 37 and 39; Maurice Blanchot, "Literature and the Right to Death," in *The Station Hill Reader*, 381, 384, 385, 387, and 399.

26. Deleuze, *The Fold*, 27.

27. Garden Guides, http://www.gardenguides.com/128093-meaning-lilac-flower.html.

28. Copjec, "The Phenomenal Non-Phenomenal," 179.

29. Perec's *Life A User's Manual*, which is propelled by its main protagonist Bartlebooth's gambit to make his own watercolor paintings disappear (along with the puzzles that were created from them), to return color to the whiteness of the original page, contains a description of a place called Crazy House, "an old Gothic fortress turned upside-down on its chimney pots, with windows back-to-front and furniture on the ceiling." Georges Perec, *Life: A User's Manual*, trans. David Bellos (Boston: David R. Godine, 2009), 404.

30. Ludwig Wittgenstein, *Philosophical Investigations, including Philosophy of Psychology—A Fragment xi (Philosophical Investigations, Part II)*, revised 4th edition, ed. P. M. S. Hacker and Joachim Schulte, trans. G. E. M. Anscombe (Malden, Mass.: Wiley-Blackwell, 2009), §85, 44e.

31. My thanks to Will Daddario for bringing this drawing to my attention.

32. The line of thinking that extends in the "modern age" from Cartesian radical doubt to Kantian transcendentalism has reached its most recent iteration in the "New Realism" belief expounded by the contemporary German philosopher Markus Gabriel in his book *Why the World Does Not Exist* (Malden, Mass.: Polity, 2015).

33. "I'm hidden in a little square room without a door [in a building that is undergoing construction]. (I had to enter through the ceiling.)" Perec writes this in his dream journal, *La Boutique Obscure*, 221.

34. Husserl, *Phantasy, Image, Consciousness, and Memory*, 619–20.

35. Jorge Luis Borges, "Death and the Compass," in *Collected Fictions*, 156.

36. Pierre Corneille, *Le Cid*, trans. Richard Wilbur (New York: Mariner Books, 2009), act 5, scene 7, 117.

37. Leibniz's principle of sufficient reason states that "for every thing, every fact, and every occurrence, there must be a reason why it is thus and so rather than otherwise." Leibniz, "Monadology," §32, paraphrased in Quentin Meillassoux, *After Finitude: An Essay on the Necessity of Contingency*, trans. Ray Brassier (New York: Continuum, 2009), 33.

38. "Spinoza's Epistemology," in *Internet Encyclopedia of Philosophy*, http://www.iep.utm.edu/spino-ep/#SH2a

39. Free Dictionary, http://www.thefreedictionary.com/Plimsoll%20mark.

40. Jorge Luis Borges, "The Secret Miracle," in *Collected Fictions*, 160.

41. Borges, "Death and the Compass," 147, 148, and 152.

42. Gilles Deleuze, *Expressionism in Philosophy: Spinoza*, trans. Martin Joughin (New York: Zone Books, 1992), 157.

43. Gertrude Stein, *Lectures in America* (New York: Random House, 1935), 79.

44. Sofia Miguens and Gerhard Preyer, eds., *Consciousness and Subjectivity* (De Gruyter online publishing, 2012), cited in Elijah Chudnoff, http://philpapers.org/rec/CHUPP.

45. Losey made *The Prowler* just before his self-exile after being named a communist by the House Un-American Activities Committee, along with *The Prowler*'s screenwriter, Dalton Trumbo, who continued to write Hollywood films

under assumed names, in the shadows. The film's producer, "Samuel P. Eagle," was in fact a pseudonym for Samuel P. Spiegel, who would become one of Hollywood's most famous producers. Spiegel was Eagle from 1935 to 1954.

46. A standard mystery and suspense trope is the reading of a number at face value and then later discovering that its true meaning can only be gleaned by misreading it. Thus, 1918 could be a date or a house address, a number total, a Bible passage, a military time marker, or, similarly colon-ized, the dimensions of a scale model (e.g., 1:918).

47. Ellroy provides video commentary on the 2011 VCI Entertainment DVD version of the film.

48. James Ellroy, *My Dark Places* (New York: Vintage Books, 1997), 270.

49. G. W. Leibniz, "Dialogue on Human Freedom and the Origin of Evil" (January 25, 1695), in *Philosophical Essays*, 114–15.

50. Leiris, *Nights as Days, Days as Nights*, 13.

51. Charles Brockden Brown, *Wieland; or The Transformation: with Related Texts*, ed. Philip Barnard and Stephen Shapiro (Indianapolis, Ind.: Hackett, 2009), frontispiece, 85 and 93.

52. The voice on the radio is actually that of the film's soon-to-be blacklisted screenwriter Dalton Trumbo, here writing under the name "Hugo Butler."

53. Kierkegaard, *The Sickness Unto Death*, 51 and 62.

54. Kierkegaard, *The Sickness Unto Death*, 36 and 37.

55. Kierkegaard, *The Sickness Unto Death*, 42, 44, 45, and 57.

56. This scene will be replayed almost verbatim in Hitchcock's *The Trouble with Harry* (1955), which I discuss in chapter 6.

57. Ricoeur, *The Rule of Metaphor*, 309.

58. Spinoza, *Ethics*, *P* §26, 50.

59. Deleuze, *Spinoza: Practical Philosophy*, 18, referring to Spinoza, *Ethics*, III, 2, scholium.

60. Spinoza, *Practical Philosophy*, 18.

61. Spinoza, *Ethics*, book 2, *P* 31, 52.

62. This scenario also occurs in *The Big Clock* and its remake, *No Way Out* (dir. Roger Donaldson, 1987).

63. Perec, *La Boutique Obscure*, 155 and 164.

Chapter 3

1. The *Life and Death of Colonel Blimp* (dir. Michael Powell and Emeric Pressburger, 1943).

2. A critical biography of Hitchcock begins with the image of Hitchcock as a magician out of whose prop trunk he drew the objects—umbrellas, door keys, tiepins, rings, and so on—from which he spun his yarns. Patrick McGilligan, *Alfred Hitchcock: A Life in Darkness and Light* (New York: itbooks/HarperCollins, 2004), 3.

3. Spinoza, *Ethics*, II/151, *P* 15, 78 and 79.

4. Nagel, *The View from Nowhere*, 33.

5. Derek Parfit, *Reasons and Persons* (New York: Oxford, 1987), 213, 221, 277.

6. Nagel, *The View from Nowhere*, 54 and 55; René Descartes, "Letter to Jean de Silhon" (1648), in *The Philosophical Writings of Descartes*, vol. 3, ed. John

Cottingham, Dugald Murdoch, Robert Stoothoff, and Anthony Kenny (Cambridge: Cambridge University Press, 1991), 331.

7. Perec, *Life: A User's Manual*, 335.

8. In *My Winnipeg*, cine-dreaming Guy Maddin says he was dyslexic as a child.

9. Parfit, *Reasons and Persons*, 222.

10. David Hume, *A Treatise of Human Nature*, vol. 1, ed. David Fate Norton and Mary J. Norton (Oxford: Oxford University Press, 2011), §§1.4.6–1.4.7, 170–71.

11. Levinas, *Totality and Infinity*, 154.

12. Kant, *Critique of Pure Reason*, 286.

13. Brian Massumi, *Parables for the Virtual: Movement, Affect, Sensation* (Durham, N.C.: Duke University Press, 2002), 16; Giordano Bruno, *De la magie*, trans. Danielle Sonnier and Boris Donne (Paris: Allia, 2013), 33, cited in Massumi, *Parables for the Virtual*, 257–58 n. 8.

14. *5 Against the House* (dir. Phil Karlson, 1955).

15. Deleuze, *Practical Philosophy*, 86.

16. Citing what André Bazin called "the mummy complex," Peter Conrad argues that Hitchcock "shows how we can 'keep up appearances in the face of death by preserving flesh and bone.'" Peter Conrad, *The Hitchcock Murders* (New York: Faber and Faber, 2000), 141–42.

17. "He might saw a woman in half, as one of his favorite real-life murderers did." So begins McGilligan's critical biography of Hitchcock. McGilligan, *Alfred Hitchcock: A Life in Darkness and Light*, 3.

18. Sigmund Freud, "A Note upon the 'Mystic Writing Pad" (1925), from Freud, *General Psychological Theory*, chapter 13 (1925), http://home.uchicago.edu/~awinter/mystic.pdf.

19. John T. Irwin, *The Mystery to a Solution: Poe, Borges, and the Analytic Detective Story* (Baltimore, Md.: Johns Hopkins University Press, 1996).

20. Jacques Derrida, "Freud and the Scene of Writing," in *Writing and Difference*, trans. Alan Bass (Chicago: University of Chicago Press, 1978), 250, 253, 254, and 267.

21. Derrida, "Freud and the Scene of Writing," 268, 272, and 289.

22. Nietzsche, *The Will to Power*, §552b, 297

23. Nietzsche, *The Will to Power*, §569 and §570, 307.

24. "Who compels us to think that subjectivity is real, essential? . . . (There might only be an apparent world, but not *our* apparent world.)" Nietzsche, *The Will to Power*, §583, 313 and §585, 317.

25. Nietzsche, *The Will to Power,* §17, 15–16, §30, 20–21, §488, 270, and §550, 294.

26. It should be noted that the subject of Levinas's focus in the sections I am quoting in this context is Husserlian phenomenology, whose influence Levinas's work reflects and progressively opposes although does not reject. Emmanuel Levinas, "Outside the Subject," in *Outside the Subject*, trans. Michael B. Smith (Stanford, Calif.: Stanford University Press, 1994), xvi ("Translator's Introduction") and 152.

27. Levinas, "Outside the Subject," 151 and 168 n. 1.

28. Levinas, "Outside the Subject," 156 and 157.

29. Levinas, "Outside the Subject," 158.

30. Simone Weil, *Waiting for God*, trans. Emma Crauferd (New York: Harper Perennial, 2009), 63.

31. Weil, *Waiting for God*, 48.

32. Emmanuel Levinas, *De la existent à l'existent*, 3rd edition (Paris: Vrin, 1986), 94 and 98, quoted and commented on by Simon Critchley in *Very Little . . . Almost Nothing* (New York: Routledge, 2004), 67.

33. Casullo, *A Priori Justification*, 90 (Kantian paraphrases) and 102.

Chapter 4

1. Moran and Cohen, *The Husserl Dictionary*, 324.

2. Nietzsche, *The Will to Power*, §521, 282.

3. Circles recur throughout the film: the clock on the wall of Neale's room at the asylum; the cake; a crater produced by a bomb that saved Neale on the train; the horoscope depicted on the sign outside of the fortune-teller's tent. Interview with Joe McElhaney. *Ministry of Fear*, Criterion Collection DVD extra, 2013.

4. Kant, *Critique of Pure Reason,* 346, 347, and 348.

5. Husserl, *Ideas I*, §46, 83.

6. Kant, *Critique of Pure Reason,* 349, 384, 392, and 403.

7. Georges Poulet, "The Dream of Descartes," in *Studies in Human Time*, trans. Elliott Coleman (New York: Harper Torchbooks, 1959), 58.

8. Freud's use of the phrase appears in his "Notes upon a Case of Obsessional Neurosis" (1909), in which he describes the case of "the Rat Man," http://www.mhweb.org/freud/ratman1.pdf.

9. Brown, *Wieland*, 131.

10. Daniel Paul Schrieber, *Memoirs of My Nervous Illness* (New York: New York Review of Books Classics, 2000), 62.

11. Brown, *Wieland*, 44 n. 17.

12. Schreber, "Memoirs," 17.

13. Philip Barnard and Stephen Shapiro, "Introduction," in Brown, *Wieland*, xxii.

14. "One speaks, to be sure, of evidence but instead of bringing it as discerning into *essential connections* with seeing [*Sehen*] in the usual sense, one speaks of a '*feeling of evidence*,' a kind of mystical *index veri* [indicator of the true] that supposedly lends the judgment an affective coloring." Husserl, *Ideas I*, §21, 39, §145, 287.

15. Brown, *Wieland*, 51.

16. Thanatophobia being akin to what J. Hillis Miller calls a "single-line labyrinth," subjective but indeterminate, like the death it has in mind. This "figure without a figure," which one encounters in Blanchot's writing, can be heard over a telephone line that goes dead. In the climactic phone call from her husband when she realizes that he is responsible for her imminent murder, Leona's single-line labyrinth is revealed as being anastomotic, the suturing of one telephonic artery of her awareness to another. Miller, *Ariadne's Thread*, 8, 154, and 232.

17. William H. Gass, *Cartesian Sonata and Other Novellas* (Champaign, Ill.: Dalkey Archive, 2009), 5.

18. Gass, *Cartesian Sonata*, 53.

19. Gass, *Cartesian Sonata*, 153.

20. Gass, *Cartesian Sonata*, 160.

21. J. Hillis Miller, *For Derrida* (New York: Fordham University Press, 2009), 52.

22. Levinas, *God, Death, and Time*, 72.

23. Jacques Derrida, *Adieu: To Emmanuel Levinas*, trans. Pascale-Anne Brault and Michel Naas (Stanford, Calif.: Stanford University Press, 1999), 9.

24. Levinas is here, as elsewhere, writing his way through Heidegger's notion of *Dasein* toward a responsibility to the other through which we gain the self. Levinas, *God, Death, and Time*, 39, and 47.

25. Leibniz, "Discourse on Metaphysics," 58.

26. P. F. Strawson, *Individuals: An Essay in Descriptive Metaphysics* (New York: Routledge, 1991), 133 and 227.

27. Thomas Nagel, *Mortal Questions* (New York: Cambridge University Press, 2012), 200.

28. Nagel, *Mortal Questions*, 60.

29. Perec, *La Boutique Obscure*, 176.

30. Husserl, *Ideas I*, §108, 212–13.

31. Perec, *Life: A User's Manual*, 422, 423, 424, 426 and 430.

32. Flann O'Brien, *The Third Policeman* (Normal, Ill.: Dalkey Archive, 2005), 51.

33. Perec, *La Boutique Obscure*, 176.

34. Levinas, *Totality and Infinity*, 138.

35. Paraphrase of a passage from Anne Carson, *Eros the Bittersweet* (Normal, Ill.: Dalkey Archive, 1998), 73, after Aristotle's *Poetics*, 21.1457b7.

36. "The ambiguous [test] materials consist of a set of cards that portray human figures in a variety of settings and situations. The subject is asked to tell the examiner a story about each card that includes the following elements: the event shown in the picture; what has led up to it; what the characters in the picture are feeling and thinking; and the outcome of the event," http://www.minddisorders.com/Py-Z/Thematic-Apperception-Test.html.

37. Nagel, *Mortal Questions*, 1.

38. Ricoeur, *The Rule of Metaphor*, 240.

39. Umberto Eco, *The Island of the Day Before* (New York: Harcourt Mifflin, 2006), 1.

40. Eco, *The Island of the Day Before*, 122.

41. Borges cites the British idealist philosopher Frances Herbert Bradley's *Appearance and Reality* (1897, p. 215) as his source in the (Borges) story "A Survey of the Works of Herbert Quain," 108–9. Deleuze, *Expressionism in Philosophy: Spinoza*, 155; Leibniz, "Discourse on Metaphysics," §26, 58.

42. Spinoza, *Ethics*, 33.

43. G. W. F. Hegel, *Phenomenology of Sprit*, trans. A. V. Miller (New York: Oxford, 1977), §32, 19.

44. Gilles Deleuze, *Proust and Signs*, trans. Richard Howard (Minneapolis: University of Minnesota Press, 2004), 4.

45. Derrida, *Aporias*, 4–5.

46. Derrida, *Aporias*, 85–86.

47. Derrida, *Aporias*, 55 and 58.

48. Derrida, *Aporias*, 49.

49. Kierkegaard, *The Sickness Unto Death*, 23, 25, 66, and 74.

50. Derrida, *Aporias*, 76.

51. Perec, *Life: A User's Manual*, 493 and 497.

52. Elijah Chudnoff, *Intuition* (New York: Oxford, 2013), 146; Jacques Lacan, *Anxiety,* trans. A. R. Price (Cambridge: Polity, 2016), 14–15.

53. Chudnoff, *Intuition*, 146 and 147.

54. Georges Perec, *I Remember*, trans. Philip Terry and David Bellos (Boston: David R. Godine, 2014).

55. Paul de Man, *Aesthetic Ideology*, ed. Andrzej Warminski (Minneapolis: University of Minnesota Press, 2008), 46 and 47.

56. De Man, *Aesthetic Ideology*, 39.

57. "That the voice appeared to come from the ceiling was to be considered as an illusion of the fancy." Brown, *Wieland*, 64.

58. O'Brien, *The Third Policeman,* 144.

59. Perec, *La Boutique Obscure*, 20.

60. Perec, *La Boutique Obscure*, 121.

61. Ricoeur, *The Rule of Metaphor*, 250; Nietzsche, *The Will to Power*, 265 and 266; Miller, *Ariadne's Thread*, 41, 43, 44, and 133.

62. Deleuze, *The Fold*, 125.

63. Husserl, *Ideas I*, §81, 157.

64. Ivor Armstrong Richards, *Coleridge on Imagination,* 3rd edition (London: Routledge and Kegan Paul, 1962), 154.

65. Ricoeur, *Time and Narrative*, vol. 3: 132 and 133; Husserl, *Ideas I*, §77, 139.

66. Kant, *Critique of Pure Reason*, 180.

67. P. F. Strawson, *The Bounds of Sense: An Essay on Kant's Critique of Pure Reason* (New York: Routledge, 1975), 38, 39, and 53.

68. Jacques Derrida, *The Beast and the Sovereign,* vol. 2, trans. Geoffrey Bennington (Chicago: University of Chicago Press, 2011), 50, paraphrased in Miller, *For Derrida*, 63; Jacques Derrida, *Learning to Live Finally—An Interview with Jean Birnbaum*, trans. Pascale-Anne Brault and Michael Naas (Hoboken, N.J.: Melville House, 2007), 33; Jacques Derrida, "Circumfession," trans. Geoffrey Bennington, in *Jacques Derrida,* by Geoffrey Bennington and Jacques Derrida (Chicago: University of Chicago Press, 1993), 26.

69. Vilém Flusser, *On Doubt*, trans. Rodrigo Maltez Novaes, ed. Siegfried Zielinski (Minneapolis, Minn.: Univocal, 2014), 40 and 41; Husserl, *Ideas I*, §81, 157.

70. Casullo, *A Priori Justification*, 26 and 27.

71. Husserl, *Ideas I*, §117, 232.

72. Spinoza, *Ethics*, *P* 10, 76 and *P* 12, 77.

73. Spinoza, *Ethics*, II/148, *P* 10, 76 and II/293, *P* 21, 171–72; Nietzsche, *The Will to Power*, §659, 348.

74. Paul Ricoeur, *Time and Narrative*, vol. 3, trans. Kathleen Blamey and David Pellauer (Chicago: University of Chicago Press, 1990), 17 and 278 n. 20.

75. Ricoeur, *Time and Narrative*, 3 and 5.

76. Ricoeur, *Time and Narrative*, 49 and 280 n. 25.

77. Edmund Husserl, *The Phenomenology of Time-Consciousness*, trans. James S. Churchill (Bloomington: Indiana University Press, 1964), 51; Ricoeur, *Time and Narrative*, vol. 3: 30, 35 and 36.

78. Ricoeur, *Time and Narrative*, vol. 3: 19, 36, and 168.

79. Husserl, *The Phenomenology of Time-Consciousness*, 99.

80. Chudnoff, *Intuition*, 55 and 56.

81. See René Magritte, *Collective Invention* (1935).

82. Deleuze, *The Fold*, 27.

83. Deleuze, *The Fold*, 32 and 90; *The Street with No Name* (dir. William Keighley, 1948) is a film noir.

84. Deleuze, *The Fold*, 24, 90, and 91.

85. Deleuze, *The Fold*, 76 and 78.

86. Deleuze, *The Fold*, 76 and 78.

87. Deleuze, *The Fold*, 78.

88. Leibniz, *Discourse on Metaphysics*, 65; Perec, *Life: A User's Manual*, 142 and 143.

89. "That we were always perceiving in folds means that we have been grasping figures without objects, but through the haze of dust without objects that the figures themselves raise up from the depths, and then fall back again, but with time enough to be seen for an instant." Deleuze, *The Fold*, 94.

Chapter 5

1. Roland Barthes, "The World as Object," in *Critical Essays* (Evanston, Ill.: Northwestern University Press, 1972), 3–12.

2. Ricoeur, *The Rule of Metaphor*, 296.

3. Deleuze, *Proust and Signs*, 97 and 98. Jack Carter's travel (train) reading in the neo-noir *Get Carter* (dir. Mike Hodges, 1971) is Raymond Chandler's *Farewell, My Lovely* (1940). The disposable paperback's back cover features a close up of a woman's wide-eyed stare at the reader (the expendable Carter, whose assassin travels with him anonymously on the train). Her stare disambiguates the first-person subjective camera shot, which defines and encapsulates the film version of Chandler's novel, *Lady in the Lake* (1947), which marks subjectivity as the site of death.

4. I discuss *The Voyeur*, a murder mystery set on an island (eye-land) in Spencer Golub, *Infinity (Stage)* (Ann Arbor: University of Michigan Press, 2001), 101–4.

5. M. Davies and M. Coltheart, "Introduction," in *Pathologies of Belief* (Malden, Mass.: Blackwell, 2000), 32.

6. Jorge Luis Borges, "Tlan, Uqbar, Orbis Tertius," in *Collected Fictions*, 68.

7. Ellroy, *My Dark Places*, 111.

8. Ricoeur, *The Rule of Metaphor*, 289.

9. Shakespeare, *Hamlet* (3.1).

10. "I doubt, therefore, I am. I doubt that I doubt, therefore I confirm that I am. I doubt that I doubt, therefore, I doubt that I am. . . ." Flusser, *On Doubt*, 5, 6, and 26.

11. Slavoj Žižek, "Why Does a Letter Always Arrive at Its Destination?" in *Enjoy Your Symptom! Jacques Lacan in Hollywood and Out* (New York: Routledge, 2007), 11, 12, 24–25.

12. *Cause*'s director Tay Garnett had by this point already directed *The Postman Always Rings Twice* (1946).

13. Jacques Derrida, *The Animal That Therefore I Am*, trans. Marie-Louis Mallet (New York: Fordham University Press, 2008), 68.

14. Derrida, *The Animal That Therefore I Am*, 52. Derrida is in turn citing Plato's *Phaedrus*, ca. 370 BC.

15. Lewis Carroll, "Advice from a Caterpillar," chapter 5 of *Alice's Adventures in Wonderland*, in Martin Gardner, *The Annotated Alice* (New York: Wings Books/Random House, 1960), 67 and 69.

16. Discussed in Derrida, *The Animal That Therefore I Am*, 138.

17. Derrida, *The Animal That Therefore I Am*, 10 and 11.

18. "Dennis Potter: Under the Skin, An Interview," on the DVD version of *The Singing Detective* (1986); Nagel, *The View from Nowhere*, 69.

19. Nagel, *The View from Nowhere*, 113–14.

20. Nagel, *The View from Nowhere*, 118 and 119.

21. Alain Badiou, *The Century*, trans. Alberto Toscano (Malden, Mass: Polity Press, 2005), 101, 106, 107.

22. Karen Ng, "Hegel's Logic of Actuality," *The Review of Metaphysics* 63 (September 2009): 170.

23. Sigmund Freud, "Notes upon a Case of Obsessional Neurosis" (1909), in *Collected Papers*, vol. 3, trans. Alix and James Strachey (London: Hogarth, 1925), 293–383.

24. Nietzsche, *The Will to Power*, §584, 316.

25. In his analysis of *Casablanca*, Richard Klein refers to Bogart as "the Face," which is withheld from the spectator who first sees his hand holding a cigarette and reaching for an ashtray. Richard Klein, *Cigarettes Are Sublime* (Durham, N.C.: Duke University Press, 1995), 164.

26. Klein, *Cigarettes Are Sublime*, 108.

27. Klein, *Cigarettes Are Sublime*, 90 and 110.

28. Derrida, *The Animal That Therefore I Am*, 127.

29. Levinas, *Totality and Infinity*, 191, 201 and 204.

30. Levinas, *Totality and Infinity*, 118.

31. Levinas, *Totality and Infinity*, 59.

32. Levinas, *Totality and Infinity*, 118 and 119.

33. "I encounter the other not as his representation but as his invocation of me." Miller, *For Derrida*, 112.

34. Levinas, *Alterity & Transcendence*, 126 and 175.

35. Perec, *La Boutique Obscure*, 85.

36. Beginning in 1918, the American author Robert Ripley collected oddities from around the world, which he displayed in various formats under the title "Ripley's Believe It or Not!" The entertainment gambled on our desire to test our secular beliefs as to what is and is not true in and about the world. Kant, *Critique of Pure Reason*, 326 and 327.

37. Oscar Wilde, *De Profundis* (1905), in *De Profundis, The Ballad of Reading Gaol and Other Writings* (Ware, Eng.: Wordsworth Editions, 1999), 73.

38. G. W. Leibniz, "Second Letter to Clarke," in *Philosophical Essays*, 327; Jorge Luis Borges, "Pierre Menard, Author of the *Quixote*," in *Collected Fictions*, trans. Andrew Hurley (New York: Penguin, 1999), 94.

39. All references are to Oscar Wilde, *The Importance of Being Earnest: A Serious Comedy for Trivial People*, ed. Russell Jackson (New York: W.W. Norton, 2004), http://site.iugaza.edu.ps/rareer/files/2014/11/Oscar-Wilde-The-Importance-of-Being-Earnest.pdf.

40. Ricoeur, *The Rule of Metaphor*, 142.

41. Ricoeur, *The Rule of Metaphor*, 80. Nietzsche suggested that "*between* two thoughts *all kinds of affects* play their game: but their motions are too fast, therefore we *fail* to *recognize* them, we *deny* them." It could be counter-argued that because the display of Wilde's wit in *Earnest* was so profligate, the censorious reader/spectator felt honor-bound to revile the play for what it (apparently) made him understand. Nietzsche, *The Will to Power*, 263–64.

42. Levinas, *Totality and Infinity*, 240.

43. The money "belongs," although not rightfully, to Fuller, who blackmailed the head of an insurance firm for the cash. It represents part of the profits the businessman made collecting the paper on insurance claims on bridges that were never filed.

44. Ricoeur, *The Rule of Metaphor*, 70, paraphrasing the argument of Strawson, *Individuals: An Essay in Descriptive Metaphysics*.

45. In a sense, Wilde's characters are trapped inside Nietzsche's "prisonhouse of language," which J. Hillis Miller describes as the "inextricable tangle of hypostatized presuppositions, and presuppositions of presuppositions." Miller, *Ariadne's Thread*, 49; Ricoeur, *The Rule of Metaphor*, 4.

46. Kant, *Critique of Judgment*, §451, 341.

47. G. W. Leibniz, "Leibniz's Fifth Paper," in *Philosophical Essays*, no. 29, 334.

48. G. W. Leibniz, "Leibniz's Third Paper" ("From the Letters to Clarke"), in *Philosophical Essays*, no. 29, 325.

49. Hegel, *Phenomenology of Spirit*, 3 and 4. On a possible Wilde-Hegel link, see Juliet Prewitt Brown, *Cosmopolitan Criticism: Oscar Wilde's Philosophy of Art* (Charlottesville: University Press of Virginia, 1997), xv; Philip E. Smith II and Michael S. Helfand, *Oscar Wilde's Notebooks: A Portrait of Mind in the Making* (New York: Oxford University Press, 1989), vii; and Sandra F. Siegel, review of *Cosmopolitan Criticism: Oscar Wilde's Philosophy of Art*, in *Nineteenth-Century Literature* 52, no. 2 (September 1999): 266–67, 268.

50. Søren Kierkegaard, *Three Discourses on Imagined Occasions*, in *The Essential Kierkegaard*, ed. Howard V. Hong and Edna H. Hong (Princeton, N.J.: Princeton University Press, 2000), 166, 167, and 169.

51. E. M. Cioran, *A Short History of Decay*, trans. Richard Howard (New York: Arcade, 2012), 11.

52. Cioran, *A Short History of Decay*, 9 and 14.

53. Cioran, *A Short History of Decay*, 13.

54. Søren Kierkegaard, *Repetition*, in *Fear and Trembling/Repetition*, ed. and trans. Howard V. Hong and Edna H. Hong (Princeton, N.J.: Princeton University Press, 1983), 154, 157, 160, and 163.

55. Kierkegaard, *Repetition*, 68 and 69.

56. Kierkegaard, *The Sickness Unto Death*, 133; Marcus Pound, "Lacan, Kierkegaard, and Repetition," *Quodlibet Journal* 7, no. 2 (April–June 2005), http://www.quodlibet.net/articles/pound-repetition.shtml.

57. Kierkegaard, *The Sickness Unto Death*, 159.

58. Kierkegaard, *The Sickness Unto Death*, 169.

59. Danielewski, *House of Leaves*, 67; Nagel, *The View from Nowhere*, 72 and 73.

60. Nagel, *The View from Nowhere*, 73.

61. Zachary Rufa, "Mise en scene" class, Brown University, April 2012; Ricoeur, *The Rule of Metaphor*, 308.

62. Husserl, *Ideas I*, §89, 177, §90, 179, and §99, 201; Nagel, *The View from Nowhere*, 73.

63. On the branching of the labyrinth, see Miller, *Ariadne's Thread*, 19. Nagel points out contra Bishop George Berkeley's immaterialist argument (objects are because we perceive them as our ideas) in *A Treatise Regarding the Principles of Human Knowledge* (1710) that "even if I employ a visual image to think about the tree, that does not mean I am thinking about a visual impression of a tree, any more than if I draw a tree, I am drawing a drawing of a tree." Nagel, *The View from Nowhere*, 93.

64. Levinas is citing Husserl's *Ideas*. Levinas, *Totality and Infinity*, 124.

65. Miller, *Ariadne's Labyrinth*, 132.

66. Cioran, *A Short History of Decay*, 210.

67. Simone Weil, *Gravity and Grace*, trans. Arthur Wills (Lincoln, Nebraska: Bison Books/University of Nebraska Press, 1997), 86 and 99.

68. Andreas Philppopoulos-Mihalopoulos compares Niklas Luhmann's working definition of ipseity as "unity of difference" to Merleau-Ponty's phenomenological "difference of difference." Andreas Philippopoulos-Mihalopoulos, "Suspension of Suspension: Notes on the Hybrid," in Niels Akerstrom Andersen and Inger-Johanne Sand, eds., *Hybrid Forms of Governance: Self Suspension of Power*, 27. The source of Merleau-Ponty's argument, although it is not cited by page, is *The Visible and the Invisible*, trans. Alphonso Lingis (Evanston, Ill.: Northwestern University Press, 1968). Niklas Luhmann, *Law as a Social System*, trans. Klaus A. Ziegert, ed. Fatima Kastner, Richard Nobles, David Schiff, and Rosamund Ziegert (Oxford: Oxford University Press, 2004), no page number given.

69. Unitary or fixed selfhood is "a long-exploded myth" that has been re-exploded by philosophers and linguists from the empiricist Hume to Derrida and beyond, yet it persists. Likewise, "character exists only as displacement, not as the solid ground of its various manifestations." Miller, *Ariadne's Labyrinth*, 116–17, 118.

70. Miller, *Ariadne's Thread*, 31; Philippopoulos-Mihalopoulos, "Suspension of Suspension," 25.

71. Miller (after Nietzsche), *Ariadne's Thread*, 46.

72. Miller, *Ariadne's Thread*, 26.

73. Philippopoulos-Mihalopoulos, "Suspension of Suspension," 25.

74. Philippopoulos-Mihalopoulos, "Suspension of Suspension," 25.

75. In Michael Almeyreda's film *Hamlet* (2000), the protagonist first sees the image of his dead father ghosting alongside himself on a video monitor.

76. At one point, Laure stays in hotel room no. 214. The number 2 represents the Bardo dream state, and 1 represents birth and 4 death.

77. Eyal Peretz, *Becoming Visionary: Brian De Palma's Cinematic Education of the Senses* (Stanford, Calif.: Stanford University Press, 2007), 161–63.

78. Perec, *Life: A User's Manual*, 33.

79. Moran and Cohen, "Time Consciousness," in *The Husserl Dictionary*, 326.

80. Moran and Cohen, "Signitive Act," in *The Husserl Dictionary*, 300; Levinas, *The Theory of Intuition in Husserl's Phenomenology*, 67.

81. Nietzsche, *The Will to Power*, §521, 282.

Chapter 6

1. The story was previously filmed as *The Street with No Name* (dir. William Keighley, 1948), minus *Bamboo*'s Japanese locale.

2. Gass, *Finding a Form*, 339.

3. Carlos Fuentes, *Terra Nostra*, trans. Margaret Sayers Peden (New York: Farrar, Straus and Giroux, 1976), 445.

4. Gass, *Finding a Form*, 351–52.

5. Gayle Greene, *Insomniac* (Berkeley: University of California Press, 2008), 1.

6. All of the deleted scenes that are described appear as bonus features on the unrated 2003 DVD edition of *Swimming Pool.*

7. Gass, *Finding a Form*, 330.

8. Gunsmiths may have repurposed broken pistols as "the earliest true lighters." Jack Pendarvis, *Cigarette Lighter (Object Lessons)* (New York: Bloomsbury Academic, 2016), 27.

9. Sigizmund Krzhizhanovsky, *Autobiography of a Corpse*, trans. Joanne Turnbull (New York: New York Review of Books Classics, 2013), 11.

10. Miller is referring to Jacques Derrida, *The Postcard: From Socrates to Freud and Beyond*, trans. Alan Bass (Chicago: University of Chicago Press, 1987). J. Hillis Miller, "Derrida's Disinterrance," *MLN* 121, no. 4 (September 2006): 900 and 905; Miller, *Ariadne's Thread*, 66 and 67.

11. J. Hillis Miller states that we are kept from falling into "a copse of undergrowth" by metaphors, which "name the unnameable, present the unpresentable, and therefore serve simultaneously as decent covering and as revelation or unveiling." In this sense, *The Trouble with Harry*, with its corpse at the foot of a copse, is one long extended metaphor of what metaphor is and does. Miller, *Ariadne's Thread*, 111.

12. Jacques Derrida, *Spectres of Marx: The State of the Debt, the Work of Mourning, and the New International*, trans. Peggy Kamuf (New York: Routledge, 1994), cited in Miller, *For Derrida*, 29.

13. J. Hillis Miller likens Derrida's notion of *disinterrance* to *différance*, "that is, to a temporality of differing and deferring, without present or presence: a kind of intertemporal interspace. Miller, *For Derrida*, 29.

14. *Merriam-Webster Dictionary*, http://www.merriam-webster.com/dictionary/corpse.

15. IMDb, http://www.imdb.com/title/tt0048750/.

16. Edmund Husserl, *Phenomenological Psychology*, trans. John Scanlon (The Hague, Neth.: Martinus Nijhoff, 1977), §23, 103.

17. Derrida differentiates between the other in the sense of another specific person (*autrui*) and "the wholly other" (*autre* implicitly suggesting *tout autre*), which disposes with the concept of likeness to me. Arnie's disinterment action in the plot (which effectively keeps Harry's corpse disinterred) recalls Kafka's statement, "What we call the way is only wandering." Kafka paraphrased in Miller, *For Derrida*, 50 and 115.

18. Harry's body is what Derrida calls a "remainder effect," like "sentences fixed on paper," subject to various postmortem interpretations. Derrida feared what would become of his writing, his remains, after he died. Miller, *For Derrida*, 79.

19. Gass, *Finding a Form*, 149 and 152.

20. The second Mrs. de Winter first sees "Manderley with adjacent landscaping and a sky backing" as "perhaps the largest scale miniature that had ever been built. It almost filled an entire de-soundproofed stage and it was used for close views." Steven Jacobs, *The Wrong House: The Architecture of Alfred Hitchcock* (Rotterdam: nai010 Publishers, 2014), 179. As "the second," the one who disambiguates the role of "Mrs. de Winter," perhaps she was able to glimpse the miniature because she was metaphorically disposed to see it as being a comment on her (own) inadequate performance/performance of inadequacy.

21. Barry Stroud, *The Quest for Reality: Subjectivism and the Metaphysics of Colour* (New York: Oxford University Press, 2002), 27.

22. Nagel eventually partially disowned the "Proustian exhaustiveness" that Parfit brought to the concept of series-persons since it likely became self-limiting for Nagel in his attempt to reconcile subjective and objective views of the world. This does not, however, obviate the concept's usefulness in relation to narrative metaphor. Nagel, *The View from Nowhere*, 45, n. 11; Parfit, *Reasons and Persons*, 290 and 291.

23. Parfit, *Reasons and Persons*, 210; Nagel, *The View from Nowhere*, 58–59.

24. Nagel, *The View from Nowhere*, 55, 57, 57 n. 1, 58.

25. Nagel, *The View from Nowhere*, 63–64.

26. Nagel, *The View from Nowhere*, 58.

27. Atop Mount Rushmore near the conclusion of *North by Northwest*, which Hitchcock joked he wanted to title *The Man in Lincoln's Nose*, Cary Grant as Roger Thornhill remarks to Eve Kendall regarding one of the giant heads, "I don't like the way Teddy Roosevelt is looking at me."

28. Cary Grant's own talent was for ambivalent self-abstraction, which led him to reject many roles he thought were unsuitable to the audience's expectations of his self-made persona.

29. Maurice Blanchot, "The Narrative Voice," in *The Station Hill Blanchot Reader*, 462, 463, and 464.

30. Georges Perec, *Portrait of a Man Known as Il Condottiere*, trans. David Bellos (Chicago: University of Chicago Press, 2015), 32–33.

31. Joseph Kesselring's play *Arsenic and Old Lace* (1939) enjoyed a highly successful Broadway run (January 10, 1941 to June 17, 1944) totaling 1,444 performances.

32. Conrad, *The Hitchcock Murders*, 220.

33. Conrad, *The Hitchcock Murders*, 56.

34. The nervous Mayor in Gogol's play *The Inspector General* (1842) accidently dons a hatbox in place of his hat.

35. This wraparound story structural possibility again recalls Gogol's *The Inspector General*, which begins and ends with the public reading of a letter that contains the plot of the play.

36. Brandon and Phillip serve as rough drafts for Bruno Antony and Guy Haines (the latter played by Farley Granger, who was also *Rope*'s Philip) in

Hitchcock's *Strangers on a Train*, as well as for the trunk murderer Lars Thorwald in *Rear Window* (1954) and Robert Rusk in *Frenzy* (1972). The abstract expressionist painter Mark Rothko likened his own paintings to trunk murders. Conrad, *The Hitchcock Murders*, 78.

37. Parfit, *Reasons and Persons*, 205.

38. *Ripley's Game* (2002), adapted from Patricia Highsmith's novel of the same name. Cowritten and directed by Liliana Cavani.

39. Perec, *Portrait of a Man Known as Il Condottiere*, 13 and 17; Miller, *Ariadne's Thread*, 250.

40. *Rope* (1929) by Patrick Hamilton. Thomas De Quincey, "Postscript to On Murder Considered as One of the Fine Arts," in *On Murder* (New York: Oxford University Press, 2009), 97.

41. De Quincey, "On Murder Considered as One of the Fine Arts," 17.

42. Perec, *Portrait of a Man Known as Il Condottiore*, 98.

43. Ibid., *Portrait of a Man Known as Il Condottiore,* 99 and 103.

44. Quine, *Word & Object*, 198; Perec, *Portrait of a Man Known as Il Condottiere*, 65.

45. Parfit, *Reasons and Persons*, 201.

46. Levinas, *Theory of Intuition in Husserl's Philosophy*, 111; Husserl, *Ideas I*, §141, 282.

47. Levinas, *Theory of Intuition in Husserl's Philosophy*, 111.

48. Renée Grinnell, "Circumstantiality," http://psychcentral.com/encyclopedia/2008/circumstantiality/.

49. Badiou, *The Century*, 54.

50. Badiou, *The Century*, 51.

51. Bill Krohn, author of *Hitchcock at Work* (2003), speaking on the DVD *Suspicion*'s extra "Before the Fact: Suspicious Hitchcock."

52. Nagel, *The View from Nowhere*, 65–66.

53. This skeletal image appears in "A Conversation with Peter Bogdanovich," one of the film's DVD special features (Columbia Pictures, 2000).

54. Rita Hayworth died at age sixty-eight from complications connected to Alzheimer's disease, a condition that had severely affected her memory and caused emotional instability for some twenty years prior to her being diagnosed.

55. I have been describing the cover of Joseph McElroy's *Actress in the House* (New York: Overlook, 2004); Perec, *Life: A User's Manual*, 83.

56. "Welles celebrated their engagement by sawing Hayworth in half in a magic show." He also demanded that her signature red-dyed hair be re-dyed blonde for *The Lady from Shanghai*, "making her look like a photographic negative of herself." Peter Conrad, *Orson Welles: The Stories of His Life* (London: Faber and Faber, 2003), 232.

57. Peter Conrad suggests that O'Hara may indeed have died "while trying to forget the story that he retells as he sails through limbo." Conrad, *The Hitchcock Murders*, 364–65.

58. "Since the objective self, though it can escape the human perspective, is still as short-lived as we are, we must assume that its best efforts will soon be superseded." Nagel, *The View from Nowhere*, 86.

59. Cioran, *The Trouble with Being Born*, trans. Richard Howard (New York: Arcade Publishing, 2013), 55.

60. Levinas, *God, Death, and Time*, 17, 19, 20, and 21.
61. Levinas, *God, Death, and Time*, 9, 14, and 90.
62. Strawson, *Individuals: An Essay in Descriptive Metaphysics*, 103.
63. Deleuze, *The Fold*, 112.
64. Deleuze, *The Fold*, 120.
65. Georges Perec, *Species of Spaces and Other Pieces*, trans. John Sturrock (New York: Penguin Books, 1999), 16 and 17.
66. Marina Tsvetaeva, "Attempt at a Room," in Marina Tsvetaeva, *Phaedra: With "New Year's Eve" and Other Poems*, trans. Angela Livingstone (London: Angel Books, 2012), 118.
67. Cioran, *The Trouble with Being Born*, 17.
68. Critchley, *Very Little . . . Almost Nothing*, 74; Simon Critchley, "I Want to Die, I Hate My Life—Phaedra's Malaise," *Theory and Event* 7, no. 2 (2004): 5.
69. Emmanuel Levinas, *God, Death, and Time*, 18, 20, 21 and 25.
70. Cioran, *The Trouble with Being Born*, 30.
71. Cioran, *The Trouble with Being Born*, 6.
72. "Ah, what corrupting counsels do I hear!" Phaedra spits at Oenone just prior to dismissing her (4.6.84). Jean Racine, *Phaedra*, trans. Richard Wilbur (New York: Mariner, 1984). For a discussion of pain (as performance) behavior, see Golub, *Incapacity: Wittgenstein, Anxiety, and Pain Behavior;* Cioran, *The Trouble with Being Born*, 91.
73. Allen Shawn, *Wish I Could Be There: Notes from a Phobic Life* (New York: Penguin Books, 2008), 216.
74. Roland Barthes, *On Racine*, trans. Richard Howard (New York: PAJ Publications, 1991), vii.
75. Racine, *Phaedra*, 10.
76. Krzhizhanovsky, *Autobiography of a Corpse*, 10.
77. Emmanuel Levinas, "Is Ontology Fundamental?" https://frenchtheorysheffield.files.wordpress.com/2014/01/levinas004.pdf, 121–22 and 123.
78. Leiris, *Nights as Days, Days as Nights*, 125 and 125–26.
79. Cioran, *The Trouble with Being Born*, 15.
80. Cioran, *The Trouble with Being Born*, 132.
81. Ricoeur, *Oneself as Another*, 119.
82. Cioran, *The Trouble with Being Born*, 90.
83. Cioran, *The Trouble with Being Born*, 125–26.
84. Cioran, *The Trouble with Being Born*, 17, 34, and 91.
85. Nietzsche, *The Will to Power*, §853, 451.
86. Cioran, *The Trouble with Being Born*, 48.
87. Cioran, *The Trouble with Being Born*, 21.
88. Kierkegaard, *The Sickness Unto Death*, 66–67.
89. Cioran, *The Trouble with Being Born*, 66 and 84.
90. Barthes, *On Racine*, 121.

INDEX